Advance Praise for *The Cartoons That Shook the World*

"A significant contribution to understanding the events around the Danish cartoons crisis, which will undoubtedly be subjected to continuing fascination and manipulation. Klausen offers an understanding of the Danish context that no other researcher can match."
—Jørgen S. Nielsen, University of Copenhagen

"The Danish cartoon crisis has been described as a deep cultural clash. This fine scholarly study presents it instead as a domestic political conflict among Danish citizens that spread to the international political arena. There were many losers, Klausen argues, but no winners. This is, by far, the best analysis of these events, and certainly the most thorough.
—Martin Schain, author of *The Politics of Immigration in France, Britain and the United States*

"The 'cartoons that shook the world' have polarized opinions and values in a war of words waged around the globe. Jytte Klausen's timely book brings facts and comparative data to make sense of a debate too often biased by passion, fantasies, and false representations."
—Patrick Weil, author of *How to Be French: Nationality in the Making since 1789*

THE CARTOONS THAT SHOOK THE WORLD

JYTTE KLAUSEN

THE Cartoons That Shook the World

YALE UNIVERSITY PRESS   NEW HAVEN & LONDON

Set in Scala and Scala Sans types by Keystone Typesetting, Inc., Orwigsburg, Pennsylvania. Printed in the United States of America.

Library of Congress Cataloging-in-Publication Data
Klausen, Jytte.
The cartoons that shook the world / Jytte Klausen.
  p. cm.
Includes bibliographical references and index.
ISBN 978-0-300-12472-9 (clothbound : alk. paper)
1. Morgenavisen Jyllands-posten. 2. Muhammad, Prophet, d. 632—Caricatures and cartoons. 3. Caricatures and cartoons—Political aspects—Denmark. 4. Muslims—Denmark—Politics and government—21st century. 5. Protest movements—Denmark—History—21st century. 6. Caricatures and cartoons—Political aspects—Islamic countries. 7. Christianity and other religions—Islam—Case studies. 8. Blasphemy (Islam)—Case studies. 9. Denmark—Relations—Islamic countries. 10. Islamic countries—Relations—Denmark. I. Title.
  PN5289.A253M675 2009
  363.4—dc22   2009020363

A catalogue record for this book is available from the British Library.

This paper meets the requirements of ANSI/NISO Z39.48-1992 (Permanence of Paper).

10 9 8 7 6 5 4 3 2 1

CONTENTS

PUBLISHER'S STATEMENT
After careful consideration, Yale University Press has declined to reprint in this book the cartoons that were published in the September 30, 2005, edition of *Jyllands-Posten*, as well as other depictions of the Prophet Muhammad that the author proposed to include. We recognize that inclusion of the cartoons would complement the book's text with a convenient visual reference for the reader, who otherwise must consult the Internet to view the images. As an institution deeply committed to free expression, we were inclined to publish the cartoons and other images as proposed by the author. The original publication of the cartoons, however, was an occasion for violent incidents worldwide that resulted in more than two hundred deaths. Republication of the cartoons has repeatedly resulted in violent incidents, as recently as 2008, some three years after the original publication and long after the images had been available on the Internet. These facts led us to consult extensively with experts in the intelligence, national security, law enforcement, and diplomatic fields, as well as with leading scholars in Islamic studies and Middle East studies. The overwhelming judgment of the experts was that the republication of the cartoons by Yale University Press ran a serious risk of instigating violence; many of the most senior experts advised that publishing other illustrations of the Prophet Muhammad *in the context of this book about the Danish cartoon controversy* raised similar risk. In excluding depictions of the Prophet Muhammad, we hope that Jytte Klausen's excellent scholarly treatment will be read and noticed by those seeking deeper understanding of the causes and consequences of the Danish cartoon controversy.

AUTHOR'S STATEMENT
Muslim scholars, friends, and political activists and leaders urged me to include the cartoons in the book with the purpose of encouraging reasoned analysis and debate on the cartoon episode. I agreed with sadness to the Press's decision not to print the cartoons and other hitherto uncontroversial illustrations featuring images of the Muslim prophet. But I also never intended the book to become another demonstration for or against the cartoons, and I hope the book can still serve its intended purpose without illustrations.

ACKNOWLEDGMENTS

I am grateful to Carsten Juste, Tage Clausen, and Ervin Nielsen for their help and permission to use material from *Jyllands-Posten*'s archives and to Flemming Rose for his help and generosity. I also thank Uffe Ellemann-Jensen, Adam Kuper, Abdul Haqq Baker, Ufuk Gökçen, Yael Lempert, and Tim Winter for their help and insight. The manuscript benefited from comments from Tarek Masoud, Steve Simon, Jørgen S. Nielsen, and Jonathan Laurence. Ünver Rüstem, Kjeld von Folsach, Richard Bulliet, and Sofie Lene Bak drew my attention to the complicated history of pictorial representation and to political cartoon events in the past, and I thank them for help in obtaining examples. Adam Jaffe and Steven Burg from Brandeis University helped me with travel expenses and released me from other obligations so I could write, for which I am very thankful. I am grateful also to the Norman Fund and Brandeis University for financial help with the production of the book. Jonathan Brent, Sarah Miller, and Laura Jones Dooley at Yale University Press have been wonderful editors. They have been consistently enthusiastic and supportive.

Alexandra Bowie and Kishwer Falkner provided correct grammar and encouragement. They are great friends. My family has put up with my travel and absentmindedness for a long time. They have my love and gratitude.

Introduction

ON SEPTEMBER 30, 2005, a Danish newspaper, *Jyllands-Posten,* published twelve cartoons featuring the Prophet Muhammad. Five months later, thousands of Muslims inundated the newspaper with outpourings of anger and grief by phone, email, and fax. A dozen countries launched a trade boycott against Danish goods. Consulates and embassies were torched. Danes were advised against travel in Muslim countries, and Danish diplomats and aid workers were withdrawn from several countries to protect their safety. The conflict spread when newspapers around the world reprinted the offending cartoons. Cyber attacks and spammed death threats followed as demonstrations spread across the Arab and Muslim world. Meanwhile diplomats from the Islamic countries turned to the United Nations for help against the Danes and to stem the escalation of protests. These are the uncontested facts, but why it all happened is in dispute.

This book is about the cartoons and the protests against them. The protests—which eventually stretched from the Middle East to Asia, Africa, and Europe and left only Latin America untouched—unfolded with little or no coordination except that provided by the events themselves and the global media's attention. The ubiquity of the cartoons lent an illusion of cohesion to the protests in the streets in London, Lahore, Beirut, and Damascus, but the protesters shared no consensus on exactly what was the problem with the cartoons or regarding the aims and means of the protests. Many

Muslims, perhaps most Muslims—whether they protested or not—agreed only that the cartoons maligned Muslims and their religion.

The cartoons achieved global celebrity. Eighty percent of respondents in a thirteen-country public opinion survey conducted by the Pew Global Attitudes Project in 2006 had heard about the cartoons, a number that rose to 90 percent in Jordan and Egypt and in the western European countries surveyed. The Pew survey showed an overwhelming inclination to attribute fault to the other side. Muslims thought Western arrogance was at fault; "Westerners" thought that Muslims were at fault.[1] Pew's choice of terminology is unfortunate. European Muslims are also "Westerners." The term "Muslim" is also problematic, if only because it refers to a religious identity—or, perhaps, a religious heritage that people sometimes choose to recognize as an identity—which is as complex and diverse as Christianity. The term is sometimes used, still more loosely, to describe an ethnicity or even geography. Alternative labels that do not seem overly generalizing are nonetheless difficult to find. Parsing the terminology too closely invites tedious discussions of the proper classification of Muslim atheists or, for that matter, of Muslim converts. And the cartoon controversy did in fact rouse dualist impulses. To be sure, not all people of Muslim origin agreed on the issues, as this book will make abundantly clear, but in the case of the cartoons international opinion *was* highly polarized between Muslims and non-Muslims. Actors in many countries and on different sides mobilized on the basis of appeals to "Muslim" identity. As shorthand, I shall sometimes use the terms "Muslims" and "the West" as public opinion surveys and opinion leaders did at the time, but always with the appropriate reservations.

It is hard not to marvel at how twelve little cartoons could cause so much trouble. Motives matter greatly in any effort to explain the decisions that contributed to the escalation, but the psychology of the moment is hard to reconstruct later. Anger and pride certainly influenced the behavior of some of the main actors, but so did deliberate political calculation and motives other than the public ones.

The emergence of a significant European Muslim minority is relevant. In 1950, there were perhaps three hundred thousand Muslims in western Europe. Today, demographers estimate Europe's Muslim population at around fifteen million, and about half have either been born in Europe or immigrated after 1985.[2] On any given day, European papers will carry news about Muslims behaving badly. Popular anxieties over immigration in general and Muslims in particular sway more voters than even economic concerns. In the heat of controversy it was forgotten that large majorities of Muslims are very supportive of European political institutions—elections, governments, and the police—and, according to some opinion surveys, more trusting of those institutions than is the general population. Yet many Europeans believe that Muslims are at war with Western values. Radicalism and extremism are minority phenomena among a minority, appealing to between 6 and 10 percent of the 2 to 6 percent of Europe's national populations who are Muslims, depending on the country and which survey you consult.[3] It suggests that about one hundred thousand Muslims support Islamist extremism, a fragment of western Europe's four hundred million people.

An obvious but neglected fact is that Muslim migration also has large-scale consequences for the originating Muslim countries. The governments in Ankara and Cairo worry greatly about the inevitable backflow to the countries of origin of undesirable ideas developed in Europe and the consequences of extremism among alienated Muslims. European publics and governments worry about the influence of Muslims on European norms and habits, and the Muslim publics and governments worry about the influence of European ideas and customs on Muslims. And everyone regarded the cartoons as an opportunity to draw a line in the sand, albeit for different reasons.

Genuine cultural misunderstanding and lack of information about "the other side" played a role. The Danish cartoonists and editors had little understanding of how the cartoons would be seen by Muslim publics. The press and opinion leaders in Muslim countries failed to appreciate that the cartoons were typical expressions of European anticlericalism. It is untrue, as was sometimes said, that "Danes would never do this to Jesus or their queen," although it *is* true that egregious examples of mockery of Jesus or the queen provoke an outcry and are routinely condemned and occasionally censored. But the essential fact is that the cartoons and the protests against them confirmed existing prejudices on both sides. The cartoons became "things to think with" because of their deceptive iconographic simplicity.

FROM THE RUSHDIE AFFAIR TO THE CARTOON CRISIS

Names carry connotations and expectations, and finding the right name for the cartoon controversy is not uncomplicated. As it dragged on, the cartoons became intricately linked with the word "crisis," which I have also used here.[4] But was it a "crisis"? And if so, for whom was it a crisis?

The cartoons did indeed set off an international row, and the personal security of the cartoonists and the newspaper's staff was put at risk. The protests were deeply upsetting to Danes, but the Danish media went overboard, nominating the events as the most serious international crisis to occur to the nation since German occupation in 1940. Both the world and the Danes have experienced more serious calamities since World War II. Danes over fifty remember the 1973–1974 oil crisis, when the country was singled out for particular penalties by the Arab oil-producing countries because of a prime minister's incautious words about Israel and ended up freezing and with carless Sundays.[5] The 1962 Cuban missile crisis involved a sudden escalation of international relations that built up over a few days and signaled a reordering of the international balance of power.

The cartoons did not precipitate a shock to the international balance of power or the economy. Territory was not lost. People died, but not in Denmark, and the deaths were caused by street violence and rough policing rather than military action or assassination attempts. The cartoons and the protests they unleashed were nonetheless far from trivial. The outcome of the cartoon conflict is still under negotiation—in the United Nations and in European and Muslim intergovernmental organizations— but the cartoons certainly have lasting consequences for the alignment of the international system on matters of trust and perception. The cartoons were launched to make a stand for free speech, but from Islamic art collections to Arab satellite television, new rules—formal and informal— apply that undoubtedly shrink the space for speech and artistic expression. They have also introduced a new vocabulary for thinking about global and domestic relations among faith groups and the importance of religion in international relations.

The real novelty of the cartoon crisis derived in part from the role of new media. Satellite TV, cell phones, blogs, and the online chat rooms made Danish print journalism, usually available to only five million Danes and a few Nordic friends, globally accessible. The cartoons took on a life of their own. They became avatars. And facilitated by Microsoft and Al Jazeera, people all over the world could act out their grievances in a transnational political theater unfettered by the normal constraints on political expression.

The new format was itself a causal factor. Had *Jyllands-Posten* not published the cartoons in the paper's online edition—and kept them there—only regular subscribers would have seen them. And when the crisis reached its zenith six months later, the offending pages would have been composted and available only in a few libraries in Denmark.

In some ways the cartoon conflict resembles the Dreyfus Affair, which began in 1894 with the wrongful conviction of a French Jewish junior officer, Alfred Dreyfus, on treason charges. An *affaire*—or in the English spelling, an affair—had become defined as a protracted political scandal that raises questions of conscience and loyalty or is emblematic of deep political divisions. The false accusations against Dreyfus represented an attack on truth and universalism and revealed the persistence of anti-Semitism in France contrary to official public values. A moral drama that engaged the press and the intellectual elite in many countries, the affair ended only in 1915, when Dreyfus was cleared and had his rank restored.[6] Analogously, Muslims argued that the cartoons revealed the presence of entrenched Islamophobic sentiments in European societies (not just Denmark) and called for a wider recognition that anti-Semitism and Islamophobia are similar expressions of religious hate. It is conceivable that the "cartoon affair" may one day end with some symbolic act of restitution to Muslims and a new recognition of religious pluralism in European states.

The Rushdie Affair is another parallel and, some would argue, an antecedent to the cartoon conflict. Salman Rushdie published his novel *The Satanic Verses* in 1988, and in February 1989, Iran's leader the Ayatollah Khomeini (who died four months later) issued a fatwa against the author and offered a reward to Rushdie's murderer. Muslims in Britain staged angry demonstrations, and commentators compared book-burning Muslims to Nazis burning books. Diplomatic relations between Britain, where Rushdie lived, and Iran were frozen for a decade. Rushdie has lived under police protection ever since.[7]

The demonstrations and book burnings that followed in Pakistan and many major cities in the Islamic world suggested a degree of Muslim unanimity and anger at Western ways not hitherto seen. Demonstrations and counterdemonstrations were held in the major cities in Pakistan, Iran, and India. Bookstores were burned, even in the United States, and the publishers threatened. Three translators of Rushdie's books were attacked, and one died. Few bookstores dared to exhibit the book openly.

The Rushdie Affair is widely regretted among Muslim leaders in Europe and in the Islamic nations, and when the cartoon conflict began, it was on many peoples' minds as an example of what they wanted protests to *avoid* becoming. Muslim governments used diplomatic means to press their complaints against *Jyllands-Posten* and the Danish government at the United Nations. Islamic clerical authorities called on Muslims to protest and sometimes used language they later regretted, but they, too, wanted peaceful protests. No widely influential religious authority issued edicts during the cartoon controversy calling for punishment of the editors and the cartoonists, by death or otherwise. Mahmoud Ahmadinejad, the Iranian president elected in June 2005, who carried on the Ayatollah's political project, put things in a different perspective by calling for a cartoon arms race. He called for a competition among Muslim cartoonists to lampoon the Holocaust. It was a curious response but accorded with Ahmadinejad's history of Holocaust denial.

Strictly speaking, the twelve drawings at the center of the conflict are mostly caricatures and not cartoons. In contemporary parlance, a cartoon is a story told in one or more panels using graphic pictures, either with words or alone. Political cartoons tell a story or make a comment on current events. Some of *Jyllands-Posten*'s drawings were cartoons in this sense. One made fun of the newspapers' editors, but because the artist, Lars Refn, used a caption in Arabic script to make his point, the joke was lost on Danish readers. People who read Arabic were hardly any wiser because the pictorial references were unintelligible.

Caricatures are wordless line drawings that use exaggerated physiognomic features to make a statement about the fundamental nature of a person or a thing. Their intent is to satirize, mock, or ridicule—which is also what the newspaper said in its editorial statement that day that it aimed to do. Flemming Rose, the paper's culture editor, notoriously wrote that in democratic societies "you must be ready to put up with insults, mockery, and ridicule." Yet *Jyllands-Posten*'s chief editor, Carsten Juste, has angrily denied that the paper aimed to "caricature" the Prophet and accused commentators who described them as such of misrepresenting the paper's intentions. And it is true that the paper did not specify what sort of drawings it hoped to get from artists when it commissioned the drawings. Artists were simply asked to "draw Mohammad as you see him," but then it is also true that the paper sent the invitation to the members of the union of newspaper illustrators who specialize in caricatures. "Drawings" seemed the more neutral term until Osama bin Laden used it to justify attacking European targets by darkly hinting at a violation of Koranic prohibitions against depiction.

Why quibble over words? Who after all has heard of the "caricature affaire"? For lack of an uncontroversial alternative, I shall continue to speak of the "cartoon crisis."

FACTS AND INTERPRETATION

The story of how the cartoon protests developed from small-scale local demonstrations to global uproar only to subside without a proper conclusion is fraught with unintended consequences and misunderstanding. The difference between genuine misunderstanding and deliberate misrepresentation is often difficult to establish. And when it comes to judging consequences and responsibility, things get even murkier. Facts are sometimes slippery, and what was once thought to be a fact about the cartoon controversy often turned out to be a misrepresentation or true but insignificant in the larger picture.

An example of a contested fact is a visit by a delegation of Danish imams and mosque activists to Cairo in December 2005. It is a fact that the visit took place, and it is known who participated and also that the visit was arranged through the Egyptian embassy in Copenhagen. The activists brought along a dossier that included copies of the cartoons from *Jyllands-Posten* and other cartoons from Danish papers purporting to depict Muslims or the Prophet Muhammad. The dossier also included three cartoons of a very insulting and sexual nature never published in Denmark.

The dossier turned up at various important junctures at meetings in the Middle East, where angry resolutions against the Danes were passed, and traveled back to Europe in the briefcases of Muslim association leaders who had attended those meetings. The presence of the cartoon dossier at such events would suggest that the activists and their misguided decision to include the "false" cartoons were responsible for spreading the conflict and inflaming people's views. The imams unwisely bragged about their success, and many Danes believed, as did international journalists, that they were responsible for getting Egypt involved.[8] But Egypt had been building a diplomatic offensive against the Danes for months, and the imams would never have made it to Cairo if they had not been invited there. Danes did not know about the scale of the diplomatic protests because the Danish government did not make the key official protest letters public until much later and even today has still not released the full record of contacts. The part played by the local imams seems less significant when viewed in this context.

The list of doubtful facts and misconceptions is long. It was often said that Islam prohibits the depiction of Muhammad and that Muslims were angry because the prohibition was violated. One need not spend much time in Islamic art collections to know that the Prophet's life and biography are the subjects of many illustrations. Stories about Muhammad's life have been regarded as inspirational, and his beauty and strength are often extolled. The representations are regarded as pictures of the human prophet and not of the divine, "the beauty of which no human eye can capture," according to the Koran. Christians have painted and drawn Muhammad without Muslims protesting in the streets. Radical clerics with an interest in the politicization of Koranic interpretations aside, few Muslims cited religious law as the reason for their protest.

Jyllands-Posten's defenders lauded the paper for its uncompromising attitude to free speech, but the cartoonists and the editors did not think that free speech is an absolute right. Some of the cartoonists agreed with the paper's critics that it was picking on Muslims in unacceptable ways. Carsten Juste himself rejects the argument that free speech is absolute. "Of course we practice self-censorship," he has said. He argues instead that he and the paper had inadvertently offended the feeling of many Muslims in ways he had not expected.

It is also not true that the right to insult a religion or its adherents is an uncontested part of the Western secularist canon. Fifty-two percent of the British non-Muslim public expressed sympathy for angry reactions of Muslims to the cartoons.[9] Religious Christians and Jews are also concerned about blasphemy and the room for religious values in public life. On the other hand, there were Muslims who argued that it was about time that Muslims learned to appreciate free speech. Some added that it was the fault of Muslims themselves that Danes understand so little about Islam that they equate the faith with terrorism.

The conflict did not pit an uncompromising Western appreciation for free speech against a pious Muslim proclivity for censorship. "Westerners" guard their tongue in religious matters, and many Muslims also believe in free speech. A plurality of European states still criminalize blasphemy and speech acts ranging from incitement to violence, the defamation of religious groups, anti-Semitism and other forms for racialist speech, and Holocaust denial. The only Western country with a strong tradition of protecting free speech is the United States, but few British and American papers and weeklies published the cartoons, generally declaring them "offensive."[10] The Associated Press declined to distribute the cartoons to American subscribers. By my count in the United States five regional newspapers and some twenty student newspapers and street papers republished the cartoons. *Harper's* magazine printed them all in the June 2006 issue. The cartoons elicited a global controversy over the boundaries of free speech. *Ejour,* a Danish web site covering journalism news, found that by the end of February 2006 one or more of the cartoons had been reprinted in at least 143 newspapers in fifty-six countries. In Russia and South Africa, the courts stepped in and banned the cartoons. Meanwhile, Arab and South Asian papers republished the cartoons. Some Muslim editors faced stiff penalties, while others were not troubled by the authorities.[11]

There is one point on which everybody agrees. None of the protagonists think they won. Ekmeleddin İhsanoğlu, the secretary-general of the Organization of the Islamic Conference, who played an important role in the conflict, summed up the feelings of many diplomats, Muslim or not: "It was a bad conflict. Everybody ended up feeling worse afterwards than they did at the start."[12]

Even people who were in the thick of the conflict felt at a loss to explain why twelve cartoons could set off such serious trouble. People would sometimes try to make sense of it all by referring to the "butterfly effect," an image drawn from chaos theory which suggests that a tiny disturbance somewhere far away—Indonesia is often mentioned—sets off a chain reaction that ends with a tornado off the Florida coast.

The most common explanation relied on popularized versions of the "clash of civilizations" thesis. This is the idea that Islam and Christendom are separate and opposed civilizations, perpetually rubbing against each other. Samuel P. Huntington's remark about Islam's "bloody borders" was invoked as the explanation for the angry and sometimes violent demonstrations and threats. From this perspective the protests were represented as entirely predictable results of the atavistic opposition of Muslims to Europe's secular values. Moreover, the protests verified, ex post facto, *Jyllands-Posten*'s claim that the Muslim clerics in Europe were voices "from a dark age." That the favored medium for the delivery of obscurant edicts and threats was the very contemporary Internet was overlooked.

Interviewing protagonists in the course of researching this book it struck me that a film made by the Japanese film director Akira Kurosawa, *Rashomon*, in 1950, provided an appropriate framework for telling the story. The film shows the same event from the vantage point of different actors. Each understood the facts differently, and was poorly equipped to understand the motives that drove the actions of others. However, their actions were based on their particular understandings of what was going on. The moral was that interpretations are more consequential than objective realities.

ABOUT THIS BOOK

As a Dane living in the United States, I quickly became absorbed by the events. In early 2006, I found myself being asked to explain how the "good Danes" had turned into hate-filled racists with no respect for human rights. I was more accustomed to being asked to tell the story of how the Danes rescued some seven thousand Jews during the Holocaust. Both stereotypes were wrong, I said, this is all about politics, on both sides.[13] In retrospect I would allow more room for fumbling and misunderstanding, but I still think we need to regard the crisis as a political conflict rather than as a colossal cultural misunderstanding.

I grew up reading *Jyllands-Posten* regularly. It was—and still is—the newspaper my family reads. The paper has a national readership today, but its name reflects its provincial origin. It is, literally, the record of events for the peninsula known in English as Jutland. Its main offices are in Århus, Denmark's second largest city. The buildings are located on the outskirts of town in an area zoned for industrial use and resemble a well-kept, small manufacturing plant. Inside everything is white and pleasant.

In Denmark who you are used to determine which papers you read

and what party you voted for. Working-class families read the social democratic papers and voted accordingly. Bankers, doctors, lawyers, managers,
and the wealthy read the conservative paper and voted for the Conservative Party. And the provincial bourgeoisie and the better-off farm families
read *Jyllands-Posten* and voted for Venstre. The party's name literally
means "left," but there is nothing left-wing about the party. The designation was determined by the seating arrangements in parliament in the
days of limited suffrage. There were two parties. The conservatives were
known as "Højre"—the right—because they sat on the right side of the
benches, and the farmers' party was know as "Venstre" because they sat
on the left. Today Venstre is known in English as "the Liberals." It is the
party of Anders Fogh Rasmussen, the prime minister who would not say
sorry. *Jyllands-Posten* was created as an independent paper in 1871 and for
many years supported the Conservative Party. In 1971, it declared itself
"liberal" and had in recent years been supportive of Fogh Rasmussen's
governments.

The crisis was distressing for me, not just as a native of Denmark. I had
just spent the preceding three years interviewing more than three hundred
Muslim leaders in western Europe about their views of how Islam can be
integrated in Europe.[14] The people I spoke with were not fundamentalists
or terrorists, and they did not support the codification of Islamic religious
law in Europe or anywhere else. Instead, they routinely evoked human
rights as the core of their belief system and spoke in straightforward and
practical terms about the need to build a European Islam.

I had loyalties on both sides in this conflict. As accusations and coun-
teraccusations started flying, my first objective became to unravel the
sequence of events that produced the escalation of conflict. This turned
out to be no easy task.

The cartoons and their iconographic meanings are discussed at various points in the book. The cartoons are still available on many Internet
sites, but the longevity of such sites is unpredictable and they are often
marred by obscene commentary and misleading translations of the Danish captions.[15] In 2006, Borders and Waldenbooks refused to sell an issue
of *Free Inquiry*, a monthly magazine, because it republished the cartoons.
It was a meaningless gesture because the images were at the time freely
available over the Internet. It was also a misinterpretation of what angered
Muslims about the cartoons and an unwise decision for other reasons.

Several books have been published in Danish about the events. They are cited when I build on their accounts. Many of my sources come from confidential interviews with people who were involved in the protests. Sometimes people spoke to me as private persons and expressed views contrary to their official positions. I have only on a few occasions used such statements, and then the identities of the authors are shielded. I have used anonymous sources more often than I wanted to, but it is a testimony to the delicacy of the circumstances of the protests that there is little room for dissent on all sides in the conflict. Alarmingly, this applies in equal measure to my Danish and my Muslim friends and contacts.

The cartoon conflict involved diplomats and civil servants, government leaders and ministers, elected officials and party leaders, journalists and editors, activists and ordinary citizens, and religious leaders ranging from self-appointed "sheikhs" to well-known public intellectuals. At the organizational level, the scope of involvement was also unusual. Among those who were drawn into the conflict were European governments and courts, parliaments and presidents in Muslim countries, the European Union, the United Nations, pan-Islamic associations, small mosques and Al-Azhar, the national Churches and the Vatican, clandestine political groups, reputable and disreputable clerics, intergovernmental organizations, newspapers and universities across the world, and groups that were set up just for the purpose of protesting against the cartoons or against the protesters.

A chronology of events can be found on page 185. It is intended to assist readers who may find keeping track of the dateline of events difficult as the chapters unwind the loopy chains leading to the breakout of global protests in February 2006. Readers may read it first or go straight to chapter 1, which begins where it all started, the Sunday issue of *Jyllands-Posten* in September 2005.

CHAPTER 1

The Editors and the Cartoonists

ON SEPTEMBER 30, 2005, Carsten Juste, editor in chief of the Danish newspaper *Jyllands-Posten,* wrote a seven-hundred-word editorial to explain why the newspaper was publishing twelve drawings of the Prophet Muhammad that day. The Muslims who publicly represent Islam are beset by a "sickly oversensitivity" to criticism, he wrote. "Any provocation against one of these self-important imams or mad mullahs is instantly interpreted as a provocation against the Prophet himself or the holy book, the Koran, and then trouble ensues. The Islamic spiritual leaders feel called upon to gripe and an army of intellectually underequipped followers respond and do what is interpreted as the Prophet's command and ultimately kill the offenders." Juste also described these Muslim clerics as being voices from "a dark and violent middle age" and expressed his hope—his tone suggested it was unlikely—that there was a large, silent, and more reasonable majority among Muslims who preferred peaceful coexistence and who would eventually reject this "stubborn adherence to a dark past."[1]

The twelve cartoons were printed on one page under the headline "The Face of Muhammad." The page was placed in the newspaper's culture section and printed along with an essay by Flemming Rose, the culture and book review editor, who argued that *Jyllands-Posten* was striking a blow for freedom of speech and against self-censorship motivated by political correctness. The choice of headline proclaimed the newspaper's intention to violate the Muslim taboo against the pictorial representation of Muhammad. Not all the cartoons depicted the Prophet. Some mocked far-right politicians; others portrayed Muslims as victims.

It has sometimes been said that the cartoons were the result of a competition. In fact, the editors were conducting an experiment. They solicited drawings of the Prophet Muhammad from all the members of the union of newspaper illustrators (in Denmark everyone belongs to a union) in order to establish whether illustrators would refuse to participate. Prompting this experiment was a rumor, circulated earlier during the summer, that an author of children's books named Kåre Bluitgen had been unable to find an illustrator for a book about Muhammad. The editors wished to see whether such fear was widespread and if illustrators would therefore refuse the commission.

The aggressive tone taken by the newspaper's editorial was commonplace in contemporary Danish discourse. Indeed, several commentators observed later that the editorial simply repeated what some Danish politicians and commentators had been saying for years. Over time, the boundaries of permissible language had shifted.[2] What once would have been considered offensive speech about "other people" was now justified as standing up to piety or simply as speaking one's mind.

THE GENESIS OF THE CARTOONS

After some discussion among the newspaper's different section editors, it fell to Rose to send a letter inviting the forty-two members of the union of newspaper illustrators to submit drawings. The letter went out on September 19. In it Rose mentioned the rumor that illustrators had been afraid to draw Muhammad for Bluitgen's children's book and explained that *Jyllands-Posten* had decided to take a stand for free speech by asking the illustrators to "draw Muhammad, as you see him."[3] He promised that the paper would print all the drawings that were submitted as a demonstration against intimidation and self-censorship. The illustrators were promised the paper's usual fee of about $160 for their trouble.

Although forty-two artists were invited to contribute to the experiment, only fifteen responded. Of these, three turned down the commission. One said that the assignment was too vague, a second that both the pay and the project were ridiculous, and a third that he was afraid to participate.[4] Twelve drawings were submitted. The editors were in a bind. A plurality of the illustrators had not even responded. There was no way to determine why they did not answer, and so the results of the experiment were inconclusive. Yet because *Jyllands-Posten* had promised the illustrators who did respond that their drawings would be published, it was difficult to cancel the project.

Not all the cartoons backed the editors' claim that Denmark had succumbed to fear-induced political correctness, but Flemming Rose was untroubled by this. When I interviewed him for this book, he told me that, after all, Danes hardly ever agree on anything. Even though some cartoonists clearly had not followed "the program"—they did not draw the Prophet—Rose decided, "in the name of pluralism," as he put it in the interview, to publish all the submissions.[5]

Carsten Juste had second thoughts because of the inconclusive result of the experiment and delayed the project for a week. He decided to move the cartoons from the news section—where they had originally been scheduled to appear—to the culture section, where readers' expectations about content are different. The twelve cartoons that had been submitted were then published.

The Danish summer ends in August, and the cartoon editorial was timed for the end of the "silly season" of summer reportage. The feature was supposed to be a summertime prank with a serious edge, but readers did not see the cartoons as a joke. The editors' bombast and the sensational headline invited a different reading of the page.

Rose's essay did not differ much from Juste's editorial. He explained that over the summer he had become increasingly concerned about self-censorship and cited incidents that showed that artists, comedians, authors, and translators were afraid—or should be afraid—to treat Muslims as they would members of any other religious group. This was evidence in Denmark of a growing political correctness that treated Muslims with exaggerated respect. And political correctness was a mere step from totalitarianism.

Flemming Rose had been a foreign correspondent in Moscow before becoming an editor at *Jyllands-Posten*, and he had been back in Denmark only since 2000. He justified the idea of the cartoon challenge by comparing it to Russian dissidents' use of humor against the Soviet state. "It is no coincidence," he wrote, "that people in totalitarian societies are imprisoned for telling jokes or for satirizing dictators. It is usually done with the argument that people's feelings have been hurt. Things have not gone that far in Denmark, but the examples that have been given show that we are on a slippery slope and nobody can predict where self-censorship will end." The demand made by some Muslims for special regard was incompatible with a secular democracy and free speech. In a free society, Rose concluded, "everybody must be willing to put up with sarcasm, mockery, and ridicule."

Rose cited several examples of the new censorship: the writer who had been unable to find an illustrator for a children's book about Muhammad; a stand-up comedian who had said he was afraid to make fun of the Koran in the way he would happily mock the Bible; a group of imams who had asked the prime minister, Anders Fogh Rasmussen, to tell the press to moderate its criticisms of Muslims; the fact that three summer cabarets had put on shows lampooning George W. Bush and Fogh Rasmussen but none had made fun of Osama bin Laden. Rose's other examples did not involve Denmark. The Tate Gallery in London had removed a piece of artwork to avoid offending Muslims. An unnamed translator of the Dutch-Somali politician Ayaan Hirsi Ali's essays wanted to remain anonymous. (In fact, Hirsi Ali's first book, *The Caged Virgin,* had an anonymous Dutch ghostwriter, as did her second book, *Infidel,* which was published after the cartoon crisis.)[6]

The essay's examples combined serious and trivial, even doubtful, instances of both censorship and self-censorship and ignored the motives behind them. Self-censorship may be caused by a credible fear of retaliation and bodily harm, but it may also follow out of respect for other people's religious beliefs or from a desire not to hurt people's feelings.

Rose also ignored recent instances of censorship and self-censorship that did not involve Muslims. Six months earlier, in Birmingham, England, Sikhs had demanded the closure of a theater performance that depicted sexual abuse in a temple. The theater protested that the performance was fiction, but Sikh community leaders managed to shut the show down. They received support from other religious leaders. The Roman Catholic archbishop of Birmingham, Vincent Nichols, said: "Such a deliberate, even if fictional, violation of the sacred place of the Sikh religion demeans the sacred places of every religion."[7] This was a problematic example of artistic censorship due to religious sensitivity, but the protagonists were a Catholic archbishop and paternalistic Sikh elders, not the "sickly sensitive" Muslim clerics who bothered *Jyllands-Posten.*

Rose could rightly have included another incident closer to home on his list. In October 2004 a lecturer from the University of Copenhagen was abducted and beaten up by a group of Muslim men while he waited for a bus. His crime was to have recited from the Koran during a class in religious studies. The lecturer was not Muslim, and the attackers were punishing him because, as they said during the assault, apostates are prohibited from reading from the Holy Book. Hizb ut-Tahrir, an extremist organization, was blamed for the attack, but the police never solved the crime. Although the attack on the lecturer caused much concern among academics, it hardly fitted Rose's prescription for resistance to multicultural political correctness through "mockery and ridicule."

The initial response in the Danish press to *Jyllands-Posten*'s editorials and the cartoons was that the brouhaha about self-censorship was nonsense. Danes were not afraid of pious Muslims. This lasted until the first report of a death threat against some of the cartoonists.

In the days that followed the publication of the cartoons, few Danish newspaper columnists applauded Juste and Rose for their willingness to stand up to political correctness. Most people groaned that the newspaper was at it again, bashing Muslims. The instinct was to split the blame: Muslims should behave themselves, but the newspaper had crossed the line. A conservative newspaper, *Berlingske Tidende,* wrote a patronizing editorial chastising *Jyllands-Posten* for its "gag" but also explained that it is good for Islam and for Muslims to be criticized. *Politiken,* a competing and more liberal newspaper, attacked the veracity of Rose's account of spreading self-censorship. Its journalists called the same members of the union of illustrators whom Rose had written to and asked them if they would agree to illustrate the children's book about Muhammad. This time, twenty-three responded that they would and six that they would not because they wished to respect Muslims' feelings. One reported being afraid, and one was not sure.[8] *Politiken* concluded on this basis that distrust of *Jyllands-Posten*'s motives rather than fear of Muslims had caused most artists not to respond. (Rose says that perhaps as many as half of the illustrators had exclusive contracts with other publications, which prevented them from publishing a drawing in *Jyllands-Posten.*)

Jyllands-Posten's story began to fall apart. The cabaret managers who were chided for not making fun of Osama bin Laden protested that they simply found President Bush and the prime minster better material for summertime entertainment. Kåre Bluitgen could not identify the illustrators whom he claimed had declined to illustrate his book.

The comedian Frank Hvam protested that he had been misquoted. It seems, however, that he was quoted accurately but now wanted to correct his statement. Hvam had used a common colloquial expression for ridicule, saying he was "afraid to take the piss on the Koran" as he would on the Bible. Rose quoted Hvam's actual words in the newspaper, and the unfortunate expression was later mistranslated on many foreign-language web sites as if Hvam wanted to "piss on" the Koran. Even in Denmark comedians cannot urinate on holy books as public entertainment, and the colloquial expression is so common that all Danes knew that Hvam merely wished to "make fun" of scripture. Months later, French right-wing extremists turned up at a demonstration organized by Dansk Front, an ultranationalist group, and filmed themselves pissing on the Koran. The film was posted on YouTube and now migrates from Spanish to Russian to Japanese ultranationalist sites every time it is shut down.[9]

THE RIGHT TO RIDICULE AND MOCKERY

The argument that mockery, sarcasm, and ridicule are democratic values will not appeal to all believers in free speech, and it contradicts the more familiar argument that civility is a basic requirement of democracy.[10] In northern Europe, however, rudeness is sometimes regarded as authenticity and is even seen as a civic virtue when directed against pompous and arrogant figures of authority. The Dutch are perhaps even more inclined than the Danes to regard insult as a legitimate form of argument. This was the view of Theo van Gogh, the filmmaker who was assassinated for his deliberate provocation of Muslims.[11]

The cartoons were nonetheless not exactly a quintessential expression of Danish democratic values, as Rose and others have suggested. Denmark has legal prohibitions against both blasphemy and racial hate speech. There are limits to what you can say about people and their religion.

When I interviewed Rose, he explained that he had two reasons for publishing the cartoons—as a test of the extent to which self-censorship had spread among Danish illustrators and to demonstrate resistance to

Islamic orthodoxy by depicting the Prophet. That was as he had described his motives before. He now added: "If one person stands up against the repression, the fear of breaking a taboo rests on that person, but if five hundred stand up, the fear is diluted and reprisals are made more difficult."[12] Cartoons are a form of political speech, but Rose neglected the fact that the courts have treated artistic representation with less leniency than the written or spoken word.

Rose's plea for humor as resistance to repression suggested a parallel between communist authoritarianism and the fledging political assertiveness of Islamist groups in Denmark. The parallel implied was preposterous. The Soviet dissidents were up against the crushing power of the communist state, and their humor was directed at the authorities. Danish Muslims are a divided and marginalized minority amply subjected to criticism.

The editorial decision to print the cartoons has been scrutinized. How could the newspaper's editors not have foreseen the consequences? They did not. Juste says that had he known what would have happened, he would never have gone ahead. Rose says that he would still have done what he did. Reconstructions of the editorial process throw up moments of missed warnings. It is also clear that the cartoons were by no means the result of a deliberate and collective act of heroism that the newspaper's admirers later made it out to be.

Members of the editorial staff cautioned Juste that Muslims would be very hurt by the project and that *Jyllands-Posten* should not make light of those feelings. Rose says that he never heard of the concerns.[13] This is not surprising. Rose's office is in Copenhagen, and the people with concerns were in Århus, hours away. Rose never participated in the meetings at which second thoughts were discussed.

Juste dealt with his doubts by moving the cartoons to the culture section. The placement would signal to readers of the print edition that they should not take the exercise too seriously. Yet Juste's own editorial contradicted that message, and moreover, no one who consulted the newspaper's web site had a clue that the cartoons were intended as cultural expression rather than as editorial opinion or "news."

No one at the newspaper focused on the impact of using drawings instead of words to express editorial content. And no one foresaw that the cartoons would acquire an independent and long-lasting life in cyber-

space. Incomprehension and ignorance about Muslim feelings with respect to the Prophet aside, the editors also failed to notice that several of
the cartoons were malignant representations of stereotypes in the manner of European anti-Semitism. The headline, "The Face of Muhammad,"
aggravated matters. The translation into English was unambiguous. It
framed the entire exercise as a provocation. Given the packaging, it is not
surprising that many people failed to notice that some drawings in fact
neither depicted the Prophet nor insulted Islam.

The remedy would have been to subject each drawing to editorial
evaluation and decide to publish some and not others. The editors, however, had placed themselves in an impossible position. The content of the
drawings was never discussed for the obvious reason that it would have
gone against the premise of the experiment. As Rose wrote in his letter to
the illustrators, the purpose was to break a taboo. The illustrators had
been invited to draw the Prophet as "you see him." A normal process of
editorial assessment, in which the editors made substantive decisions
about quality and content, was out of the question because it would have
seemed like censorship.

THE CARTOONISTS

The cartoonists had very different ideas about their tasks. Several mocked
Rose's suggestion that Danes were facing a looming gulag of self-censorship. Two mocked the children's author as a self-promoting jokester. One
suggested that Muslims are the victims rather than the perpetrators of a
public mugging. Several made no effort to depict the Prophet. Among those
who did, one is self-consciously neutral, whereas the others use iconography
that ranges from racialist essentialism to self-righteous prejudice.

The cartoons were marketed as "humor against tyranny," but what
some people find funny, others do not find amusing at all. It is fair to say
also that laughter was not foremost on the mind of all the contributors.
One journalist at *Jyllands-Posten* enthusiastically described the cartoon
editorial as "democratic electroshock therapy" for the Islamists.[14]

A quick Internet search will produce a link to the cartoons that lists the
cartoonists' names, but academics have been hesitant to name the illustrators.[15] The monthly newsmagazine *Harper's* published a review essay in
June 2006, by the cartoonist Art Spiegelman, in which each Danish cartoonist was named and graded using ticking bombs in place of stars for ar-

tistic skill and humor.[16] For their part, some of the cartoonists have been extremely averse to publicity, while others have complained they are not being credited for their work. Several have spoken publicly about their ideas and their drawings, and I have cited these artists here by name.

In his submission, the illustrator Lars Refn drew Muhammad as a youth teasing the editors at *Jyllands-Posten*. The caption identifies the boy as "Muhammad—seventh grade" from a suburban school district outside Copenhagen known for its largely immigrant-origin student body. The boy wears a soccer shirt in the colors of a local team named Fremad, which means forward. The echo of socialist slogans is not accidental. The club was associated with the socialist labor movement. In the drawing, Refn has changed the name of the club to Future. Today the club is multiethnic. The boy grins while scribbling something on the blackboard in Arabic. Refn had an Iranian friend help him with the script, which was eventually translated. "The journalists at *Jyllands-Posten* are a bunch of reactionaries," writes the boy (in Farsi). Refn was the first cartoonist to receive a death threat and to be moved to a safe house.

Several drawings refer to current Danish personalities or to standard Danish tales or anecdotes. In one cartoon Kåre Bluitgen, the children's author, wears a turban and holds a piece of paper on which a stick figure is drawn. The stick figure is identified as "Muhammad" and is supposedly an illustration for Bluitgen's book. The joke is on him. An orange bearing the words "PR Stunt" falls into Bluitgen's turban. To have an orange drop into your turban is a Danish expression for receiving undeserved good luck. Another cartoon similarly suggests that Bluitgen made up the story about Muslim intimidation to get attention. It puts Bluitgen in a police lineup of suspects who appear to have committed a mugging. The lineup includes Jesus, Buddha, what appears to be a hippie, a "mad mullah," and Pia Kjærsgaard, the leader of the Danish People's Party. The victim—a Muslim, presumably, but it could be everyman—is scratching his chin and saying, "I cannot recognize him." These and other drawings employed such specific Danish references that no one outside the country could possibly make head or tail of them.

The cartoon of the Prophet with a bomb in his turban and the Shahada—the Muslim declaration of faith: "There is no god but God, Muhammad is the Messenger of God"—inscribed on the bomb-turban became the iconic focus for the protests. This was the cartoon Muslims cited as evidence of the Danes' disrespect for Islam. Yet it was not the conclusion the artist had intended. Kurt Westergaard, who drew the cartoon, was angry that there were illustrators who were "afraid" and wanted to prove there was no need to worry about such matters in Denmark. He intended his drawing to show that radical Muslims use the Prophet's name to justify violence. He did not for a minute consider that Muslims would interpret his drawings the other way around, as intended to show that the Prophet is the source of violence.

The distinction is conceptual and cannot be inferred from the drawing. Danish readers, accustomed to Protestant disparagement of Roman Catholics for placing the laws of the church above the mercy of God, would recognize the drawing as a classic anticlerical statement. Muslims might agree with that message, but they read the cartoon as an attempt to blame terrorism on the Prophet and the faith—and, by implication, as charging all Muslims with being terrorists because of their faith. This was at once blasphemous and libelous.

Four of the cartoons, including Westergaard's, used language that to many people—but curiously not Danes—recalled the language of anti-Semitic caricature used in Germany and elsewhere in Europe in the 1920s and 1930s.

One drawing without a caption places a green crescent and star on a face with the immediately recognizable physiognomy of a "Semite."[17] Although that term is used today mostly in the context of "anti-Semitic," which most people recognize in the meaning of "anti-Jewish," the root of the word designates people who speak Semitic languages and includes both Arabs and Jews.[18] Strictly speaking, then, the usage can connote both Jews and Arabs. The anti-Semitic style exaggerates what supposedly are the physiognomic features of an Arab or a Jew to produce a decidedly racialist caricature.

Anti-Semitic cartoons from the Nazi era and from present-day Arab papers can be found in a number of online archives, including the Holocaust Museum in Washington, DC. Anti-Muslim caricatures convey a different message, but the use of physiognomy to portray the Prophet's violent or treacherous inner qualities is unpleasantly similar to the racialist *Rassenschander* of Nazi iconography.

بســـم الله الرحمـــن الرحيـــم
والصلاة والسلام على سيدنا محمد 'صلى الله عليه وسلم'
"لن ترضى عنك اليهود ولا النصارى حتى تتبع ملتهم"

By Name of GOD

For all PIGS whose share in opinion, drawing and publishing those drawing of our PROPHET, we tell you ' BY GOD WILL WE WILL KILL ALL UNBELIVERS; which mean YOUUUUUUUUU '.

We promise you that we will reach TO you in your home sterility and fighting you; since we announcing AL-JHAD in your country, at that moment you ALL will know that is ' THE HELL IS YOUR END '.
NO BODY INSULT OUR PROPHET AND GET AWAY WITH OUT PUNISHMENT.

Where ever you are just look around you because in some day in some place you will find INSURGENT MUSLIM lurking you with a knife to jabbing your straying heart.

SO REMEMBER THIS SHARP SPEARHEAD BECAUSE YOU WILL TASTE IT.

FIGURE 1. Death threat sent to *Jyllands-Posten* on February 5, 2008, from a Yahoo account, probably from Saudi Arabia or Yemen. Used with permission from *Jyllands-Posten* and Danmarks Mediemuseum. Source: Danmarks Mediemuseum, special collection DMM 571-10-57000.

A third cartoon depicts Muhammad with a Semitic nose and an unruly gray beard but equips the Prophet with a menacing sword. The sword is used simultaneously to threaten the viewer and to hold back two apparently pretty, though veiled, young women. The caricaturist has superimposed the black cutout from the women's attire on the old man's eyes. The black bar employs a graphic gag to suggest that the women can see but not be seen, while the Prophet is altogether blinded. The black bar also recalls the way some newspapers conceal the identity of criminal suspects in photographs.

The illustrator Franz Füchsel evoked the Arabian Nights and the tales of Ali Baba in his submission. The color scheme is typical of his work, though to the uninitiated eye it may suggest an Orientalist depiction of the lair of a sheikh. The caption presents a stark contrast to the drawing. The Prophet holds back holy warriors with drawn swords. "Take it easy, friends," he tells them, "it is just a drawing made by an infidel from southern Jutland." People from this part of Jutland are known in Danish folklore as jokers. The caption does not seem to run counter to the Muslim image of the Prophet as a man who in his own life practiced moderation and humor. Its problem is its lurid and racialist iconography.

Self-righteousness is the dominant sentiment in some of the cartoons. Arne Sørensen drew a cartoon of himself hunched over the drawing board, with the window blinds down, shaking his head as he draws an angry-looking man with bushy eyebrows, a beard, and a kaffiyeh, the scarf worn by some Arab men. One drawing shows roughly sketched veiled women and includes a haiku deriding the idiocy of keeping women wrapped up and under lock and key.

Four of the cartoonists used Christian images and concepts—even if anticlerical, as in Westergaard's case—to depict the Muslim Prophet. Two cartoonists drew the Prophet as a Jesus look-alike, in the style of popular biblical illustrations aimed at the devout. In one, Muhammad is pulling a donkey in the desert and wearing hippie sandals and holding a walking stick. In another, however, the illustrator places horns, not a halo, on the Prophet's head.

Jens Julius Hansen drew a benign-looking Prophet standing on a cloud and turning away smoldering suicide bombers. "Stop, stop, we have run out of virgins," he says. Here Hansen seems to confuse Muhammad with Saint Peter: Muhammad does not guard the gates to heaven.

The cartoonists responded to the global protests against their work with a mixture of incomprehension and anger. They felt let down by Danes who criticized them as well as by the newspaper that got them in trouble. Several have since described themselves as "small people" caught in a big machine. "It is unreal that Osama bin Laden has a view about somebody like me," one cartoonist said in an interview.

The illustrators did not think they did anything wrong or different from what they usually did when they drew the cartoons. "I have always only made tasteful drawings," one cartoonist explained to a newspaper.[19] Another had a nervous breakdown. A third is grateful to his neighbors, who looked out for him and recommended escape routes. After the death threats began, the police advised the cartoonists not to speak to the press. A few disregarded the advice, but others took it to heart, and as a result, the views and motives of the cartoonists were not known during the controversy. Some have since said that they regretted their silence at the time.

The cartoonists described the drawings as carried out in haste, and a few artists have expressed regret that they did not put more effort and thought into the job, considering how much attention the cartoons got. Füchsel reflected how strange it was that something that took him ten minutes could cause such a furor. "I have teased the pope and Bush, so I thought I could tease Muslims, too." But he was also angry about the clerics' statements. "They [Muslims] live here, work here, and many have fled from regimes and laws in the countries they come from. Yet they come here and call us infidels and want the laws they have fled put in place here. The imams who preach that we have offended them are themselves guilty of the oppression of women." Füchsel can be forgiven for having hard feelings. One anonymous caller warned him to expect a big "bang" on his next birthday, which, as he put it, spoiled the day when it came around. He told the journalists he has a drawer full of letters, faxes, and emails with death threats, because "you never know if some day one of the senders will carry out his threat." The police generally advise recipients of harassing letters to hold on to the evidence.

The illustrators had mixed feelings about their celebrity. At one point they received an offer for "millions from a millionaire in America" for all the cartoons. The promised money never materialized, and several attempts to auction the cartoons failed. Füchsel says he sold his cartoon to "a mailman from Copenhagen" for a modest sum, which he donated to a charity. Kurt Westergaard tried to sell the original drawing of the man with the bomb in the turban but concluded, "Nobody wants it." "We are all disappointed. This is documentation for our national history. Now the drawing is in a bank box. I have promised the bank not to say where it is. My wife says that if a rich sheikh wants to buy it for ten million dollars to burn it in Mecca, that's okay, too."

I met Westergaard on a visit to *Jyllands-Posten*'s offices in Århus in October 2007. I mentioned that I hoped to reprint the cartoons and confessed that I had no money to pay for the privilege. That got Westergaard started on how cartoonists and illustrators are the proletariat of the publishing world. He was only half-joking. Cartoonists, according to Westergaard, are the blue-collar workers of the intellectual production chain. Editors and writers around the world have filled their pages with stories about the cartoons but have never paid the artists. We—writers and publishers and politicians—sponge off the cartoonists by taking their work and extracting "surplus value" from them when we get the credit and the pay for writing about them. All he got out of the whole thing was eight hundred Danish crowns, which is what *Jyllands-Posten* paid for the original cartoon. I conceded that he had a point.

The cartoonists subsequently enjoyed some restitution. Ten of the original drawings have been placed in the Royal Danish Library to be used by scholars only, and *Jyllands-Posten* has donated its archives, containing all the threatening emails and faxed death threats and many, many letters to the editors, to Denmark's media museum. In May 2008, *Jyllands-Posten*'s charitable foundation awarded each cartoonist a stipend worth about ten thousand dollars. Westergaard has retained the rights to his drawing. In April 2009, Westergaard and a friend started to sell numbered reproductions of the cartoon, which they likened in importance to the *Mona Lisa*. The receipts go to a charitable organization that promotes freedom of the press.

Rose told me he was disappointed that the *New York Times* and the *Washington Post* did not reprint the cartoons, because, he says, once people see them, they see that they are not as bad as their reputation would indicate.[20] In researching this book, I carried along to my interviews with Muslim leaders and diplomats a copy of a dossier produced by the protesting Danish imams with the cartoons and other material they had included to document their complaints. (The dossier and its role in this story are described in detail later.) My purpose was to find out who had seen the dossier, but carrying the dossier around also gave me an opportunity to discover the objections to the cartoons. In my experience, Muslims generally say they are more affronted when they see all the cartoons than they were when they were following a second-hand discussion in the media coverage. Muslims—irrespective of religious convictions—react to what they perceive in the cartoons as a tone of irascible contempt. Rose's observation about the cartoons "not being as bad" when you see them as they appeared in the newspaper is probably true in the case of non-Muslims, who tend to wonder what the fuss was about once they see them fully.

Still, Rose is right that the international media's practice of partially reprinting the cartoons hurt *Jyllands-Posten*'s cause. Westergaard's cartoon with the bomb in the turban came to epitomize the cartoons, and the other drawings that criticized the newspaper—Refn's drawing, for example—received no attention. As a result, the global media frenzy reduced the message of the cartoons into a simple insult against Islam.

THE NEAR ENEMY

When the cartoons became famous and traveled the world on the Internet, they were seen as smears directed against the world's 1.3 billion Muslims and their faith. The iconography of the cartoons and the editors' belligerent tones were instantly recognizable as typical things Westerners have been saying about Muslims since 9/11. Yet in September 2005 the Danish editors had their minds set on a few local "mad mullahs" with whom the newspaper had a history of feuding. One of the mullahs was Sheikh Raed Hlayhel, who has since moved to Lebanon but in 2005 lived ten miles across town from *Jyllands-Posten*'s offices in Århus.

Jyllands-Posten first wrote about Hlayhel six months before the publication of the cartoons. Journalists from the paper had visited a mosque in Copenhagen where they heard Hlayhel give the Khutbah, or Friday sermon. The usual preacher was Ahmed Abu Laban, a charismatic imam of Palestinian origin who also played a leading role in the protests against the cartoons. The differences between Laban and Hlayhel were evident to people who know about radical Islamism, but most Danes could not tell the two sheikhs apart.

In his sermon, Hlayhel described women as "the devil's work" and held them responsible for the corruption of men. He instructed the thousand men attending prayers that day to go home and make their women cover up so that only their hands and faces would show. *Jyllands-Posten's* journalists taped the sermon; the newspaper then published a transcript of the sermon together with a highly critical story.[21] An outcry followed. Government ministers and local officials condemned Hlayhel for denigrating women and weighed in with pronouncements about bedrock Danish values. Hlayhel protested that he had a right to freedom of speech and could say what he wanted.

Hlayhel, who is Lebanese, has a master's degree in Islamic thought from a university in Medina, Saudi Arabia. He espoused a radical Salafist theology and harbored an ambition of becoming the leader of Danish Muslims when he lived in Århus. He now lives in Tripoli, Lebanon. (Salafism is a movement in Sunni Islam that advocates theological purification. Some Salafists take politically extreme positions, as does Hlayhel.) In the days after the publication of the cartoons, Hlayhel and another cleric from the same mosque, Ahmed Akkari, took the lead in putting together an action committee of imams and mosque activists from four mosques.

Ahmed Akkari came to Denmark from Lebanon as a boy with his family in the 1980s and has seldom been out of the papers since. At first, he was portrayed as a victim. The family members were refugees from the Lebanese civil war, but after years of administrative delay, Danish authorities denied their application for asylum and forced them to return to Lebanon. Danish newspapers took on the case of the family and battered the government with criticism sufficiently to force a reversal of the decision. In 1994 Akkari and his family were allowed to return to Denmark, and Akkari became a Danish citizen in 2005 just before the cartoon controversy erupted.

The young man's public image suffered a quick reversal of fortune at the hands of *Jyllands-Posten*. In May 2005, the newspaper featured a long and laudatory interview with Akkari discussing his role as a Danish imam —he speaks flawless Danish—and the problems of Muslims in Denmark. Soon afterward, the newspaper published a second story about Akkari, revealing that while working as a teacher, he had written in a Muslim youth paper—government subsidized even—that women who did not wear the headscarf deserved to get a "kick in the back."[22] The story Akkari had written was a silly report of a Danish teenager whom he claimed to have seen kicking a Muslim girl. Akkari wrote that he had not intervened because the girl was not wearing a headscarf and therefore "deserved" to be kicked. An outcry erupted. The local mayor demanded Akkari's dismissal as the spokesman for a Muslim group seeking to build a mosque and refused to meet with the group.

According to a search of *Jyllands-Posten*'s web archive, between 1999 and October 2007, the newspaper published nearly three hundred stories featuring Akkari. (The digital archive does not go past 1999.) Likewise, a search for Hlayhel's name pulls up two hundred stories between the first mention of his name, in February 2005, and October 2007. Not all the stories about Akkari were negative, but after the "kick in the back" story, the coverage was invariably unfavorable. These searches are a primitive measurement of attention because they bring up any story mentioning their names, including letters from readers in response to stories. Yet the sheer volume of mentions reveals an intense preoccupation by *Jyllands-Posten* with the two clerics.

Danes pride themselves on their internationalism, but a paper with a daily circulation of about 160,000 copies written in a language that can be read only by five and a half million Danes is by necessity focused on bringing the news home. It is a truism that all news is local news. The topsy-turvy world of Islamic domination and beleaguered resistance alluded to in the editors' editorials on the day the cartoons were published was an admonition that bad things from abroad were coming home to roost, as personified by the well-known, controversial clerics. Their names were not mentioned that day, but it was hardly necessary. Everyone knew whom the editors were writing about.

The irony is that Danish Muslims are for the most part politically placid and disinclined to support Islamic radicals and extremists. There are about two hundred thousand Muslims in Denmark. Muslims of Turkish origin are the largest subgroup, making up about one third of the Muslim population.[23] Turkish Muslims were among the first wave of labor migrants, arriving before 1974. Recent immigrants are more likely to be political refugees and from North Africa and the Middle East. The newspaper's attack on the "mad mullahs" stereotyped all Danish Muslims as radical extremists who have fled from trouble in Arab countries.

DOUBLE STANDARDS

The charge that the editors practiced a double standard became a problem for *Jyllands-Posten* when the British newspaper the *Guardian* revealed that a few years earlier *Jyllands-Posten* had refused to publish cartoons portraying Jesus on the grounds that they would offend its readers. The editor had written to the cartoonist, Christoffer Zieler, "I don't think *Jyllands-Posten's* readers will enjoy the drawings. As a matter of fact, I think that they will provoke an outcry. Therefore, I will not use them."[24] The two episodes revealed how far the newspaper had shifted its position on religious questions.

In order to prove that the newspaper did not apply a double standard, Flemming Rose announced on CNN in an interview broadcast on February 8, 2006, that he would publish the winning entries from a competition announced by Mahmoud Ahmadinejad, the president of Iran, soliciting cartoons that ridiculed the Holocaust. Rose was stung by the accusations of a double standard and of having singled Muslims out for insult. To demonstrate his willingness to insult every religion equally, he held up two drawings before the camera that he described as "possibly" offensive to Jews and Christians. The drawings were from the newspaper's archives. Rose intended to use historical material to prove that *Jyllands-Posten* treated other religious groups disrespectfully, too, but he never had time to make this clear. Viewers thought the newspaper had commissioned new cartoons to insult Christians and Jews along with Muslims.

When the CNN interviewer mentioned the Zieler story and asked Rose what he thought of the Iranian Holocaust cartoon competition, Rose answered: "I can tell you that my newspaper is trying to establish a contact with that Iranian newspaper, and we would run these cartoons the same day as they would publish them."[25] As it happened, he had not cleared his proposal with Carsten Juste, his chief editor, and there was an uproar in Denmark, in other European countries, and in the United States. The Iranian cartoons did not appear in *Jyllands-Posten.*[26]

Carsten Juste has repeatedly complained that religion has too much space in society today and that freedom of speech has been curbed. Juste and Rose have drawn different lessons from the cartoon crisis. Still, the two editors agree that there are limits to free speech and that they are responsible for negotiating a balance between responsible and free speech. Juste describes the editorial process as a process of self-censorship. You choose what to put in the paper and what to leave out, which photo to run, whether to print bad words. In our interview, Juste insisted that the cartoons were not contrary to the paper's ethical guidelines and did not represent a departure from their established practice. Had he changed his mind about publishing the cartoons, I asked him. "Would we do it again? No, of course not. Not given what we now know. We now have new information and that leads to new ethical considerations." He added, "I also still believe that it is true what we wrote: Everyone has to accept being subject to satire."[27] Parsing his words carefully to make clear that regrets emerged only later, Juste explained that after talking to Muslims from around the world, who had called in to the newspaper's office, he had come to appreciate that the newspaper had caused hurt feelings by printing the cartoons. It was the reason he decided to issue a letter of apology in January 2006.

Flemming Rose, who wrote the irascible paean to mockery, sarcasm, and ridicule as the foundation stones of a free society, also acknowledged that there are limits. "We do not ridicule particular people, only ideas," he explained. Strange as it sounds, this seemingly innocuous view may be the source of controversy. Muslims would have been more tolerant of the cartoons if they thought they were mocking the mullahs rather than Islam itself. Rose saw nothing wrong with printing the cartoons and still does not. The twelve cartoons were very different, he pointed out in an interview, and they "sent different messages" about how the illustrators approached the issue of the (unproven) taboo against drawing Muhammad. He added, nonetheless, "If I had received twelve drawings that all were like Kurt Westergaard's [the bomb in the turban cartoon], I might have had second thoughts."[28]

THE POLITICS OF APOLOGY AND FORGIVENESS

Would the Danes say sorry? Eventually it all boiled down to something as simple as an apology, if one believed what was said in the media at the time. Like other aspects of the conflict, the issue was politically manipulated and an occasion for appealing to domestic audiences. The question of the need for an apology also provoked genuine intercultural misunderstanding. Americans think it is the decent thing to say sorry when bad things happen. The English might even apologize for things they have not done just to make people feel better. Muslims think that an apology is a way of showing respect for the other party. In international diplomacy, an apology can be an expedient device for getting a concession. Danes, however, take the narrower view that an "apology" is only for cases when you intentionally do something you know is wrong. If you accidentally kick a soccer ball through a window because the wind blows the ball that way, you are not obliged to apologize. It was beyond your control. Whether the ball lands in the window because your aim is bad or because you intended to break the window for reasons of mischief calls for different degrees of apology. An apology is an admission of guilt, and a loss of face is involved.

Danes strongly resisted apologizing for the insult caused by the cartoons. And even if an apology was called for, who was responsible for making it? The Danish government refused to apologize because, as Anders Fogh Rasmussen, the prime minister, said repeatedly during the conflict, "You cannot apologize for something you have not done." The newspaper did it, and consequently the government was under no obligation to make an apology. Danish public opinion was strongly against apologizing to Muslims.

On January 28, 2006, Juste did issue an apology in an open letter to Muslims everywhere. The letter was posted first on the newspaper's Internet site, and a few days later English and Arabic versions were posted on *Jyllands-Posten*'s web site and on that of a Jordanian newspaper. Danish consulates and embassies in the Middle East also posted the letter.[29]

Juste used the word "apology" but did not apologize for having published the cartoons. There had been a misunderstanding, he wrote, and he wanted to set the record straight. The drawings were an exercise in free speech, which, perhaps because of a "culturally based misunderstanding," had been interpreted to be part of a campaign against Muslims in Denmark and the rest of the world. Any offense caused, he wrote, was unintentional. "In our opinion, the twelve drawings were sober. They were not intended to be offensive, nor were they at variance with Danish law, but they have indisputably offended many Muslims, for which we apologize."[30] For all the problems with the wording of his apology, Juste showed courage in making it. Fortunately, the Danish tin ear for how to say you are sorry did not matter. The Islamic governments and diplomats declared Juste's letter a sufficient response.

No one in any official capacity had asked the government for an apology in the first place. The Muslim diplomats and the letters and diplomatic communiqués from Egypt, the Organization of the Islamic Conference, and the Arab League did not state that an apology was required. They requested an official acknowledgment from the Danish government that you could not say racialist or denigrating things about Islam and a pledge that Denmark would apply existing laws to the Islamophobic statements made by a minister and other members of parliament and a member of parliament from the Danish People's Party, the small far-right party whose parliamentary support Fogh Rasmussen's government depended on. But many ordinary Muslims wanted an apology. It was the dominant theme in the many calls and emails to the government—the foreign ministry alone received some 717,000 email requests by early March 2006, when the computers were equipped with a filter to sort them out—and to *Jyllands-Posten*'s offices.[31] It was also the driving theme in many op-ed pages and letters to the editor in the Middle East and Pakistan.

Muslim leaders came to regret their advocacy of forgiveness after Juste's apology when the cartoons had an encore performance in 2008. In mid-February 2008 the Danish police arrested three Muslim men for plotting to kill the cartoonist Westergaard and his wife. The next day, seventeen Danish newspapers reprinted Westergaard's bomb-in-the-turban cartoon in a show of "solidarity." The Danes' concept of solidarity was lost on the authorities in Cairo, where I was visiting at the time to conduct interviews for this book. "It just shows that they haven't learned anything," many people said. People who two years earlier had advocated that the Danes "be forgiven" now lost face, because the Danes were showing that they really were not interested in being educated. Sore feelings remain on all sides. Commitments were made that cannot easily be abandoned. The effects of the trade boycott linger. Danish businesses that had just started to recover after the first cartoon episode reported that markets were now lost. In April 2008, a spokesman for the hard-hit dairy product seller Arla announced that sales in the Middle East had come to a complete halt in 2006 and that they had reached less than half of pre-boycott sales in 2007.[32] Novo Nordisk, a pharmaceutical company, and Danfoss, a producer of advanced machinery, also reported large losses and canceled contracts in 2006. The Danish foreign ministry reported that all exports to the Middle East fell 24 percent in 2006 and were reduced by as much as 75 percent in some countries. A moderate recovery in 2007 did not restore sales fully. The reprinting of Westergaard's cartoon in February 2008 revived the consumer boycott of Danish products in Jordan, Saudi Arabia, and the Gulf states. This time, however, the reaction was muted on the part of the intergovernmental organizations and the Arab governments.

Carsten Juste retired as editor in chief of *Jyllands-Posten* in May 2008. When asked by another newspaper what he was most proud of having done as editor in chief, he did not mention the cartoons.[33] Flemming Rose left the newspaper at the same time to write a book about the cartoons, free speech, and globalization. Rose returned to the newspaper in February 2009 as editor of the culture and opinion pages.

Jyllands-Posten has twice tried to use legal means to stop critics.[34] In October 2006, Carsten Juste filed a complaint of scholarly misconduct against a Danish professor, Tim Jensen, who had said that the newspaper had published the cartoons to deliberately provoke Muslims. Juste charged that Jensen had expressed his private opinion and that his assertion was not based on research. Things got murkier when it turned out that *Jyllands-Posten* had consulted Jensen about what might happen if it published the drawings and Jensen had advised the newspaper not to publish them. The second complaint was against an attorney who represented the Muslim organization that took *Jyllands-Posten* to court. The attorney had released a press statement detailing his court argument, which included a request that the newspaper address a rumor that it had solicited additional cartoons from the paper's in-house illustrators—among them Kurt Westergaard— after it decided that the illustrations initially submitted in response to Rose's invitation were "too tame." Juste and Rose sued the attorney for defamation because he had put the question into a press release. (Court proceedings are public in Denmark.)[35] Whatever the merits of the legal case, the editors had trouble shaking off the charge that they exercised double standards by trying to silence their critics.

CHAPTER 2

The Path to a Showdown

UNBEKNOWN TO THE EDITORS and the Danish public, Denmark was headed toward a diplomatic train wreck within ten days of the publication of the twelve cartoons. For this was when the government of Egypt decided to make an international issue of the cartoons. Many rivulets eventually merged to form the flood of worldwide protests in February and March 2006, but the main source of the flood sprung forth during those first weeks in October 2005 in Cairo.

In Copenhagen, eleven ambassadors representing Muslim countries to Denmark sent a letter shortly after the publication of the cartoons to Prime Minister Anders Fogh Rasmussen protesting against what they described as "an on-going smearing campaign in Danish public circles and media against Islam" (box 1). One of the envoys was Mona Omar Attia, the Egyptian ambassador. The Egyptian government immediately involved also the Arab League and the Organization of the Islamic Conference, both of which also dispatched letters to the Danish government. At the same time the clerics who had been targeted by *Jyllands-Posten's* cartoon editorial started an action committee. They turned to Attia to solicit help from Muslim countries. In time, they received assistance. When no response was forthcoming from the Danish government, the OIC and the Arab League passed resolutions condemning the cartoons. In November 2005 the different streams met up. By the end of 2005, the

Box 1. Official letter sent October 12, 2005, to Prime Minister Anders Fogh Rasmussen from ten ambassadors representing Muslim and Arab countries and the Palestinian representative in Copenhagen.

His Excellency Mr. Anders Fogh Rasmussen, Prime Minister, Kingdom of Denmark

Excellency,

The undersigned ambassadors, Cd'a.i. and Head of Palestinian Delegation accredited to Denmark take this opportunity to draw your attention to an urgent matter.

This pertains to on-going smearing campaign in Danish public circles and media against Islam and Muslims. Radio Holger's remarks for which it was indicted, DF (Danish People's Party) MP and Mayoral candidate Louise Frevert's derogatory remarks, Culture Minister Brian Mikkelsen's statement on war against Muslims and Daily Jyllands-Posten's cultural page inviting people to draw sketches of Holy Prophet Mohammad (PBUH) are some recent examples.

We strongly feel that casting aspersions on Islam as a religion and publishing demeaning caricatures of Holy Prophet Muhammad (PBUH) goes against the spirit of Danish values of tolerance and civil society. This is on the whole a very discriminatory tendency and does not bode well with the high human rights standards of Denmark. We may underline that it can also cause reactions in Muslim countries and among Muslim communities in Europe. In your speech at the opening of Danish Parliament, Your Excellency rightly underlined that terrorists should not be allowed to abuse Islam for their crimes. In the same token, Danish press and public representatives should not be allowed to abuse Islam in the name of democracy, freedom of expression and human rights, the values that we share.

We deplore these statements and publications and urge Your Excellency's government to take all those responsible to task under law of the land in the interest of inter-faith harmony, better integration and Denmark's overall relations with Muslim world. We rest assured that you will take all steps necessary.

Given the sensitive nature of the matter, we request an urgent meeting at your convenience. An early response would be greatly appreciated.

Please accept, Excellency, best wishes and assurances of our highest consideration.

Fugen Ok Ambassador of Turkey, Mohammad Ibrahim Al-

Hejailan Ambassador of Saudi Arabia, Ahmad Danialy Ambassador of the Islamic republic of Iran, Javed A. Qureshi Ambassador of Pakistan, Mona Omar Attia Ambassador of Egypt, Perwitorini Wijono Ambassador of Indonesia, Latifa Benazza Ambassador of Algeria, Sead Maslo Ambassador of Bosnia and Herzegovina, Mohammad E.R. Rimali Libyan Embassy, El Houssaine Oustitane Charge d'Affaires a.i. of Morocco, Maie F.B. Sarraf Head of Palestinian General Delegation.

Cc: H.E. Mr. Per Stig Møller, Foreign Minister, Royal Danish Ministry of Foreign Affairs, Copenhagen, Denmark.

Muslim intergovernmental organizations came out in favor of a trade boycott, which was initiated around Christmas time 2005. In February 2006 came the riots. The long story of these events and intersections follows in subsequent chapters.

The conflict moved through different phases with different actors driving events. This chapter takes a development perspective on the conflict without attempting a full chronological history. Conspiracy theories are rife about how things turned out so badly for Muslims or the Danes, depending on which side you are on. The facts are complicated, but the Muslim diplomats did not intend to unleash the furious demonstrations that occurred in February 2006. The separate initiatives by mosque activists in Copenhagen and diplomats in Cairo eventually merged, even if only briefly. Rather than the result of a master plan to arouse the Muslim masses, the Egyptian government's actions were inspired by short-term considerations and rested on incomplete information about the imams' political agenda.

On December 3, 2005, a delegation from the Danish action committee of imams and mosque activists arrived in Cairo at the invitation of the Egyptian foreign ministry. The delegation brought along a dossier with copies of the twelve cartoons and translations into Arabic of *Jyllands-Posten*'s editorials. The fateful dossier also included other documentary material produced by the imams, including three pictures of what they described as representations of Muslims and their prophet. When the Islamic countries met in Mecca, Saudi Arabia, on December 7–8, 2005, and a decision was made to escalate the conflict, the dossier featured prominently albeit unofficially in the deliberations.

Other sources fed the protests. The demonstrations that occurred in February and March 2006 were sponsored in part by radical Islamist parties and in part by various governments, chiefly Iran and Syria. Early warning signs that extremist groups were employing the cartoons for the purposes of domestic destabilization had been overlooked. As early as November 2005, independently of events in Cairo and Copenhagen, the cartoons had attracted the attention of radical leaders in India and Pakistan. In February 2006 demonstrations erupted in Europe's capitals, this time fed by European newspapers' reprinting of the cartoons. This chapter provides an overview of the development of the conflict and some of the main intersections of local, regional, and international protests.

CYCLES OF PROTEST

Social movements are generally associated with a predictable pattern of mass mobilization.[1] An initial phase of mobilization is followed by a period of escalation and contagion as competing groups take up the demands of the movement. The momentum ebbs when the contestants become divided and radicalized, and toward the end of the cycle violence often ensues as the most extremist groups attempt to assume control. The movement may then collapse or moderate in response to countermobilization by opponents, suppression, or cooptation. The cycle of protest ends when parties and interest groups take up the demands of the protesters and make the claims amenable to the normal procedures of political representation and bargaining. Social scientists find that movements never really die but are carried on in routinized forms and inspire innovations in claims-making that enter into normal political language. Often leaders of the protest movement enter normal politics as the demands of the movement become incorporated into representative mechanisms.

The Western press perceived apparent unity in February 2006 among the cartoon protesters and described the protests as if they were the result of a global social movement. Nonetheless, deep divisions existed at all times between the Middle Eastern governments and the religious authorities, as well as between the European Muslim associations and the Muslim diplomats. Belatedly, even Al-Qaeda and the Taliban entered the fray with predictable results. Setting aside for the movement the question of whether the cartoon protests were actually the result of what we might call a global social movement, the developmental model of social movement theory can be used to describe the different phases of the protests.

In the case of the cartoons, the mobilization phase started the day they were published, September 30, 2005, and ended when violent street protests erupted across the world in February 2006. Over those four months a great deal happened that was not known to the public. Most was known to the governments in both Copenhagen and Cairo, but no one put all the pieces together, which explains in part why the demonstrations and riots in February seemed to appear out of nowhere. In reality, they were the result of a process of deliberate, albeit uncoordinated, escalation.

As soon as the cartoons were published, newspaper sellers called the paper's offices to say that they would not distribute that day's paper. Large numbers of Danish Muslims let *Jyllands-Posten* know that they objected to the cartoons. A coalition of imams and mosque activists from four Danish mosques quickly formed with the purpose of planning and organizing a protest movement: fourteen days after the publication of the cartoons, they held a demonstration in front of City Hall in Copenhagen. But after that, the protests petered out in Denmark. There was no groundswell of support for the mosque activists and imams who led the charge against the newspaper and the government in Denmark.

The imams and the activists had strong roots in various streams of Sunni radicalism but had not previously joined forces. The ethnic, even clannish, and theological tensions that are characteristics of Sunni radicalism in general were all represented in the inner circle of this little group but were temporarily overridden by a shared revulsion against the cartoons.

The effort by Egypt and the OIC to coordinate government action and mobilize Muslim public opinion against Western Islamophobia in December 2005 soon gave way to a new phase of mass mobilization and radicalization. From January through March 2006 there were demonstrations, some orderly, some violent, across the Middle East, the Caucasus region, South and Southeast Asia, and Africa, as well as in many European cities. The cartoons were condemned in Friday sermons across the Middle East and in many mosques in Europe. On February 3, 2006, Sheikh Yusuf al-Qaradawi, a charismatic preacher based in Qatar, lambasted the cartoons in his televised Friday sermon and called for "a day of rage." Al-Qaradawi, an Egyptian-born scholar and preacher linked to the Muslim Brotherhood who is revered by many Muslims in Europe and the Middle East, accused Islamic states of choosing the United States over the Prophet and thundered against "our feeble governments." His anger was genuine, but he hardly intended the consequences.

When papers across the world—mostly in Europe but also in Russia, in countries in Africa and Asia, and in a few predominantly Muslim countries—reprinted the cartoons, the conflict escalated as Muslims in those countries started to demonstrate against these papers, too. The issue ceased to be about the Danes and what they did. The escalation into violence was occasioned by the direct involvement of Syria and Iran and by the cooptation of the cartoon issue by extremist Islamist movements in Pakistan and Africa.

The contagion and radicalization associated with the increasingly violent demonstrations in February caused the Muslim governments, the intergovernmental organizations, and the religious authorities that had been responsible for stepping up the diplomatic protests throughout the fall to lose control.

The shifts in momentum brought along another change. Diplomatic protests and resolutions gave way to violent street demonstrations and death threats, some virtual and others real. As the international demonstrations reached a high point in February and March 2006, *Jyllands-Posten*'s computers and telephones were jammed with protests, and Denmark's consular offices were attacked in a number of cities in Islamic countries. Stunned Danes initially rallied behind the government. However, critical voices from the business establishment and the opposition in parliament finally pointed out that Fogh Rasmussen's policies were partly responsible for the crisis.

The escalation of the protests in February coincided with the beginning of the Ashura, when Shiites mark the death of the third imam, Hussein Ibn Ali, the grandson of the Prophet, whom Shiites regard as Muhammad's rightful successor. A demonstration against the cartoons took place in Lebanon, when five hundred thousand people turned out for the Ashura commemoration and heard Sayyed Hassan Nasrallah, Hezbollah's leader, blame George W. Bush and Zionists for the insult to the Prophet committed by the Danes. The procession turned into a demonstration against the cartoons.[2] The link to the "crusader nations"—the term lumps the United States with Israel and Europe as joint enemies of the Muslim *ummah*, or Muslim nation—became a theme for the extremist Shiite and Sunni leaders.

In Pakistan, the Jamaat-i-Islami party started using the cartoons against Pervez Musharraf's ruling coalition as early as November 2005, when the first reports of a fatwa against the Danish cartoonists were made. Allegedly, the Jamaat's youth organization issued a five-hundred-thousand-rupee (about $8,500) bounty for the execution of any of the cartoonists sometime in mid-November. Party leaders later denied the report, but rumors of a bounty kept circulating.[3]

Franchises of Holiday Inn, Kentucky Fried Chicken, Pizza Hut, and McDonald's were torched even though the American government publicly scolded the Danes for failing to respect religious sentiments. In Pakistan's Northwest Territories, a stronghold of Islamic radicals, protests turned against President Pervez Musharraf and the West.

COUNTERPROTESTS AND CONTAINMENT

The street protests in the Muslim world exposed rifts among Danish Muslims as well as internationally. When European Muslim associations took up the cartoon protests, the authors Ayaan Hirsi Ali and Salman Rushdie cheered on the Danes and *Jyllands-Posten*. They and ten others released a "manifesto" comparing Islamism to totalitarianism and called for resistance to multiculturalism that would grant Muslims special consideration on religious grounds.[4] At the same time, organizations focused on obtaining civil recognition and minority rights for Muslims in Europe criticized the cartoons' Islamophobic derision of Muslims and their faith. Hizb ut-Tahrir and other extremist Islamists in London seeking the new caliphate joined the sheikhs in Pakistan in calling for the cartoonists' beheading. In Denmark thousands of Muslims protested against both the imam coalitions' attempt to speak for them and the cartoons.

Toward the end of January 2006, Prime Minister Fogh Rasmussen changed course and tried to contain the conflict. In an interview on the satellite news channel Al Arabiya, he explained that "the Danish people had no intention of offending Muslims" and condemned "every expression and act that offend people's religious feelings."[5] The same statement might have been made back in October with no harm to Danish pride or values. Yet emotions still ran high in Denmark over the question of an apology. When Muslim leaders and diplomats quickly expressed satisfaction with Rasmussen's "apology," back home the prime minster denied that he had apologized.

Meanwhile, Muslim diplomats and governments sought to contain the anti-Western clerics and parties and further their own agendas by involving intergovernmental organizations and appealing to universal human rights.

At the peak of the crisis, in February 2006, Javier Solana, the foreign policy coordinator for the European Union, undertook a weeklong trip to discuss the cartoons and interreligious dialogue in meetings with governments of Muslim countries. The agenda was set at a meeting in Doha, Qatar, on February 26, 2006, where Kofi Annan, secretary-general of the United Nations, compared the cartoons and the Danish editors to Islamic extremists and asked, "How effective are our voices of moderation and reconciliation, when it comes to countering narratives of hatred and mistrust?" It was a sad truth that "incidents like the caricatures of the Prophet, or a death threat to the artist who drew it, make far more impact on the popular imagination than pious statements by foreign ministers and secretaries-general."[6] The occasion for the meeting was a second preparatory meeting of a new UN agency, The Alliance of Civilizations. The idea for the strangely named agency, a joint Spanish-Turkish initiative, predated the cartoons, but the cartoons became the alliance's first major issue. (Jorge Sampaio, former president of Portugal, was appointed as the first high representative of the agency in April 2007.)

In the end, few intergovernmental organizations were left untouched by the cartoon crisis and escaped having to make statements or pass resolutions. Ömer Orhun, a Turkish diplomat from the Organization for Security and Co-operation in Europe, who was engaged in shuttle diplomacy related to the cartoons for about eight months, expressed frustration and disbelief over the escalation of the conflict, when I asked him about the experience. "Those silly things!" he exclaimed, "I spent so much time on them and for what?"[7]

A NEW SOCIAL MOVEMENT?

Social movements are conventionally defined by social scientists as leaderless expressions of collective claims either against governments or elites that are perceived to be repressive or against unfair social conditions (shortages or reduced living circumstances, for example) that require political change or redress. Social movements are also characterized by rapid growth, the involvement of both old and new political actors, and the use of new technologies or repertoires of protests and dissemination of information.[8]

The Muslim activists in Denmark who started the action committee against the cartoons faithfully copied tactics familiar to Danish action committees: writing letters to the press, using community groups to build a network for recruitment to demonstrations, staging sleep-ins and raising consciousness about the injustice done to Muslims by sending speakers to Friday prayers at mosques. The demonstrators addressed themselves to the Danish government and called for a public policy response.

And yet this was also a very different kind of political activism, because it was quickly internationalized. The Danish activists at the center of the protests came from four mosques known as centers of theological orthodoxy and had personal ties to extremism. (Their political biographies are discussed in chapter 4.) They appealed for support to foreign governments and broadcast their cause on the Internet. Several members of the group had contacts in the Middle East that they used to create leverage against the Danish government and to get on Al Jazeera, the international news network.[9]

The language of protest was also foreign to Danish and European ears: some of the clerics were quite literally more comfortable speaking Arabic than Danish. But their objectives were also novel. This was not a campaign against the capitalist exploitation of natural resources or other issues recognizable within the normal European politics of left versus right.[10] Demands were made in the name of the ummah, or community of believers, and in defense of the Prophet Muhammad, God's messenger. The most frequently used acronym was PBUH (Peace Be Upon Him), the traditional blessing that Muslims append to the mentioning of the Prophet's name following a Koranic injunction to shower blessings on the Prophet, rather than the more familiar acronyms from the lexicon of Marxist abbreviations to which Scandinavians are accustomed.

The unfamiliarity of the claims and the language used to justify them was one reason that the cartoon crisis triggered anxiety in a public and a media already conditioned to look with suspicion on the presence of a substantial number of Muslims in Europe's traditionally Christian societies.[11] Many people found it difficult to distinguish clearly between the clerics' demands for respect and recognition of their religious norms and revolutionary demands for Islamic rule.

There were hints of violence from the start. Four days after the publication, the police arrested a seventeen-year-old local youth for making a death threat against one of the cartoonists. The young man's mother called the police. Another seventeen-year-old local youth was arrested for the same reason two weeks later, and the police assigned security details to the cartoonists and put two of them in safe houses.

The mosque activists' decision to align themselves with the Muslim government and intergovernmental organization also proved controversial among Danish Muslims, who, though for the most part agreed on the substance of the protests and perceived the cartoons as another insult in a long-running campaign against Muslims in Denmark, also strongly opposed the activists' goals and strategies. The idea that Muslim countries have a role to play in Danish domestic Muslim affairs is anathema to a population of immigrants who regard their exclusion from Danish society as their primary problem and a substantial number of whom are refugees from persecution in those very states.

The cartoon protests, however, were also from the start a matter of international relations. For the first six months of the cycle the actors were primarily diplomats and government officials. Popular mobilization followed rather than preceded the involvement of governments and diplomats. We have to stretch our understanding of the nature of a "social movement" considerably to consider the coordinated actions of state actors—diplomats, religious authorities, parliaments, and foreign ministers—as an example. The global scale of the protests obscured that the number of people involved in direct popular protests was limited in most countries, even in Denmark. In fact, only in appearances did the cartoon protests resemble a social movement.

In one respect, at least, a hypothesis associated with social movement theory holds. Sociologists have found that protest movements often introduce new repertoires—or styles—of protest, which subsequently become "mainstreamed" as innovations in standard political activism. The cartoon controversy introduced cell phones and the Internet as new means of global political mobilization, communication, and even the deployment of virtual violence, which turns out to be difficult to distinguish from actual violence when you are the recipient of an emailed death threat. Chat rooms, text messaging, and the Internet proved an unmanageable source of political mobilization and rapid radicalization. But that, too, turned out to involve a mix of new repertoires with time-honed ones rather than a shift to a completely new paradigm of global protests. The largest demonstration in the Middle East was organized by Hezbollah on the day of the Ashura. It is a religious *cum* political holiday when everyone —families, young and old, men and women—traditionally march in a procession in a well-established manifestation of Hezbollah's strength.

The use of new communication technologies nonetheless also created unanticipated possibilities and unusual alliances. On February 3, 2006, a Friday, the cell phones of Muslims across Europe and in the Middle East rang to report that the Danes planned to burn the Koran the next day in Copenhagen. A small Danish neo-Nazi organization had planned the event and broadcast it on far-right web sites with limited traffic. Sheikh Mahmoud Fouad Albarazi, one of the imams from the Danish mosque coalition, tearfully announced on Al Jazeera that "the Danes will burn the Koran." News of the Danes' intended sacrilege spread like wildfire through Europe and the Middle East through the organized use of a "viral" campaign using text messaging and the Internet. The police prevented the bonfire of the Koran, but the reports inflamed demonstrations in far-flung places. The campaign may well have been a first example of the international usage of "flash mob" techniques to encourage civil disorder and violence. The probability that Muslim and neofascist extremists acted in concert—relying on what may be described as implicit coordination—makes it even more disquieting. Twitter and Facebook, the now ubiquitous web-based networking platforms available to the Iranian protesters in June 2009, were not yet available across the Muslim world in February 2006.

DESCENT INTO EXTREMISM

The street demonstrations ebbed in March and early April 2005. The conflict then entered a new stage, heralded by Al-Qaeda's belated entry into the fray. On March 5, 2005, Al-Qaeda's second-in-command, Ayman al-Zawahiri, issued the group's first statement on the cartoons. The jihadi cooptation of the protests marked a significant shift, ratcheting up the radicalization of the protests. Al-Qaeda now regularly invokes the cartoons to illustrate that the West is sinful and that its so-called democracies violate the sacred. In a message released in March 2008, on the fifth anniversary of the invasion of Iraq, Osama bin Laden singled out the cartoons as part of a "new crusade" launched by Pope Benedict and threatened reprisals against Europeans.[12] On June 2, 2008, a car bomb exploded outside the Danish embassy in Islamabad, Pakistan. The next day Al-Qaeda claimed responsibility for the bombing and described it as a revenge for the "insulting drawings."[13]

Danish newspapers treated the June 2008 bombing as another case of Muslims victimizing Danes. In Pakistan, meanwhile, the car bomb was interpreted as a message from the jihadis to the Pakistani government that they will kill fellow Pakistanis on any pretext to get their way.[14] Two years and eight months separated the publication of the cartoons and the detonation of that car bomb in Islamabad.

The embassy bombing killed eight people and injured twenty-four. All were Muslim. One victim was a Danish citizen of Pakistani origin. Afterward Al-Qaeda issued a press release about the martyrdom of a "brave hero" who carried out God's punishment: "This should serve as a warning to the infidel countries, in terms of crimes against the Prophet Muhammad, peace be with him. They must immediately apologize, otherwise this will only be the first step in the fight. We congratulate the Islamic nation with this successful strike against the enemies of Allah, the staff at the Danish Embassy. This operation also contributes to the crucial role of Pakistani mujahideen, who participated in the preparation of this operation."[15]

The Pakistani freedom fighters included three fifteen-year-olds who were later arrested for the attack. In an interview with a Pakistani television journalist, Al-Qaeda's "number three," Abu Mustafa al-Yazid, again brought up the cartoons, identified the bomber as a Saudi Arabian "martyr," and bragged that no Muslims had been killed in the attack. This was untrue, and in fact since the 9/11 attacks and the Madrid train bombings on March 11, 2003, 95 percent of Al-Qaeda's victims have been Muslims.[16]

The cartoons were in fact incidental to the action. The Islamabad car bombing was part of a new wave of such attacks, and it was the second time in 2008 that Al-Qaeda had targeted foreigners in the Pakistani capital. Nor was it the first time that Scandinavians had been the victims of terrorist attacks. In January 2008 the Taliban attacked a hotel in Kabul where a Norwegian delegation was staying, ostensibly in order to discourage Norway's military involvement in Afghanistan.

Al-Qaeda's rhetoric has found a mirror image in Europe. Radical right-wing groups denounce the "Islamicization" of Europe and claim that the reaction to the cartoons demonstrates that Muslims cannot fit in. Many people believe that the embassy bombing only proves what the

Danish cartoonist who drew the prophet with a bomb in his turban was saying. But if we ignore Al-Qaeda's rhetoric regarding the "crusader nations," there is nothing exceptional or particularly "Islamic" about the descent into terrorism. The 1968 European social movements—students, feminists, ecologists—also spawned both terrorists and a new generation of parties and political leaders. The Italian protest movements between 1968 and 1972 described by Sidney Tarrow in his now-classic discussion of the mobilization cycles of political protest movement likewise devolved into violent extremism and terrorism.[17] A difference is that it is not yet clear if the cartoon conflict produced any new political actors. Muslims across the world were annoyed, even angry, but most people took in the news from the comfort of their living rooms. The issue was new, but the main actors were already present on the global political scene.

The comparison between the cartoon conflict and protest movements born out of political alienation or repression does not hold. Social movements usually are born out of social grievances, and their political energy derives from repression or blocked avenues for mediation and a shared focus on gaining redress from states. The Danish cartoons triggered an emotional grievance. But they were foils for the deliberate manipulation of political actors—both national and transnational, state actors and nonstate actors—who were already engaged in battle. The demands for redress—an apology from the Danes or a severing of all ties with the West—were symbolic and not intended to alleviate social hardship. The grievance was about feelings and the demands for redress focused on restoration through symbolic action.

THE INTERNATIONAL MEDIA MOVEMENT

Media coverage played a significant role in the escalation of the conflict. Editors perceived that they were faced with an existential choice: to reprint or not to reprint the cartoons. On January 10, 2006, the cartoons were reprinted in a small Norwegian magazine, *Magazinet*. Oddly, it was an important milestone in the escalation of the conflict. "We saw it [*Magazinet*'s reprinting] as the beginning of a campaign against us," said Ufuk Gökçen, the special adviser to the OIC's secretary-general, Ekmeleddin İhsanoğlu.[18] *Magazinet* was a conservative Christian paper with a circulation of about five thousand. Norway's larger papers had reprinted some of the cartoons months earlier, in October, as part of their generally negative news coverage of events in Denmark.

But in fact there was no campaign, in the sense of a coordinated movement with a joint leadership, although editors certainly found it difficult to locate the line between reporting the news and making news. The reprinting movement got under way in February 2006 after the large demonstrations in the Middle East and reports about a spreading trade boycott against Danish goods, but there were early birds who printed the cartoons right away and received little notice. One of the first papers to republish a cartoon was an Egyptian newspaper, *Al-Fagr,* on October 17, 2005, three months before most western European papers declared their solidarity. The issue was confiscated from the newsstands and months later it was also removed from the paper's web site, but bloggers scanned the pages with cartoons, and they are still available on the Internet.[19] Its editor has not been prosecuted. The Moroccan daily *Al-Nahar Al-Maghribiyya* reprinted two cartoons shortly after they were published by *Jyllands-Posten* but apparently attracted little attention. In Bosnia-Herzegovina a newsweekly also reprinted the cartoons in November 2005. The Dutch weekly *Elsevier* and newspaper *De Volkskrant* also reprinted all twelve cartoons in October. They reprinted them a second time when all the other newspapers across Europe got involved.

Newspapers that did reprint the cartoons generally used only Westergaard's caricature of the Prophet with the bomb in the turban, which everyone seemed to understand, although the newspapers sometimes obscured the picture in one way or another. The newspapers also almost invariably proclaimed that publication of the cartoon or cartoons was a statement of solidarity with the Danes or a stand for freedom of the press.

Was there a real threat of censorship? Many Europeans took it for granted that newspapers should be free to publish satirical drawings of anything they pleased. And the menaces against *Jyllands-Posten* should not be understated. The Danes were threatened with a trade boycott, and the presence of credible death threats against some of the cartoonists—and a couple of bomb threats against the newspaper's offices—were enough to frighten everybody. On the other hand, the public was divided and did not unconditionally support the argument that the freedom to mock and insult religious people is part of the European canon of basic values. And if the intended message was to tell Muslims to back off, the message they received was a different one: Europeans have no respect for Muslims.

Journalists and editors in Europe latched on to a shared interpretation of what was going on—Islamic states were trying to censor what Europeans can say and write—and acted in concert based on this shared perception. Journalists and editors believed that they were making a stand against censorship. Some editors concluded that what happened to the Danish paper could happen to any paper. The Musketeers' motto, "One for all, and all for one," suddenly became an operational editorial principle. Others worried that they would be accused of political correctness if they did not themselves republish the cartoons. However, the torrent of republication was interpreted differently by European editors and many Muslim observers. Muslims read the newspapers' decision to reprint the by-now-ubiquitous cartoons as a coordinated campaign of denigration.

Each time the cartoons were reprinted they set off a domestic chain-reaction of protests and counterprotests. This had the curious effect of making the Danish cartoons the object of localized contests over free speech norms and respect for religious values. Since European—and American—traditions and legal frameworks vary widely on these issues, distinct cross-national differences emerged in how the papers, and the governments and courts, reacted to the cartoons. Where national laws prohibit blasphemy and the feelings of Christians are generally recognized, as has been the case in Denmark, Muslim associations would try to use blasphemy laws to drive home their point about Muslims' right to respect. Where laws favored antidiscrimination norms, as in Britain, where the concept of Islamophobia is well established, Muslim associations complained about racialism. And sometimes both charges were made. In the United States, the First Amendment provides broader constitutional protection of speech than anywhere in Europe, but norms restraining the media's treatment of minority groups and religion made the newspapers reluctant to reprint the cartoons.

During two weeks in February, the cartoons were reprinted across the world. Russian, African, Latin American, and Asian and Australian papers, even the *Times* of India, reprinted the cartoons. Counts vary as to how many newspapers reprinted the cartoons, and estimates are even more difficult to obtain beyond the print media. A Danish web site that covers journalism news found that by the end of February 2006 one or more of the cartoons had been reprinted in at least 143 newspapers in fifty-six countries.[20]

The *Editor's Weblog*, an online publication of the World Editor's Forum, published a media analysis on February 6, 2006, that is still available online.[21] It found that almost 2 percent of the world's news outlets reproduced the cartoons. Among them were twelve or more papers, magazines, or news stations in Arab and North African Muslim countries. It noted that the British and American media stood apart by not reprinting the cartoons: "Only three regional newspapers of more than 1,400 newspapers in the States and zero newspapers but a student daily in the UK [took] the risk."

In the United States, the *Philadelphia Inquirer* published Kurt Westergaard's drawing of the man with the bomb in the turban, but the *New York Times* and the *Boston Globe* explained that they would not publish the cartoons because they were a provocation and added nothing constructive to public debate. The *New York Sun,* a paper known for its strongly pro-Zionist views, published two of the drawings and was criticized by a State Department spokesman, Justin Higgins, for inciting ethnic hatred.[22] The major American television networks announced that they would not show the cartoons, although CNN showed the pages of the newspapers that had published the cartoons. CBS's Bob Simon went to Copenhagen to film a segment for *60 Minutes* and concluded that "the lines between fantasy and reality aren't sharply defined around Denmark."[23] The Associated Press declined to distribute the cartoons to U.S. subscribers. By my count five regional newspapers and some twenty student newspapers and street publications republished the cartoons. And, as mentioned earlier, *Harper's* magazine published the cartoons with an essay by Art Spiegelman.

The British media overall did refrain from joining the reprint movement. The *Economist* called the cartoons a "schoolboy prank" and cited former Danish foreign minister Uffe Ellemann-Jensen as saying that the Danes suffered from the mistaken belief that free speech meant you were obligated to say anything you thought.[24] But the BBC did broadcast pictures of the cartoons. Proclaiming that the network would show only "responsible glimpses" of the offending material, the BBC nonetheless became one of the most important sources of misinformation about the cartoons.[25] Two BBC news programs covered the sacking of the editor at *France Soir* and showed the newspaper's page with the cartoon on February 2. The BBC also ran a news clip of one of the Danish imams holding a picture and presented it as one of the cartoons as part of a story about the imams' visit to Cairo. Yet the picture the imam was holding was not a drawing but a photo downloaded from the Internet of a man wearing a pig snout, which the Danish imams had added to their documentary material even though no Danish paper had ever printed this image. The BBC later apologized for both broadcasts.

Left-wing and right-wing papers were equally likely to republish the cartoons. The important difference was instead regional: papers from Germany, the Netherlands, Italy, and France were particularly inclined to declare solidarity with *Jyllands-Posten,* whereas American and British editors hesitated and were more likely to decide that the cartoons had crossed the line of decent criticism. Many of the European papers used the occasion to condemn Muslims' political influence in their home countries.

A French satirical magazine, *Charlie Hebdo,* published all the cartoons on February 8, 2006, but with a different caricature on the cover. *France Soir,* a conservative paper, also reprinted the cartoons, with the result that the paper's owner dismissed Jacques Lefranc, the editor. (Lefranc was rehired the next day when the employees at *France Soir* protested.) *Le Monde* equivocated, reproducing one drawing that had appeared in another French newspaper while expressing distaste for the exercise. Another French paper, *Liberation,* reproduced two cartoons in solidarity with the editor at *France Soir* and stressed that the reason for publishing them was to protest the dismissal of Lefranc.

German publications were sympathetic to *Jyllands-Posten's* troubles, but they also voiced criticism of how Denmark treats its Muslim minority. Josef Joffe, the publisher and editor-in-chief of Germany's *Die Zeit,* an intellectual weekly, defended the Danes but then also published several critical stories about the government's diplomatic ineptitude and the tone of Danish debates. The German *Tageszeitung* criticized the xenophobic tone of Danish public debates while also condemning censorship. The *Frankfurter Allgemeine* and *Süddeutsche Zeitung* characterized *Jyllands-Posten's* actions as a provocation and distanced themselves from the angry Danes. In February, more Dutch papers republished the cartoons: *De Telegraaf, Trouw, Het Parool,* and *NRC Handelsblad* all carried selections. Among Europe's other large papers, the Italian *Corriere della Sera* and the Spanish *El Mondo* and *El País* also carried partial reprints of the cartoons.

Stories generated stories as the global media started to cover itself. To publish or not to publish became the story, but the editors who published the cartoons often also condemned them. The editors generally said the same thing: The cartoons were offensive—so therefore we show just a little bit of them—but the Muslim countries should not try to interfere with what we print. A cynic might argue that a bandwagon effect explains much of the solidarity. The newspapers were fearful both of Muslim reactions and of accusations of appeasement, and in consequence they rarely printed the cartoons in full. Often they were published under the guise of covering the news and reprinted only partially or obscured by pixilation.

During the phase of international protests, newspapers in Arab and other Muslim countries also reprinted the cartoons.[26] In these countries the act involved a risk unparalleled elsewhere. The authorities sometimes ignored the provocation and at other times responded harshly. Middle Eastern papers that printed the cartoons in 2005 were generally spared legal action. This changed after the cartoons became a matter of international conflict. In Algeria, three weekly newsmagazines reprinted the cartoons in February 2006.[27] Two of the magazines are regarded as Islamist and presumably reprinted the cartoons to ensure that their readers were suitably enraged. The editors of all three publications were imprisoned. Two satellite television stations, Canal Algerie and A3, showed the cartoons for a few seconds during coverage of events at *France Soir*. The journalists were fired.

In Jordan, Amman's newspaper *Al-Shihan* reprinted three cartoons, including the one featuring the bomb in the turban; the editor in chief, Jihad Momani, was arrested. Another Jordanian newspaper, *El Mehwar*, also reprinted the cartoons. *Le Journal Hebdomadaire*, a French-language Moroccan weekly, republished a photograph from the AFP (an international wire service) showing the page with the cartoons as they were printed by *Jyllands-Posten* in a practically unreadable format. Three Yemeni newsmagazines reprinted the cartoons.[28]

Publication of the liberal Saudi Arabian newspaper *Shams* was suspended for two weeks by the Ministry of Information and Culture on February 20, and the paper was charged with "committing the journalistic stupidity of reprinting the blasphemous cartoons, which have infuriated the Muslims all over the world." It is difficult to ascertain why *Shams* printed the cartoons. Its editors claim that the paper reprinted the cartoons to mobilize the campaign in Saudi Arabia against Denmark, but the claim was probably a smokescreen intended to ward off the censors. The suspension took place three weeks after *Shams* published the cartoons accompanied by a clerical opinion, or fatwa, stating that it was "acceptable to print information offensive to Muslims if it helps to acquaint them with an issue." *Shams* was launched in 2005 by the publisher of the *Al-Hayat Arabic Daily,* an Arabic-language newspaper published in London and owned by a Saudi prince named Khaled bin Sultan.[29]

Outside the Arab and Islamic world, the courts intervened only in Russia and in South Africa. The South African High Court issued a pre-emptive order barring newspapers from printing the cartoons after receiving a complaint from an Islamic religious law council, Jamiatul Ulama.[30] The council is connected to the conservative Deobandi movement in Islam and is sometimes described as related to the ultrafundamentalist movement, the Tabligh.

Carsten Juste and Flemming Rose followed the republication movement closely and were pleased with it, but few editors endorsed the ideas that motivated *Jyllands-Posten's* original editorial. Most commentary on the cartoons ignored the mixed editorial content by turning them into a symbol of a simple dichotomy between free speech and Muslim fundamentalism. Rose expressed disappointment with his own profession when I interviewed him. Journalists cared too little about getting the facts right. Rose's sympathies were with the Middle Eastern papers, where the editors took great risks to make a stand for free speech.

A FAILURE OF DIPLOMACY

In early February 2006 the OIC and the Egyptian government declared an end to the conflict over the cartoons. *Jyllands-Posten* and the Danish prime minister had apologized, and Muslims were behaving badly in the streets, they said. The time had come to hand the matter over to the United Nations.

However, the controversy continued to be fueled through the Internet and by Iran and extremist Sunni groups stretching from the Maghreb to the Philippines. In February and March 2006, death threats rolled by the thousands across Denmark in the form of chain letters and spam, clogging up web sites and computers with little or no connection to *Jyllands-Posten* or the Danish government, although the newspaper and the government were also hit hard. The flood of email threats to the editors and the cartoonists thinned out by late spring 2006, but occasionally events related to the cartoons caused new flare-ups. By summer 2006, Danish diplomatic offices started to report that the crisis was over.

The cartoons linger as a nuisance in East-West relations. The diplomatic agenda for combating Islamophobia has left the European governments uncomfortably exposed to charges of discrimination. The American press was disinclined to take up *Jyllands-Posten*'s cause, and the cartoons became primarily a European liability. Yet the United States did not escape becoming ensnared in the controversy. The charge of anti-Muslim bias in Western media was a slingshot at the Bush presidency's "Freedom Agenda" for promoting democracy in the Middle East, and in Egypt in particular.

The cartoons live on in a deadlocked debate over the balance between free speech, civility, and the propriety and reach of blasphemy laws. On March 27, 2008, the UN Human Rights Council adopted a resolution urging countries to take action against the defamation of religion and particularly "attempts to identify Islam with terrorism, violence and hu-man rights violations." The vote on the resolution saw China and Russia side with the representations of Islamic countries arrayed against Canada and the European representatives. (The United States is not a member of the council.) Two months later, a joint meeting of the World Association of Newspapers and World Editors Forum condemned the Human Rights Council's efforts to suppress free speech in the name of religion. As this book goes to print, a new administration in Washington, DC, has rejoined the Human Rights Council but is debating participation in Durban II, an upcoming meeting in Geneva, Switzerland, to follow up on the World Conference against Racism, Racial Discrimination, Xenophobia and Re-lated Intolerance held in Durban, South Africa, in 2001. The proposed declaration for the Geneva meeting included a proposal put forward by the OIC to make "defamation of religion" a human rights violation.

The existing framework for international representation and conflict resolution is intergovernmental and, in the case of the United Nations, contingent on the consent of member states. But the Danish government refused to participate in mediation. European governments are disin-clined to hand over the representation of minorities to nonstate actors and even more so to other states. The protesters, however, paid little attention to national boundaries. They created instant epistemological transna-tional communities and communicated by means of digital representation and other unmediated channels of communication outside governmental control.

Israel is one of the few states to have successfully made claims to represent expatriate coreligionists. Dr. Aly El Samman, a member of the Supreme Council of the Egyptian religious authorities and the president of its interreligious dialogue council, cautioned Muslims during the crisis that it took a long time for Jewish communities in Europe to obtain legal protection against anti-Semitism.[31] He could have added that it took the ultimate catastrophe, the Holocaust. Israel was created as a homeland for Jewish refugees *from* Europe. European Muslims are emigrants from Muslim countries, and many are refugees, too, but *to* Europe. The Muslim countries hardly have a moral claim to represent Europe's Muslims. The comparison between Muslims and Jews in Europe is frequently made, but it does not always sustain the argument the speakers hope to make.

Diplomatic mediation also failed for another reason. No mechanism exists for the negotiation of matters of global civility and respect for the feelings of others, beyond the established framework for the adjudication of human rights. One outcome of the conflict was that the offense of the cartoons became framed as a violation of human rights, but it was not a comfortable fit.

The diplomats—Danish diplomats, those from the United Nations and other human rights organizations, and those from Islamic countries and pan-Islamic associations—failed to respond appropriately because they were tied down by diplomatic rules and allegiances to the agendas of governments crippled by domestic political conflicts. In the late phases of the protests, the diplomats were equally powerless to stop protests from feeding on protests. Danish diplomats were handicapped by the expression of angry anti-Muslim sentiments in Denmark itself. Muslim diplomats had to operate against the background of antigovernment riots at home.

The "clash of civilization" paradigm so dominates many people's thinking—including that of officials—that even though Muslim countries and Europe and the United States are allies in the fight against terrorism and extremism, the perception is that an undeclared war is being waged between them.

THE AFTERMATH

The cartoons became a touchstone, a point of reference for a wide range of statements that were seen as denigrating Islam. Pope Benedict's lecture on September 12, 2006, at the University of Regensburg, in which he quoted a fourteenth-century Byzantine emperor who described Islam as a "a faith spread by the sword," was linked to the cartoons by both the European media and by offended Muslims. The words were not the pope's own description of the nature of Islam, but Muslims perceived that the pope shared the emperor's sentiment. The speech revived Roman Catholic doctrine that holds all other faiths to be "false faiths," and Jews had reason to be offended as well.[32] Protestants might have been offended, too, if they cared enough to take umbrage.

The cartoons became a standard reference for real and perceived conflict over what you "can say" about Muslims. A Berlin opera house's decision to cancel a restaging of Mozart's opera *Idomeneo* in December 2006 because the severed heads of Jesus Christ, Buddha, Moses, and Muhammad were to be used as props was also classified as a cartoon incident.[33] The cancellation was preemptive. No protests or threats had been issued against the performance. The opera was placed back on the calendar after Berlin's Muslim associations protested the cancellation, which they described as groundless. Nonetheless, Muslims are still blamed for the management's decision. A Swedish artist's mass production of plywood cutouts of "Muhammad as a vagrant dog" was a deliberate copycat action and intended as a provocation, which is also how the Swedish government treated it. And the incarceration of an English teacher, Gillian Gibbon, in Sudan on charges of blasphemy because she allowed her kindergarten class to name a teddy bear "Muhammad" was the act of ambitious ultrareligious jurists.

In March 2008, Geert Wilders, a Dutch parliamentarian, released a much-hyped sixteen-minute short film that compared the Koran to Hitler's *Mein Kampf.* Wilders also embraced the Danish cartoonists' cause and proclaimed months before the anticipated premiere that he intended to insult Muslims because learning to accept insults is part of the acclimatization process needed to turn Muslims into proper Dutchmen and women. The pre-release publicity backfired. The Dutch government did everything the Danes had not done. It apologized in advance and in principle, but avoided speaking about specifics. If the film violated Dutch laws against racialist speech, the Dutch prime minister announced, Wilders would be subject to an investigation and possibly brought up on charges. Dutch amateurs flooded YouTube with spoofs of his peculiar self-presentation.[34]

After all this, Wilders was unable to find a Dutch broadcaster for his film. The public networks turned it down, and although a private network agreed to take it on, it asked that Wilders pay for security expenses in connection with the film's release. This Wilders rejected, claiming a lack of funds. In the end, the film was released on a London-based Internet site. The Pakistani government hired a Malaysian company to close down Internet access in Pakistan to YouTube, where Wilders was expected to post his film, and the company accidentally shut down access to the entire Internet for clients across the Middle East and South Asia. Weeks later Wilders used another provider to post his film, and he appeared disappointed when it failed to produce the demonstrations or international protest he anticipated.[35]

The Danes who were responsible for the cartoons disassociated themselves from Wilders. *Jyllands-Posten* published ambiguous stories about him, portraying him at times as a freedom fighter and then as a xenophobic extremist. To Wilders's disappointment, Fogh Rasmussen refused to meet with him. And Kurt Westergaard, the artist responsible for the iconic cartoon of Muhammad as a mad Muslim with a bomb in his turban, successfully sued Wilders for copyright infringement and forced the film off the Internet until his cartoon was removed. In the end, the Dutch public prosecutor found that Wilders had not broken the law, and Wilders is reported to be making a second movie.

FROM DEATH THREATS TO FARCE

The extremist rivulets of protest roll on, but the cartoons have segued into the book of anti-Western slogans used by Jamaat-i-Islami and Al-Qaeda and its aligned organizations. A source in the Danish police told me that of the many thousands of death threats received in Denmark, about two hundred were regarded as credible and investigated. About a dozen plots were graded as serious. What constitutes a credible plot when threats arrive by email and fax? At the peak of the crisis the police increased surveillance at the airport in Copenhagen and at Danish borders. But in the end it was local access and specific knowledge about the whereabouts of the putative victim that distinguished a credible threat from spam.

The most serious threat to Flemming Rose, Carsten Juste, and the cartoonists came from where it all started: their backyard. In June 2008, Rose visited an imprisoned twenty-eight-year-old man of Tunisian origin known as K. S. who had been arrested in the plot to kill Westergaard. The same man had reportedly also discussed targeting Rose. He was friendly with Raed Hlayhel, the radical cleric from Århus, who had issued a call for retribution against *Jyllands-Posten* during a Friday sermon in the spring of 2006 and promised martyrdom to those who carried out Allah's revenge. K. S. had attended these prayers and had apparently heeded the call. Rose, sitting across from the man who reportedly wanted to murder him, now prodded K. S. to tell him what was on his mind:

ROSE: What would you say to [Kurt] Westergaard if he sat here instead of me?

K.S.: I'd say that I am sorry things have turned out this way and that his and my lives have become ruined. Perhaps I would also tell him to read about the Prophet. Many people in the West have throughout history had a different picture of the Prophet [from the one Westergaard drew].[36]

Westergaard had not had enough of the controversy. In December 2008 he and a conservative commentator, Lars Hedegaard, published an illustrated book with essays mocking Islam, Muslims, and anybody perceived as excessively friendly to Muslims. Web sites friendly with Al-Qaeda predictably posted vague threats. Hedegaard was fired from his newspaper but was offered a column in *Jyllands-Posten*. "As long as what he writes is within the law and the boundaries of good taste, he can write what he wants," said the editor. Danes, however, have had enough. Critics panned the book. In April 2009, Westergaard and Hedegaard started selling poster-sized reproductions of the cartoon to raise money for an association they started to promote free speech.

MAKING SENSE OF THE CARTOON PROTESTS

Europeans have for about a decade obsessively debated the dangers of "Islamicization." Terrorism, socioeconomic exclusion, and the self-marginalization of young Muslims into radical countercultures are serious issues. They are also complex issues. The political climate is difficult. Public opinion surveys have clearly shown that Muslims are not generally inclined to radical Islamist politics but a minority is, while the general population holds negative views about Muslims. Mistaken policies, intergenerational conflict between foreign-born parents and native-born descendants, political manipulation of issues, and many other factors that have little to do with Islam are among the causes of Europe's problems with Muslims.

Xenophobic and racialist theories are diffused into mainstream debates. Europe's Muslim immigrants are compared to occupiers. Conspiracy theories about the political agendas of Muslims and Islam's inherent enmity to European values are treated as established truths. Popular books compare Muslims to Nazis. An American, Bruce Bawer, claims Europe is having "a Weimar moment."[37] A German writer, Henryk Broder, predicts the collapse of European democracy under the weight of Muslim orthodoxy and Europeans' cowardly appeasement.[38]

The novelist Martin Amis claims that Islam is stuck in the medieval age and that Muslims will bring back the Inquisition. He contributes to the understanding of the Muslim mindset by writing poetically about the Nietzschean beauty of Islam's "cult of death."[39] In The God Delusion Richard Dawkins also compares Islam to medieval Christianity and asserts the inherent incongruity between Islamic doctrine and secular democracy. The reaction to the cartoons, Dawkins writes, shows the problem with Islam. Christopher Hitchens warns that the Vatican and the Inquisition will ride back into power on the coattails of the black-robed imams to control sex and women.[40]

Demographic fearmongering is part of the dehumanizing theories about Muslims. A popular American version is the "Eurabia" theory, which marries fears of Muslims' political intentions to parallel accounts of European's weakened "will" to reproduce and Muslim women's fertility rates.[41] One widely reported factoid cited in support of this theory is that by 2025 every third child in Europe will be born to a Muslim family and that by midcentury Europe will be "majority Muslim."

Western Europe's fifteen million Muslims are not a coherent political bloc. Muslims, like other immigrants, often cannot vote because they are not citizens and their children have poor prospects of becoming citizens.

They are disqualified from citizenship because they are too poor or for other bureaucratic reasons. (Naturalization rules generally preclude awarding citizenship to people who do not show "attachment" to national norms, cannot economically support themselves and their dependent family members, or live in social housing.) The threat of a demographic takeover is based on population predictions that assume there are currently fifty million Muslims in Europe. Mark Steyn, a widely quoted source for the fallacious numbers, also mistakenly assumes that immigrants maintain fertility at the rates prevalent in their countries of origin.[42] For example, his prediction assumes that a Somali-origin woman in western Europe will continue to have the 6.68 children that women in Somalia bear on average.

The reports of the Muslim population bomb are fantasy.[43] It is also false, as is sometimes claimed, that the statistics are distorted because illegal immigrants are not counted, perhaps, it is implied, because public statistical agencies conspire to hide the truth. Illegal immigrants are a small group and mostly do not include families. Native-born descendants of immigrants—including Muslim women—are increasingly choosing the two-child family. This means that the median fertility rate among European Muslims is presently above the European mean but is converging with the European norm.

Native-born Europeans are having more babies while immigrants are having fewer. Much of the decline in past decades is due to women postponing childbirth, which means that eventually the fertility "gap" will close again. The contribution of marginally above-average fertility rates among Muslims to the national averages is in any case slight because Muslims nowhere constitute more than between 2 and 6 percent of the overall population.[44] Muslims are a small minority in Europe, which means that the higher-than-average fertility rates of Muslims have a negligible impact on the national averages. The Netherlands provides the most recently updated figures, which show total fertility rates in 2005 of 2.9 children for Moroccan immigrants, 1.9 for Dutch residents of Turkish origin, and a national average of 1.7 children. The Dutch demographers also discovered that using a survey rather than the older method of inferring the size of immigrant-origin population groups from historical immigration statistics reduced the estimated number of Dutch Muslims from a million to 850,000.[45] Differences in fertility rates are the product of a range of factors, such as the average age of a specific population group and the propensity to marry. Demographers Charles F. Westoff and Thomas Frejka have shown that the propensity to have more children goes hand in hand with strong family values, and for both reasons European Muslims have more children than European non-Muslims. Still, the difference is on average only 15 percent. "Among married women aged 35–44 Muslims have had 2.3 births, Catholics 2.2, and Protestants 2.3," they conclude.[46]

The paranoid scenarios of unrestrained fertility and alien family practices, resistant to factual falsification, are typical of racialist fearmongering. False facts about demographic trends are seamlessly interwoven with cultural stereotypes and religious prejudice to spin tales about the failure of assimilation and Muslim propensities for totalitarian behavior because of their faith. When the Danish People's Party portrays Muslim migration as a threat to Denmark's fundamental identity as a Christian country, and Geert Wilders's film sparks fears of the "Islamicization" of Europe, they combine fantasies of a demographic time bomb and fears for the very survival of Europe.

Olivier Roy and Ian Buruma have written lucid accounts of how the French and the Dutch have reacted to the demand of Muslim immigrants for a place in their societies by asserting essential national values that are in fact recent inventions, born during the anticlerical social liberation movements of the 1970s.[47] Prejudice is always expressed in national dialects, however. In France, critics blend concerns about the suppression of Muslim women with warnings that the republican creed of secularism is endangered by women wearing headscarves. In the Netherlands, the habit of unlimited self-expression was elevated to a civic virtue, and pious immigrants were attacked for putting a social consensus at risk. In Denmark, for largely accidental reasons, corrosive and profane humor became the symbol of essential Danish values that are placed at risk by religious Muslims.

The cartoon controversy has been cited as evidence of nefarious political plots orchestrated by Muslims against Europe. In reality, however, the protests against the cartoons revealed deep fissures in the Muslim countries between secularists, electoral Islamists, and extremists. European Muslims, for their part, generally rejected the role in which they were cast in Cairo or Jeddah, but they also objected that they had the same right to respect and protection against prejudice that everybody else enjoys in European democracies.

When the violence and demonstrations, resolutions and counter-resolutions, flooded the airwaves and television screens in February and March 2006, it looked as if a coordinated global protest movement was under way. But goals varied, and the protest movement was fragmented. The governments of Muslim countries aimed to make symbolic statements and influence international debates about human rights, democracy, and Muslims, in part as a defense against criticisms of affairs in their own backyard and in part because they feared the effects of growing anti-Muslim sentiments in Europe. The radical extremists aimed to destabilize Islamic governments and turned the cartoons against them. The Danish mosque activists wanted to change things in Denmark and shake up Danish Muslims, and they sought international help for that purpose. European Muslim associations and the Muslim Brotherhood pursued legal avenues of redress in order to obtain recognition and promote the rights of Muslims in the context of national politics.

CHAPTER 3

The Diplomatic Protest against the Cartoons

SHORTLY AFTER THE CARTOONS were published, the eleven ambassadors and chargés d'affaires representing Muslim countries in Copenhagen met at a reception to mark the start of Ramadan. They discussed the cartoons and decided to write a joint letter to Prime Minister Anders Fogh Rasmussen to ask for a meeting and to voice their concerns not only about the cartoons but also about statements made about Muslims by the culture minister, Brian Mikkelsen, and by representatives of the Danish Peoples' Party, an ally of the governing party. The Pakistani ambassador was asked to write the letter because the others agreed he had the best command of English. Ten days later, after consultation between the ambassadors and with their home countries, a letter was sent to Fogh Rasmussen (box 2).

At the same time, the Egyptian government started to register its displeasure through all available diplomatic channels. Cairo instructed Egyptian envoys in intergovernmental organizations to make contact with their Danish counterparts to inform them of the government's displeasure. Ambassadors to Muslim countries were told to inform the local governments that Egypt intended to make an issue of the cartoons. At a previously scheduled meeting in Cairo, a delegation from the Danish foreign ministry was told that the Egyptians regarded the cartoons as a serious matter and as constituting an attack on Islam. The Islamic Educational, Scientific and Cultural Organization, based in Rabat, Morocco, issued a statement describing the cartoons as slanderous and offensive to the world's 1.3 billion Muslims. A few months later, ISESCO was the first to call on member states to boycott Danish goods. These diplomatic initiatives occurred within the first two weeks following the publication of the cartoons.

Egypt mobilized the considerable skills of its diplomatic corps, its foreign ministry, and the League of Arab States, headquartered in Cairo. The Arab League was founded in 1945 and today has twenty-two member states from North Africa and the Arabian Peninsula. Its secretary-general since 2001, Amr Moussa, had previously been foreign minister of Egypt for ten years and was widely regarded as the second most powerful politician in Egypt after President Hosni Mubarak. Moussa worked to raise a common diplomatic front together with Ekmeleddin İhsanoğlu, the secretary-general of the Organization of the Islamic Conference. The OIC, headquartered in Jeddah, is a pan-Islamic organization with fifty-seven members. It was founded in 1969 after an arson attack on the Al-Aqsa Mosque in Jerusalem carried out by an Australian evangelical Christian, Michael Dennis Rohan, who claimed divine inspiration. Israel was widely blamed for the attack. The OIC was formed to promote global Islamic unity and the "liberation" of Jerusalem. It has subsequently focused on the promotion of Islamic cultural and economic interests, adding combating Islamophobia to its objectives in recent years.[1] The Arab League and the OIC have overlapping memberships, though Turkey is a member only of the OIC. Turkish diplomats also took their complaints to the Organization for Security and Co-operation in Europe, a security organization spanning Asia, Europe, and North America.

Later it was often asserted that the Danes had no warning of the international reaction and were given no time to prevent a full-blown crisis. This is clearly inaccurate. However, the reasons behind the Egyptian initiative, and the motives for Danish inaction, invite examination. After all, Denmark had significant economic interests in the Middle East. Its industries have benefited from the country's reputation for international honesty and neighborly behavior, and long-term contracts to sell food products ranging from cheese to beer and insulin as well as highly specialized machinery in Middle Eastern markets are a significant source of income. Moreover, the Danish reputation in the field of human rights has won the country influence in international organizations beyond what would be expected from its size. To a small, export-oriented country, international goodwill is money in the bank.[2] The government's insistence that it could not compromise on the issue of freedom of speech had significant costs, although this was not fully appreciated at first. The Egyptians had less at stake. The risks to Egypt's balance sheet were minimal. If Egyptian consumers stopped buying Danish butter, somebody else would eventually step up and meet the demand or Egyptians would stop eating butter. The present chapter deals with Egypt's role and the diplomatic escalation during the first phase of the protests. I shall return to the Danish government's actions—and inaction—in chapter 7.

THE DIPLOMATIC INITIATIVE

The Muslim ambassadors in Copenhagen addressed their letter to Fogh Rasmussen, with a copy to Foreign Minister Per Stig Møller.[3] The letter complained of an "on-going smear campaign in Danish public circles and media against Islam and Muslims." Their main example was "the demeaning caricatures of the Holy Prophet Muhammad (PBUH)," but they also cited comments made by a radio station run by a far-right group and a parliamentarian elected from the Danish People's Party, and by Brian Mikkelsen, the cultural affairs minister in Fogh Rasmussen's cabinet. The government was urged "to take all those responsible to task under [the] law of the land." The ambassadors also requested a meeting with the prime minister. Shortly afterward, the OIC sent a similar letter to the prime minister, charging that the cartoons fitted into a broader campaign against Muslims and Islam. Neither letter requested an apology.

Fogh Rasmussen responded two weeks later by sending identical letters to the ambassadors and the OIC. "The freedom of expression is the very foundation of the Danish democracy," he wrote, adding that the government had no means of influencing the press. The request for a meeting was ignored.[4] The content of his reply was not made public in Denmark until March 2006.

Fogh Rasmussen's response ignored the charge of a quasi-official campaign to denigrate Muslims and focused on *Jyllands-Posten* and the twelve cartoons. As a consequence, Danish newspapers also ignored the broader complaint contained in the ambassadors' letter. To this day Danes assume the protest was all about the cartoons, which in effect it later was. In the view of Carsten Juste, the other incidents mentioned in the diplomats' letters were "window dressing." "It was all about the cartoons all the time," he said when I asked why nobody had responded to the general complaint.[5] Perhaps the prime minister shared this view. He would also

---

Box 2. *Official letter, October 21, 2005, from Prime Minister Anders Fogh Rasmussen to Muslim and Arab ambassadors in response to earlier letter of complaint.*

Your Excellencies

Thank you very much for your letter of 12 October 2005.

The Danish society is based on respect for the freedom of expression, on religious tolerance and on equal standards for all religions. The freedom of expression is the very foundation of the Danish democracy. The freedom of expression has a wide scope and the Danish government has no means of influencing the press. However, Danish legislation prohibits acts or expressions of a blasphemous or discriminatory nature. The offended party may bring such acts or expressions to court, and it is for the courts to decide in individual cases.

I share your view that dialogue between cultures and religions needs to be based on mutual respect and understanding. There is indeed room for increasing mutual understanding between different cultures and religions.

In this regard, I have personally taken the initiative to enter into a dialogue with representatives from the Muslim communities in Denmark.

Furthermore, I would like to see the dialogue between Denmark and the Muslim world strengthened. Indeed, one of the principal objectives of the initiative "Partnership for Progress and Reform", launched by the Danish Government in 2003, is to stimulate the dialogue between Denmark, the EU and countries in North Africa and the Middle East. The initiative explicitly aims to engage a broad spectrum of Danish institutions and organisations in partnerships with their sister organisations in the Arab world and Iran. The Partnership will in this way nurture institutional and personal friendships among our societies and increase mutual understanding of the values on which we base our societies.

Yours sincerely, Anders Fogh Rasmussen.

---

have preferred to ignore complaints against members of his cabinet and the Danish People's Party. Acknowledging them could have divided Fogh Rasmussen from his government's parliamentary base. In consequence, the political incentives in Denmark worked against addressing the full measure of the eleven envoys' complaint. It was politically convenient to reframe public discussion to matters of free speech and the newspaper's right to say what it did.

Not one of the government officials or diplomats from the Islamic countries I have spoken to thought that the other incidents mentioned in the letter did not matter. On the contrary. The word "campaign" was used because that is what they thought was going on. And it was for that reason that their letter was addressed to the prime minister rather than the foreign minister, as diplomatic protocol would normally have dictated. They held Fogh Rasmussen responsible for the actions of politicians in his government or associated with his government, as in the case of the Danish People's Party. Once the street protests started it *was* all about the cartoons, but the diplomats had reason to consider the other statements worthy of legal action. The parliamentarian from the Danish People's Party and the radio station were later both prosecuted and convicted of racial defamation.

EARLY WARNING SIGNS

Turkey also gave the Danes advance warning that the complaints about the cartoons and the tone of Danish discourse on Islam and Muslims would not go away. An incident in Copenhagen provided evidence that the cartoons were one issue among others that were causing offense. In mid-November 2005, the Turkish prime minister Recep Tayyip Erdoğan brought up the cartoons during an official visit to Copenhagen. Press accounts described Fogh Rasmussen as unyielding to Erdoğan's request that he act to defend Muslims' rights: "I will simply not compromise. This is about how a democracy works." The visit ended badly when Erdoğan walked out of the final press conference with Rasmussen because he spotted a crew from ROJ TV, a television station affiliated with the PKK (Kurdistan Workers' Party), a separatist organization. The Turkish press described the encounter as "a crisis."

ROJ TV broadcasts from Copenhagen despite long-standing objections by the Turkish government. Erdoğan had come to Copenhagen in part to discuss the Kurdish station's activities. The decision to allow the station to attend the press conference may have been a fumble but more likely was a deliberate show of resistance to Turkish wishes. (The PKK was created in 1974 as a Marxist-Leninist guerrilla organization. The party aims to create a Kurdish state in southeastern Turkey and pursues its goals though suicide attacks in Turkey. It is outlawed in Turkey, and the European Union placed the organization on its list of terrorist organizations in 2002.) Although EU member states are required to freeze the assets of listed terrorist organizations, Denmark has not done so in the case of ROJ TV, claiming a lack of evidence of any connection to the PKK. In November 2007, Turkey took military action against PKK settlements in northern Iraq. Though banned in Germany, ROJ TV continues to broadcast by satellite from Copenhagen.[6]

Fogh Rasmussen's readiness to shelter émigré groups caused problems again in early February 2006 when Danish aid workers were ordered out of Chechnya. The pro-Russian acting prime minister of Chechnya, Ramzan Kadyrov, promised to ban "everything Danish" and declared, "I am a Muslim. After what they allowed in that country in relation to the Prophet, the very word 'Denmark' annoys me." The cartoons were the last straw, he said.[7] Several years earlier, in 2002, the Danish authorities had allowed the Chechen rebels to hold a congress in Copenhagen shortly after Chechen terrorists had attacked a theater in Moscow. Akhmed Zakaev, the rebels' leader, was arrested in Copenhagen but subsequently released. Although he was later given political asylum in the United Kingdom, Russian anger against the Danes lingers.[8]

THE DIPLOMATIC OFFENSIVE

In late October 2005, months before public knowledge of the diplomatic protest movement filtered into newspapers in Denmark or in the Middle East, Egypt bumped the complaint up to the highest international level. On November 5 the deputy ambassador at the Egyptian embassy in Copenhagen, Mohab Nasr Mostafa Mahdy, said to the wire service AFP, "We have been informed by our Foreign Minister that this caricature affair will be on the agenda at a special Summit of the Islamic conference." He added that the matter was no longer resting with the embassy, which the Danes should have taken as a warning. Egypt's ambassador in Beirut, Hussein Darrar, issued a statement on November 2 that he and the Lebanese foreign minister, Fazi Salloukh, had met to discuss measures to take against the Danish government. "We have asked the Danish government to take measures, but have not received a response to our request. As a result, we have decided not to continue talks with Denmark on the issue of human rights and discrimination."[9]

During the first weeks of November, foreign ministry officials in Pakistan, Egypt, Saudi Arabia, and apparently Lebanon summoned the resident Danish envoys to meetings to convey their displeasure with the Danish government. On November 10 and 11, Egypt's foreign minister,

Ahmed Aboul Gheit, and the secretaries-general of the Arab League and the OIC sent letters to the secretaries-general of the United Nations, the OSCE, the OECD, and the EU foreign policy coordinator, as well as to two human rights agencies complaining about the Danish government's inaction (see table 1).

Back in Denmark, the government said nothing, and unofficial government sources told the press that they had "heard nothing" about a complaint to the United Nations. Clearly they did know about it. Per Stig Møller, the Danish foreign minister, wrote on November 8 to Ahmed Aboul Gheit, his Egyptian counterpart, to acknowledge previous communications regarding Egypt's complaint to the United Nations and the Council of Europe and to warn that an escalation would benefit those who talked of a "clash of civilizations."

Møller's letter contained no promise of action on the part of his government and invited the Egyptians to join the Danes' initiative in the Middle East, the "Partnership for Progress and Reform."[10] The letter was an ineffectual and arguably an improper response to the problem at hand. The partnership program, grandiosely known in Denmark as Det Arabiske Initiativ (The Arab Initiative), was started in 2003 to promote collaboration between Danish organizations and institutions and partners in the Arab world and Iran. The projects aim to promote reform and democracy in Muslim countries. An example of what is euphemistically called "cultural diplomacy," the program preaches gender equality and the need for "reform" of Islam and is at the same time supposedly good for Danish business interests in the Middle East.

The Danish government has never released a record of the diplomatic communications it received regarding the cartoons. Meetings and calls are confidential and guided by diplomatic protocol, which disallows public release without consent. For these reasons, it is difficult to establish a complete record of contacts. I have listed here a number of documented diplomatic and governmental communications of concern to the Danish government made in 2005, before the conflict escalated in January 2006 (table 1). The list is almost certainly incomplete and underestimates the number of contacts. It is based on various documents, primarily news coverage in Muslim countries accessible through the Internet and in digital newspaper archives and my interviews with officials in Cairo.

Journalists from *Politiken*, Denmark's second largest newspaper and *Jyllands-Posten*'s keenest competitor, filed a freedom of information suit

Table 1.

Diplomatic protests, communications, and resolutions addressed to the Danish
government calling for official action regarding the cartoons, fall 2005

DATE	SENDER	TYPE OF COMMUNICATION	ACTION CALLED FOR
October 12 (received October 14)	The diplomatic representatives for eleven Muslim countries and Palestine in Denmark	Letter addressed to the prime minister copied to the foreign minister	Asks for a meeting with the prime minister and an affirmation of equal legal protection for Muslims under existing laws
October 15 (received October 19)	Ekmeleddin İhsanoğlu, OIC secretary-general	Letter to the prime minister and foreign minister	Requests preventive official action, "taking all necessary measures," and offers assistance in a joint effort to promote interreligious harmony
	ISESCO	Letter to the prime minister and foreign minister	Replicates the letter from the eleven ambassadors
	OSCE	Exchange of letters with the foreign minister	Requests that the government respond to the ambassadors' request for a meeting
mid-October	Ömür Orhun, OSCE	Communication with John Bernhard, Danish OSCE ambassador	Expresses concern over Danish inaction
October 25	Egyptian foreign ministry	Meeting between Egypt's foreign minister Ahmed Aboul Gheit and Bjarne Sørensen, Denmark's ambassador to Egypt	Requests an official statement from the prime minister condemning the mockery of Islam and the Prophet; Gheit reportedly warns Sørensen of the possibility of a trade boycott; on Egypt's initiative, two more meetings regarding the cartoons follow before December 2005

Table 1. (*Continued*)

DATE	SENDER	TYPE OF COMMUNICATION	ACTION CALLED FOR
October 29	Mona Omar Attia, Egypt's ambassador to Denmark	Public letter to the prime minister, printed in Danish newspapers	Refutes the prime minister's statements that Islamic countries are demanding legal action and requests that the government express its concern over the insult to Muslims and step in to avoid escalation of the conflict
November 10	Arab League and OIC	Joint letter to Louise Arbour, UN high commissioner of refugees; the OECD; and the UN high commissioner for human rights	Accuses Denmark of failure to observe various UN resolutions
November 11	Ahmed Aboul Gheit, Egypt's foreign minister; oral communications preceded the formal mailing of the letter, which was recorded as received by the UN on November 23	Letter to Kofi Annan, UN secretary-general, circulated in October to Javier Solana, EU foreign policy coordinator, and Marc Perrin de Brichambout, OSCE secretary-general	Asks the UN to compel Denmark to affirm principles of nondiscrimination against Muslims and respect for all religions; stresses that Egypt does not expect the government to restrict free speech or take legal actions against *Jyllands-Posten*
November 15	Recep Tayyip Erdoğan, Turkey's prime minister	Official meeting with prime minister in Copenhagen; exchange confidential	Reportedly asks for a condemnation of the cartoons' publication and assurances that laws will be fully applied to the cartoons (blasphemy charge)
November 11–16	Ahmed Aboul Gheit, Egypt's foreign minister	Conversation with Per Stig Møller during Forum on the Future meeting in Bahrain	Warns of escalation of the conflict and the possibility of a trade boycott

Table 1. (*Continued*)

DATE	SENDER	TYPE OF COMMUNICATION	ACTION CALLED FOR
November 24	Doudou Diéné, UN special rapporteur on freedom of religion or belief, and Asma Jahangir, UN special rapporteur on freedom of religion and belief	Letter to the Danish government	Alleges intolerance of religious minorities (Muslims) in Denmark and requests information regarding the government's responses to the cartoons incident
November 29	Alcee Hastings, head, OSCE Parliamentary Affairs Committee	Conversation with Per Stig Møller at OSCE meeting in Vienna	Warns of an investigation of charges of religious discrimination against Muslims in Denmark
December 7	Louise Arbour, UN high commissioner for human rights	Letter to the OIC responding to an earlier request for action	Announces an investigation into the government's handling of the affair
December 7–8	OIC extraordinary summit meeting in Mecca	Statement	Condemns the insult to the Prophet and the government's failure to protect Muslims and Islam
December 19	Council of Europe Committee of Ministers	Statement	Criticizes the government for failing both to curb xenophobia and to implement recommendations regarding minority rights
December 29	Arab League Council of Foreign Ministers		Expresses surprise and "discontent" with the government's failure to respond to Muslims' concerns

Sources: Personal conversations with officials at the Arab League and the Egyptian foreign ministry; Rune Englebreth Larsen and Tøger Sidenfaden, *Karikaturkrisen: En Undersøgelse af baggrund og ansvar* (Copenhagen: Gyldendal, 2006), appendixes 4 and 5; "Muhammed-sagen," www.TV2.dk/nyhederne; www.um.dk.

and obtained a mountain of documents, but with many names and sections blacked-out. A few of these documents have been published in excerpts or in Danish translation.[11] It is possible in some instances to deduce the existence of previous communications from these letters. Frank Aaen is a member of parliament with a seat on its standing committee on foreign policy, which the constitution requires must be informed if there is any threat to Danish national interests. (Aaen belongs to a left-wing opposition party, the Unity List.) He requested the release of a list of letters and notes from conversations between the foreign minister and Muslim ministers and diplomats.[12] From this list, we know that the Egyptian government lodged direct protests on October 25 with the Danish ambassador in Cairo. This communication occurred before or coincided with Egypt's official letter of complaint to the United Nations at the end of October. During a visit to the Egyptian foreign ministry in Cairo, I was told that the first meeting with envoys from the Danish embassy had taken place during a routine visit two weeks earlier, around the time the eleven ambassadors in Copenhagen mailed their letter to the prime minister.

The diplomatic offensive soon broadened. The prime ministers or foreign ministers of Afghanistan, Bahrain, Bangladesh, Croatia, India, Indonesia, Iran, Jordan, Kuwait, Libya, Pakistan, the Palestinian Authority, Russia, Saudi Arabia, Syria, Turkey, United Arab Emirates, and the Vatican publicly condemned the cartoons and criticized the Danish government for failing to protect the rights of Muslims. National assemblies in Bahrain, Bangladesh, Egypt, Iran, Jordan, Pakistan, Syria, Turkey, and Yemen passed resolutions condemning the cartoons and blaming the Danish government for its failure to follow up on Muslims' complaints and respond to diplomatic initiatives. The Turkish parliament officially conveyed its protest to the Danish parliament. In other cases, it appears that resolutions were passed and broadcast in the national media. The Indian government was reluctant to issue formal statements but was eventually compelled to do so by its parliament. With the exception of the early diplomatic contacts through various channels to Danish government officials or envoys by Egypt, Turkey, and Pakistan, all the resolutions and statements of condemnation were passed after the OIC's summit meeting on December 7–8, 2005, in Mecca, which marked the end of what in chapter 2 I described as the mobilization phase and the start of the escalation. The meeting marked, in my estimation, the last moment when a different response from the Danish government could have forestalled the trade boycott that began in early January 2006 and the downward spiral into widespread street demonstrations and violence.

Saudi Arabia and Iran have sometimes been credited with starting the conflict, but both countries entered the fray relatively late. The date of the first contact on the matter between the Danish ambassador in Riyadh and the Saudi Arabian authorities is unclear but appears not to have taken place until January 2006. On January 23, 2006, Saudi newspapers were filled with stories about the official condemnations from the 150-member *shura* council (the religious authorities) and the government of the cartoons and the Danish government. Iran is often blamed for everything that goes wrong in the Middle East, but the Iranians were also late to take up the cartoons. The Iranian government was implicated in violent street demonstrations that took place in early February 2006 and was later responsible for one of the sideshows in the controversy when the president, Mahmoud Ahmadinejad, launched a cartoon contest against the West, calling for competitive lampooning of the Holocaust.

Eventually the parliaments and presidencies of all predominantly Muslim countries and countries with significant Muslim minorities, including India and Russia, joined the official movement to protest the cartoons and the Danish government's handling of the matter.

The OIC summit meeting in early December 2005 was an extraordinary convocation originally organized in response to Al-Qaeda's attacks on 9/11 and later terrorist attacks in Madrid and London. The agenda was to restore "the image of Islam" and "strengthen the unity" of Islamic states against extremists. A new declaration stating the principles of moderate Islam had been under preparation for two years, but the cartoons attracted much attention as the meeting proceeded. The final communiqué condemned terrorism at length and segued directly from terrorism to Islamophobia and the cartoons. It advocated that "defamation of Islam and its values" should be criminalized as a form of racism and made actionable under international law. The cartoons were unequivocally condemned: "The Conference expressed its concern at rising hatred against Islam and Muslims and condemned the recent incident of desecration of the image of the Holy Prophet Mohammad (PBUH) in the media of certain countries and stressed the responsibility of all governments to ensure full respect of all religions and religious symbols and the inapplicability of using the freedom of expression as a pretext to defame religions."[13]

The OIC communiqué marked a turning point in the controversy

over the cartoons. It broadcast the news throughout the sprawling bu-
reaucracies of the fifty-six member states and ensured that the states
joined the movement. The communiqué gave the green light to the Saudi
Arabian and Egyptian religious authorities to become involved. Any
newspaper across the Islamic world could now safely write about the
matter. The summit also put combating Islamophobia and speech offenses at the center of the continuing shadowboxing over the "clash of
civilizations" conducted in the arenas of international human rights organizations and the United Nations.

The global Muslim population knew little about the cartoons until after
the summit meeting. It encouraged the religious establishments to become
involved and various governments and parliaments in Islamic countries to
publicly condemn the cartoons. The summit also made the boycott of Danish goods feasible. The threat of a trade boycott had been mentioned in
communications between Egyptian and Danish diplomats in October, but it
became effective only in late December, when the Middle Eastern religious
establishment called on Muslims to boycott Danish goods.

Supermarkets in Saudi Arabia and the United Arab Emirates started
to remove Danish goods from the shelves on January 28–30, 2006.[14]
Egypt soon followed. Officially, the boycott was a spontaneous outbreak of
consumer anger. In reality retailers responded to the authorities, and
although many lost heavily because they had to toss their stock of Danish
goods, others reported that business improved when they advertized their
support of the boycott.[15] The French supermarket chain Carrefour, jointly
owned with a Dubai-based company, removed all Danish products from
the chain's upscale supermarkets across the Middle East. Consumer support for the boycott was nonetheless evident.

THE ORGANIZATION OF THE ISLAMIC CONFERENCE

I interviewed Ekmeleddin İhsanoğlu, the secretary-general of the OIC, a
year after the protests peaked.[16] İhsanoğlu stressed that he had never
asked for an apology from the Danish government and stated his understanding of Fogh Rasmussen's refusal to provide one. An apology was not
what the secretary-general wanted. The letter from the OIC to the Danish
prime minister was, he said, "a nice letter" that was intended as a re-
minder of the necessity of mutual understanding as a precondition for
cooperation. İhsanoğlu acknowledged that he had not seen the cartoons
when the OIC's letter was sent but claimed to have been more shocked

FIGURE 2. The French retail giant Carrefour gives Egyptian customers notice that the supermarket chain is boycotting Danish products, February 2, 2006. Photo: Getty/AFP.

than he had expected to be when he finally did see them. "How can we cooperate in cultural programs, when the Danes insult the Prophet and describe him as a terrorist?"

The accusation that Muslims wanted to censor speech angered the secretary-general. Turkey protects free speech, he pointed out. The middle class everywhere, including in Muslim countries, wants free speech. The disagreement, he asserted, is over what constitutes defamation. Every country has red lines, which you cannot step over. The problem in Europe, he continued, is that Muslims are excluded from those same considerations. İhsanoğlu was highly critical of the European—and Danish—reactions to the cartoon debacle. The argument that the publication of offensive cartoons and negative comments about Muslims was protected by free speech and expressions of specific European values implied a separation of human rights values and universal values. If a value is universal, it had to apply to both Christians and Muslims, he insisted. If Muslims do not agree with that value, it cannot be said to be universal.

Kantians would not agree in theory, and as a practical political matter the secretary-general's view also does not accurately sum up the standard operating procedure for amendments to the international catalogue of human rights. İhsanoğlu's argument implies that no norms can be agreed to in the absence of unanimous consent, but in spring 2008, the OIC proposed adding a post-cartoon rider to UN rules on racism. It passed against the votes of the West European and North American members.

On January 7, 2006, a Danish prosecutor decided not to pursue blasphemy claims against *Jyllands-Posten* that had been filed by Danish Muslim associations. Three days later, the Norwegian magazine *Magazinet* reprinted the cartoons. The two events persuaded İhsanoğlu that the cartoons were part of "a campaign against us" (the pronoun referred to Muslims.) His view of these as meaningful and interconnected decisions was startlingly different from how they were perceived in Denmark. *Magazinet* was a conservative "born-again" Christian newspaper with a circulation of about five thousand. (It does not exist anymore.) In our interview, I was incredulous that the secretary-general would think that *Jyllands-Posten*'s editors, with their anticlerical libertarian principles, and the Christian Norwegian paper—and the judicially restrained Danish public prosecutor—were in some way part of a coherent anti-Muslim "campaign." Taken aback, I asked how he and his staff had reached that conclusion. "These countries have the same constitutions, the same outlook," he said, "and when one does something the others do it, too."

It is a fair assessment. The Nordic countries have long been subject to similar political cycles, but in recent years the political gap has grown between the Danes and their neighbors, not least with reference to the treatment of Muslim immigrants. The Norwegian government quickly condemned *Magazinet*'s action. In stark contrast to his Danish colleague, Norway's foreign minister, Jonas Gahr Støre, sent an email to Norwegian embassies in the Middle East instructing them to apologize to their hosts.[17]

İhsanoğlu took a dark view of the outcome of the cartoon conflict and pointed out that all parties had walked away feeling bitter. The cartoons, and Pope Benedict's Regensburg speech, which took place a year later but which many Muslims viewed as an equivalent attack on Islam, represented a new milestone in the deterioration of Muslim-Christian relations. A decades-long strategy of promoting interreligious toleration by means of top-level meetings between the heads of the world religions and diplomatic mediation had been proven a failure. The UN-based human rights regulatory machinery also had not worked. The conclusion İhsanoğlu had reached was that top-level interreligious dialogue between the heads of religions and intergovernmental diplomacy is powerless to address deep-seated hostility and anger in society, and "the time has come to reconsider how to address these issues in an era when new information technology leaves no room for controlling what is broadcast."

The cartoons gave the OIC and İhsanoğlu a new mission: combating Islamophobia. The famously fractious leading members in the conference—Egypt, Pakistan, Saudi Arabia, and Turkey—have found common cause in the criticism of Western bias against Islam and Muslims, and the fight against Islamophobia has proved to lend itself to the procedure-focused politics of intergovernmental diplomacy. Two tangible outcomes of the new agenda are the OIC's Islamophobia Observatory, which monitors incidents in Europe and produces an annual report, and Resolution 60/150 of the Sixtieth UN General Assembly Session, which disallows the defamation of religions. The resolution was subsequently joined by a resolution from the UN Human Rights Council that condemned efforts to link Islam to terrorism and violence. The OIC proposed the resolution, which divided the members of the council into geographic alliances— isolating the European members in the minority.

The Islamophobia Observatory was established at the meeting in Mecca in 2005 and owes its inception entirely to the cartoons. It is part of a ten-year action plan, also authorized in Mecca, to monitor and counter Islamophobia. The first report credits the cartoons as the midwife for the initiative: "The most sacred symbols of Islam, in particular the sacred image of the Prophet Muhammad (PBUH), is being defiled and denigrated in the most insulting, offensive and contemptuous manner to incite hatred and unrest in society."[18]

Not surprisingly, Geert Wilders and the Danish People's Party feature prominently in the observatory's report. It relies heavily on surveys of Western Muslims' perceptions of discrimination and the general population's attitudes to Muslims carried out by Gallup and the Pew Global Attitudes Project. These are reputable surveys. It is appropriate that the OIC would use them. The remarkable part is how the report describes the OIC's new role as a protector of Western Muslim minorities. The report states matter-of-factly and with sizable hyperbole that Muslims face a "harsh" situation living in the West and that the research "vindicates" the efforts of the OIC and the secretary-general to bring these problems to the attention of the international community. But the OIC has undertaken to do more. The cartoon protests, with the direct letters and the implicit threat of complaints to the United Nations or other international organizations, are parlayed into a model for direct intervention on behalf of European Muslims with Western governments. The antics of the Swedish artist Lars Vilks, the Dutch parliamentarian Geert Wilders, and many others in recent years have each occasioned an admonishing letter and a demand for official reassurances from the affected governments to be communicated to the OIC.[19] Many European Muslims would be startled to learn that the OIC regards itself as their watchdog.

THE ARAB LEAGUE

A year after speaking to İhsanoğlu, I obtained permission to interview the secretary-general of the Arab League, the other important intergovernmental organization involved in the cartoon protests. "Make no mistake about it," said Amr Moussa when I interviewed him in Cairo, "the clash of civilizations is real."[20] Our interview took place in the Arab League's headquarters in Cairo, a beautiful colonial era building. The secretary-general's offices were bustling with well-dressed and efficient professional women. One woman wore a headscarf with her smart suit.

Egypt was under British military government from 1882 to 1936 and a monarchy until the revolution in 1952. After eighteen years of experimentation with Arab socialism, Egypt underwent economic and political liberalization under Anwar El Sadat from 1970 to 1981. Muhammad Hosni Mubarak took over when Sadat was assassinated by Islamists and has been president ever since. He was reelected to a fifth term on September 5, 2005.

Moussa served as foreign minister for ten years until 2001, when he stepped down to become secretary-general of the Arab League. The change signaled a promotion for the previously dormant Arab League, which is a vehicle for Egyptian foreign policy. Moussa is immensely popular, and tongues wagged that Mubarak's desire to put Moussa out of the way was the real reason for the change.[21] Shaaban Abdel-Rahim, Egypt's most popular singer, once produced a song with the title: "I love Amr Moussa and I hate Israel." The same singer also made a song about the cartoons: "Muhammad cartoons go to hell!"[22] Whatever the reason for Moussa's move, under his stewardship the Arab League has become a partner in negotiations with the European Union and in mediation over Palestine.

In our interview, Moussa described the cartoons as part of a "determined and coordinated campaign of insult against Islam." The real issue, he asserted, is freedom of expression: "Where does it start and where does it end?"

The secretary-general had not seen the Danish imams' folder and did not know anything in specific about the cartoons. When I asked about the eleven ambassadors' complaint about the culture minister and the other instances of offensive speech in Denmark, Moussa confirmed what Carsten Juste had said: "It was all about the cartoons." But it turned out the secretary-general did not mean that it was all about the newspaper: "Who cares about what a newspaper writes!" he said when I inquired further as to his concerns. It was a matter about respect and equity for Muslims.

According to Moussa, the issue of the cartoons should have been raised by the government and between the government and the newspaper. "The government is not doing anything to get Muslims into mainstream society," Moussa said. It was also a matter of double standards. "The Europeans follow the line on Israel and Palestine laid out by the U.S. and pay a great deal [of] attention to the threats to security posed by the radicals [Islamist extremists], but there has to be a focus on coexistence. On these issues the government is always eager to follow on top, but respect for the Koran and Islam is missing. Christians are not being defamed here. There are laws against anti-Semitism—Islamophobia is the same thing. Muslims should be treated the same way."

I observed that many Europeans are uncomfortable about the hate speech laws and the criminalization of speech associated with these laws as well as the Holocaust denial laws. What if all such laws were repealed? "Well, fine, equal treatment is the main thing." That extended to controlling the press. "The Dutch government prevented the release of that politician's [Geert Wilders] film," Moussa pointed out. It was not entirely accurate; the Dutch government merely warned that Wilders would be subject to prosecution if his film broke any laws.

Later in the interview he launched into a rambling complaint about Europeans. "Radicalization goes on—we have radicals, too, but we control them. Provocation like the cartoons will add to the fire. If the governments in Western Europe cannot control such people—the radicals on either side, how can we control the radicals here?" The main objective of the protests against the cartoons, he insisted, was to educate the European governments: "We have to be treated equally." International rules must be created, he argued, that will protect religious figures. In March 2009 the effort bore fruit when the UN Human Rights Council passed a resolution proposed by the OIC citing the cartoons as an example of a human rights violation.

DIPLOMATIC PREVENTION: A LESSON FOR THE FUTURE?

Could the escalation have been prevented? When I met the OIC's secretary-general and his special adviser, Ufuk Gökçen, a Turkish political scientist, both repeatedly stated their firm conviction that a timely statement by the Danish government would have resolved the crisis. Ömer Orhun, an OSCE ambassador, also declared the conflict was entirely preventable: "A simple but clear condemnation by Denmark on the publication of the caricatures and restraint and moderation on the part of the media in other countries not to insist on publishing these offensive drawings could have put the outrage by the Muslim communities under control."[23] This is a common view in diplomatic circles. Even Danish diplomats (speaking off the record because it contradicts the Danish government's position) believe it likely that timely diplomatic action would have altered the cause of events, perhaps forestalling the boycott of Danish goods in the Middle East.

The Danes, however, believed that the governments of Muslim countries and İhsanoğlu were responsible for the escalation of the conflict by drawing attention to the cartoons. Had there been no resolutions and diplomatic protests, the reasoning went, there would also have been no attacks on Danish embassies and a trade boycott.[24] In fact, Egypt and the Muslim diplomats cannot rightly be accused of having set off the extremist wave. Nor, however, is it probable that a timely statement of regret from Denmark would have resolved the affair.

The OIC meeting came on the heels of a meeting in Bahrain on November 11–12 of the so-called Forum of the Future, which ended in a dustup between Arab representatives and the United States over the pressure applied from Washington to democratize and promote free speech and elections in the Middle East. Throughout the fall of 2005, civil society activists and human rights advocates were preparing a new charter that would commit states participating in the so-called Broader Middle East and North Africa (BMENA) initiative to the liberalization of laws control-ling the activities of NGOs (nongovernmental organizations). The charter was a joint European and American effort but was driven by the United States' new strategic emphasis on Arab democratization as a strategy for stabilizing the region and neutralizing extremists. The calendar for the process had been set at a meeting in Rabat in December 2004, and a draft, prepared with assistance from the American Bar Association and in con-sultation with activists and organizations from the eighteen countries, was expected to be passed in Bahrain.[25] It did not happen. When the United States refused to admit an addendum proposed by Egypt that NGOs had to be legally registered in accordance with national laws, Ah-med Aboul Gheit left the meeting. The OIC's condemnations of abusive free speech in the West in response to the cartoons turned the table on the human rights agenda.

The demonstrations in the Middle East and Pakistan were often pri-marily directed *against* the Muslim governments and organizations like the OIC. The cartoons became part of an anti-Western agenda, as the OIC secretary-general remarked in our interview in February 2007. The street demonstrations in Syria, Lebanon, Iran, Nigeria, Libya, and in the large cities of Pakistan were independent events, staged by local radical move-ments or arranged by governments. In other cases, such as in Libya, the violence was sparked by local reactions to secondary events, including the republication of the cartoons in a local newspaper and denunciations by a local charismatic sheikh. The Norwegians, who had after all made an early and comprehensive condemnation of *Magazinet*'s reprinting of the car-toons, were themselves not spared threats and attacks on their local em-bassies and citizens, which suggests that it would have been difficult to stop the wave of protests.

Moreover, the complaints did not concern the cartoons alone. The OIC, Arab League, and Egyptians were making a case against Fogh Ras-mussen's practice of supporting xenophobic critics of Muslims and Islam and of tolerating émigré extremist groups. Another source of tension was Rasmussen's opposition to Turkish membership in the European Union. Finally, he was responsible for making Denmark an enthusiastic partici-pant in President George W. Bush's "coalition of the willing" in Iraq and was the only European politician to declare that the failure to find weapons of mass destruction in Iraq made no difference to the justice of the war.

CHAPTER 4

Muslims' "Day of Rage"

ON OCTOBER 14, 2005, three thousand people demonstrated against the cartoons and the government at City Hall Plaza in Copenhagen. The pictures of angry imams and bearded men screaming slogans certainly got the public's attention. The omnipresence of the clerics from the four mosques known for their orthodoxy put Danes on the edge of their seats. Newspaper columnists and politicians admonished Muslims about the need to respect Danish culture and freedom of speech, but as far as most people were concerned, when the demonstrators went home the issue had passed. That view prevailed until the demonstrations and boycotts started in January 2006.

The tone then changed. Comparisons were made to the terrorist attacks on the Madrid train on March 11, 2003, and the London Underground on July 7, 2005. The Danish People's Party and some newspapers described the imams as the "enemy within" and compared the Muslim activists to Nazis.[1] By spring 2006, demands were made in parliament to strip the imams of their citizenship on grounds of treason.

The political activities of mosques came to the attention of policy makers and the public when it was discovered that Mohamed Atta and three other 9/11 hijackers met at the Al-Quds Mosque in Hamburg. The role of radical clerics was highlighted again in connection with the Dutch youths who formed the Hofstad network to which Mohammed Bouyeri, the murderer of the filmmaker Theo van Gogh, belonged. Bouyeri and other Dutch Muslim youth involved in the network met at the El Tawheed Mosque in Amsterdam and later moved on to another radical mosque in The Hague. Abu Hamza al-Masri from the Finsbury Park Mosque in London is another notorious example of a cleric engaged in subversive activity. The inclination of the media and the Danish public was to identify the Danish imams and mosque activists in the same brand of Salafist or Wahhabi theology.

But politics rather than theology was the issue. There are devout Muslims who would agree that Muslims were behaving badly during the cartoon crisis. Abdul Haqq Baker is the chairman and imam of the Brixton Mosque in South London. He lives in London and Saudi Arabia with his family and is a devout Salafist. He has spent much of his time since the 9/11 attacks preaching against violence and political extremism. When I asked him what devout Muslims should do about the cartoons, he said that first they should stop showing them around.[2] Muslims need not look at sacrilegious images to know that Islamophobia is a problem, and as far as he was concerned, screaming in the streets was not proper behavior. Boycotting Danish goods was a legitimate response, but violence is never allowed. The cartoons were blasphemous, but Muslims should respond by averting their gaze as they would if faced with an indecently dressed woman. The cartoons were, after all, little different from pornography and the many other offensive images that daily bombard religious people— Muslim and Christian—in the West.

Scriptural interpretation and political objectives are linked in complex ways. The connection between Salafism and jihadism—the ideology of Al-Qaeda and aligned groups—is slim. Salafism is a Sunni theological movement in Islam that seeks religious revival through a return to a pure faith. "Salaf" means pious ancestor and "salafiyaah" the way of the ancestors. Salafism took a political turn as a nineteenth-century movement, which in the mid-twentieth century became associated with Islamism. In contemporary thinking Salafism and Islamism are often regarded as identical movements. But many Salafis reject the political project associated with the Egyptian-born intellectual Sayyid Qubt (1906–1966) and the Pakistani Mawlana Abdul Ala Mawdudi (1903–1979).

Wahhabism is also often equated with Salafism, in part because the Wahhabist movement (named after Muhammad ibn Abd-al-Wahhab,

1703–1792) claims to embody the principles of Salafism. But Wahhabism is a modernizing movement that seeks to find a state form compatible with the principles of the faith.[3] It is also the philosophy of power of the al-Saud dynasty, which founded the Kingdom of Saudi Arabia in 1932 when the new king, Abdul Aziz Al-Saud, got the British to cede the territory.

Today many Salafists regard the Saudi kingdom with skepticism or worse and regard politics and power as sources of corruption. Opposition takes two routes: one that recognizes a distinction between sacred and secular power in the current age and advocates that Muslims focus on living righteous lives and observe the laws of the countries where they reside, and another revolutionary opposition that aims to re-create a new and pious caliphate and considers, in the manner of the Taliban and Al-Qaeda, democracy as forbidden for Muslims because it substitutes man-made laws for God's laws.

Like the Salafists, the jihadists seek to restore Islam to a state of purity. But there the similarities end. The jihadis advocate the use of violence to bring about the Islamic state and claim it is an obligation to wage jihad against Christians, apostates, and the sitting Islamic governments.[4] They have little compunction about killing fellow Muslims who support democracy and elections because they are apostates from God's rule, which makes them worse sinners than the infidels. At the far end of the political-theological spectrum the righteous are at war first and foremost with other Muslims. The jihadis assert the principle of the unity of the faith and regard the Crusaders' capture of Jerusalem in 1099 as the original invasion of Muslim lands, which they are fighting to undo now. Therefore, their objective is the expulsion of all occupiers—designated as "the Zionist-Crusader nations"—and the Muslim rulers, who have conceded Muslim territories to the West. Egypt and Saudi Arabia are on the top of the list of enemies because they have capitulated. The radicals also regard Shiites as apostates and occasionally have advocated that they should be annihilated. Others have focused their wrath on the current Turkish state, which was created in 1924 when Mustafa Kemal Atatürk abolished the last caliph and imposed a secular constitution.

The deep fissures between the various sects and denominations in Salafism are foreign to most people. When the different political offspring —some extremist and others moderate, some violent and others peaceful —started to make demands about what Danes can not say and do about the Prophet, few Danes could tell the difference between what one or the other group said or did, or wanted to do.

Danes heard only that they were being told to change their laws and ways. Many people thought the Islamic revolution was coming. The Danish activists were mostly orthodox in their religious practices, but they were not plotting violence. Unlike Abdul Haqq Baker in London, they had political objectives beyond the cartoons, but these were often unclear and a source of divisions among the activists. They began like any other group by developing an action plan for getting Danish Muslims off their couches.

THE DANISH MOSQUE COALITION

At a meeting held in Copenhagen a few days after *Jyllands-Posten* published the cartoons, a small group of imams and mosque activists made a plan. It might have been copied from any other plan made by a Danish single-issue activist group hoping to affect public opinion through extra-parliamentary political mobilization. Customarily, Danish protesters meet in front of the city hall in Copenhagen or, if a lot of people are expected at a demonstration, in front of the parliament building. The activists self-consciously modeled their actions on what Danes usually do. Danes saw only that the activists were a group of mostly middle-aged imams and mosque regulars who were more comfortable speaking in Arabic than Danish and were making demands that seemed entirely alien to Danish political sensibilities.

Raed Hlayhel, the angry imam from the Århus mosque who had been subject to prolonged, unflattering coverage in *Jyllands-Posten* for months, called the meeting three days after the publication of the cartoons. It took place in Copenhagen, and in attendance were members from the Islamic Faith Community, the host mosque, another Copenhagen mosque, and a mosque in Odense, Denmark's third largest city. The four mosques and their charismatic clerics, known as sheikhs, formed the nucleus of the action committee. The participants passed an action plan that Ahmed Akkari, also from Århus, wrote up and emailed to "the brothers."[5] It had nineteen points. All were followed closely.

Point 1 was to find a lawyer to file suit against the paper. Points 2 and 3 listed writing letters to relevant Danish government ministers and ambassadors of Muslim countries. Points 4, 5, and 6 called on the group to contact various Islamic religious establishments and Al Jazeera. Points 7 through 10 called for a letter-writing campaign to newspapers and mosques, and inundating Danish Muslims with text messages and emails about the protests. Points 1 through 10 happened. Points 11 and 12 called for a demonstration and a Muslim one-day strike. The demonstration took place, albeit perhaps with fewer participants than the organizers had imagined, and the strike failed. Points 13 and 14 called for getting Muslims to stage a "sleep-in" for one night "someplace" in Copenhagen and getting them to burn their passports. Neither of these happened.

The remaining points called for an Internet campaign on the part of the Prophet and "sending a press release on the part of Muslims" to a wire service. Points 18 and 19 included the appointment of a spokesman. Akkari was appointed the spokesman, and the other items were easy to accomplish.

Ironically, the plan's success depended on making sure that Muslims' anger was aroused, and to do that, the activists had to make sure Muslims saw the forbidden cartoons. The cartoons were pinned up on bulletin boards in mosques and circulated with invocations to protest. The use of text messages proved to be particularly successful in getting people to log onto *Jyllands-Posten*'s web site and to vote en masse against the cartoons in an online poll set up by the paper. The culmination of the plan was the departure of two delegations to Cairo, Beirut, and Damascus with a dossier containing the twelve cartoons as well as other material assembled by Hlayhel.

TAKING THE CARTOONS PUBLIC

Stridency and disunity marred the protests from the beginning. Hlayhel gave an interview with *Jyllands-Posten* before the protests got off the ground in which he said that democracy as practiced in Denmark is worth nothing to Muslims and that the paper must apologize to the world's Muslims. He also demanded that the newspaper "retract" the drawings and threatened to complain to the government and to file a suit alleging blasphemy.

Hlayhal does not speak Danish and was so poorly informed about religious affairs in Denmark—an overwhelmingly Protestant country—that he threatened to complain to the pope. The demand for an apology was in the action plan agreed to by the other sheikhs and the coalition members, but the rejection of democracy and the other demands were

Hlayhel's additions. *Jyllands-Posten* gleefully invited Hlayhal and the other protesting imams to file suit under the criminal code's section 140, which allows for up to four months' imprisonment for blasphemy. Hlayhel behaved in character as one of the "mad mullahs" that *Jyllands-Posten* had warned about in the cartoon editorials. The more Hlayhel protested, the more Danes became convinced that the newspaper had been right and that he was a threat to their national values.

On October 12, 2005, Hlayhel was on Al Jazeera, where he contrasted the Danes' readiness to insult Muslims to their sensitivity to Jews. The subtext was that Jews are favored while Muslims are discriminated against and that the cartoons proved the existence of a double standard because the laws against Holocaust denial prohibit denigration of Jews, and no equivalent laws protect Muslims. It is a difficult charge to disprove because, in essence, it is an argument about moral equivalency. It was, moreover, a constant refrain in the cartoon controversy.

The first delegation representing the coalition of mosques arrived in Cairo on December 3, 2005. There the delegates met with the rector of Al-Azhar University, Sheikh Muhammad Sayyid Tantawy; the secretary-general of the Arab League, Amr Moussa; and other ministers and high-ranking officials and religious authorities. Among the high-ranking individuals were Ali Gomaa, the grand mufti of Cairo, and Mohammed Shaaban, from the Egyptian foreign ministry, who previously was Egypt's ambassador to Copenhagen. They were interviewed by *Al-Ahram,* an important newspaper, and other papers. Leading the delegation was Abu Bashar, an imam of Palestinian origin from Odense. The other members of the delegation were two little-known businessmen of Egyptian origin, Ahmed Mohamad Mostafa Harby and Nour-Eddin Fattah; Sarwar Shoudri, a Pakistani; and Zeki Koçer, who heads a mosque group associated with the Turkish association Milli Görüş (MG). MG was founded by Necmettin Erbakan, who was also leader of an Islamist party that was banned in Turkey after a military coup in 1980 and until 1987. Erbakan later returned to politics in Turkey and was made prime minister in 1996, until a year later, when he was forced to step down and his party, Refah Partisi (Welfare Party), was banned. MG adherents today tend to support the current Turkish government party, the Justice and Development Party.

The Egyptian ambassador in Copenhagen, Mona Omar Attia, organized the group's appointments in Cairo. The reasons for her involvement remain murky. Ahmed Abu Laban, who was then the leader of the Islamic

Faith Community in Copenhagen, took credit for taking the initiative to make connections with the Egyptian embassy and other embassies representing Muslim countries in Copenhagen. Getting help from Islamic countries' representatives in Copenhagen was one of the points on the activists' action plan, and the task of making the contacts was delegated to Abu Laban. Ironically, Abu Laban was unable to travel to Cairo because years earlier he had been expelled from Egypt for his political activities.

At the end of December 2005, after the visit to Cairo, a second delegation went to Beirut. It consisted of Raed Hlayhel and Ahmed Akkari, both from the mosque in Århus, and Kassem Said Ahmed and Mahmoud Mansour. Ahmed is from the Islamic Faith Community mosque in Copenhagen, and Mansour is from Odense. Abu Laban insisted that their delegation had no official sponsorship from the mosque coalition, but that did not prevent the group from acting as representatives. The imams met with Shia and Sunni religious leaders in Beirut. Hlayhel gave interviews to Al Jazeera and other Arab stations and to the Lebanese television station run by Hezbollah. During the visit, Akkari took a bus to Damascus to meet with the Syrian grand mufti, Sheikh Ahmed Badr-Eddine Hassoun.

The Beirut delegation also met with Sheikh Faysal Mawlawi, a judge on the shariah court in Beirut and deputy head of the octogenarian Islamic scholar Sheikh Yusuf al-Qaradawi's European Council for Fatwa and Research. Mawlawi cofounded the fatwa council with al-Qaradawi in 1997 and is a religious law expert for IslamOnline, the web site al-Qaradawi uses to broadcast his opinions. (The site also operates as a standard news site.) Everywhere they went, the imams brought along the dossier produced by Hlayhel. The importance of the meeting with Mawlawi became clear three weeks later, when al-Qaradawi beseeched all Muslims to protest against the cartoons and the smears against the Prophet's reputation. Later, the imams attended a conference organized by al-Qaradawi's International Union of Muslim Scholars in Bahrain to debate what to do about the cartoons.

THE DOSSIER AND THE "FALSE" CARTOONS

The activists carried with them a folder, assembled by Hlayhel, that contained a selection of documentary materials, including copies of the cartoons and associated commentaries. Copies were distributed at the meetings they held with government officials and clerics. The first page of the dossier is reproduced here from a scan of a copy given to me by Abu Laban (fig. 3).

• حث المسلمين على المساهمة في مخاطبة الجريدة كل بحسبه وبوسائل الاتصال المتاحة لإعلامهم أن هذا الأمر خط أحمر لدى جميع المسلمين وليس فقط لرجال الدين فيهم.
• الطلب الصريح من الجريدة بالاعتذار والوعد بعدم التكرار واحترام مقدسات المسلمين.
• حملة جمع لتوقيعات المسلمين الرافضة لعمل الجريدة من جهة، والداعمة للخطوات للمراكز الإسلامية في مواجهة هذه الحملة ومثيلاتها.
• توجيه رسائل إلى الفعاليات السياسية والأحزاب الناشطة لإطلاعهم على خطورة الموقف وكسب تأييدهم.
• الاتصال بسفارات العالم الإسلامي (في الدنمارك) لإطلاعهم على حقيقة الموقف لينضموا مسؤولياتهم.
• الاتصال بوسائل الإعلام المحلية والعالمية (لا سيما بعد تجاهلهم).
• عندما لم نجد أي جواب من القائمين على الجريدة وبعد التجاهل المقصود من رئيس الوزراء بعد أن تقدمت السفارات الإسلامية بطلب للقاء لتبادى اللقاء أخر وأثاف أن 09-10-2005 صدر عنه بيان ورد في معظم وسائل الإعلام المحلية والعالمية
• بعد أن تناولت قناة العربية هذا الأمر على تمت تناولت وثيرة الجريدة وخصصت هذه زاوية خاصة عنوانها (صور النبي). وكتبت مقالاً بالقلة العربية – وهي سابقة غربية – عنونه (الكلمة حرة) وأبرزت ما أوردته الجزيرة وكلهم أسرارا على موقفهم وضعاهم عدد الصحف يتحدث لتعالية عدد هذا الموضوع ولإشراك المريدين لهم حيث القضية أنها حرية يقبلونها فهي
• أسرت الجمعيات على إثر ذلك بياناً تابياً طالبت به العالم الإسلامي بالتدخل بعد أن القضية ولأن النبي صلى الله عليه وسلم لا يقبض مسلمي الدنمارك فقط بل مسلمي العالم فلا يجوز أن ترضى بالإساءة لرسولنا تحت أي شعار أو تبرير.
• بحث القضية على مستوى قادة العالم الإسلامي حيث أشير أشير للموضوع بوضوح في البيان الختامي.

ومما زادنا ألماً وحرقة عدة أمور:
1- أصبح الاستهزاء بالإسلام – فضلاً عن أهله – بضاعة رائجة؛ إذا أقدمت جريدة (شيء معينة) على نشر صور أشد وأكثر وذلك في 10-11-2005 ولعلها لمتصد من ذلك الشهرة الخروج بين الناس من جديد وهي (فوق أندأ أخر).
2- وصلت للمسلمين خلال هذه الفترة – لإسبانيا من سامهم اي الاعتراض على نشر مثل هذه الصور، وصلاتهم وترجحت وترغبونها بين تهديد مباشر أو كتم للإسلام تقدم مع التفاعل للروح الأفضل، فاتخاذ شاطئهم يشجيع إلا إذا أهتر، نشرت تلك صور بباب التفاعل للروح الأفضل، فاتخذ شاطئهم يشجيع إلا إذا أهتر، نشرت تلك صور بباب التعبير والرأي، وعليهم ألا يقبلوا هذه السخرية، لأن هذا أسوء يغير مم من شيء يتهلكم بهم.
3- استصحاب الدنمرك كاذبة مؤلمنية – من أصول مرسومنية. هي نفسها أصول مرسومنية للإسلام الذي قال منه مخرجه مؤخراً في هولندا؛ فكانت استصحابها وما أصلته للتعبير لا سيما عندما تحدث في مقابلة على القار الدنمركي تحدث عن الإسلام باللعة منتهجودة بإطلالات

بسم الله الرحمن الرحيم

مُقَدّمَة

الحمد لله رب العالمين، والصلاة والسلام على خاتم الأنبياء وإمام المرسلين، وبعد:
نحن المسلمين القاطنين في مملكة الدنمرك نعرض من بهمم الأمر – وكل مسلم كذلك، أحوالنا في هذه الديار التي تقع في شمال أوروبا، وهي إحدى الدول الاسكندنافية.
هذا البلد له لغته الخاصة، وعدد سكانه 5 ملايين نسمة غالبيتهم من البروتستانت، ومع أن رأيهم الصليب، إلا أنه قد عزئهم العلمانية حتى لو قلت عنهم (ملاعدة) فإنك لا تجانب الصواب.
وقد وفدت إلى هذه الديار مسلمون مهاجرون (الأتراك) واللاجئون من بلاد طحناها الحروب (البوسنة والهرسك – الصومال – العراق – لبنان) والأتاكي فإنه امتلاك الدنمرك بأجانب لا سيما من ديانة مختلفة يعكر حديثا بين 20-30 سنة. علماً أن تعداد المسلمين قد يصل إلى مائة وسبعين ألفا تقريباً.
يعاني القاطنون بينهم من أمور، على رأسها عدم الاعتراف الرسمي بالديانة الإسلامية، مما يشكل إشكالات كبيرة لظهرهم أظهرها به عدم السماح لهم ببناء مساجد، فيضطرون إلى تحويل بعض الشركات القديمة أو المستودعات إلى مصليات.
ضمن هذه الظروف، يوجد جيل يسأم عن ثاني العنصرية التي تؤرث وتغرقها بعد أحداث الحادي عشر من سبتمبر، وقد أخذت ألوانا متعددة، القاسم المشترك فيها الطعن بالإسلام (شارة تتحدث عن الحجاب – وأخرى عن موضوع الختان – وأخرى يتحدثون عن الأمراض التي تسببها الصلاة ... إلخ).
وكذلك تلك الظواهر بصور ورسومات عدة معروضة تصوير النبي صلى الله عليه وسلم بصورة مقيتة ومزرية، وملابسات هذه التصية تمثل عبارة عن امتناع الكثير من إتباع النبي ليكون على علاقة كتاب عن الإسلام – خوفاً من ردة فعل المسلمين – إما بسبب القائمين على جريدة (البولاند بوستن) أعترها منهم على علل وطلبوا إلى أربعين رسماً كاريكاتورية المزوعات تولوا القضية وأخذوها على معالجتهم إذا أرسلت الجريدة إلى أربعين رسماً لرسم النبي على تلك من باب التفاعل للروح الأفضل، فاتخذ شاطئهم يشجيع إلا إذا أهتر، نشرت تلك صور بباب (العدد الصادر يوم الجمعة 30-09-2005) ولعلها أراكت معا كالما لرئيس مجمعة أنه ينفي على المسلمين أن يقبلوا هذه السخرية، لأن هذا أسوء يغير مم من شيء يتهلكم بهم.
ولطهري الموقف تجاه تلك الجمعيات والمراكز أكبر الإسلامية فاجتمعوا يوم الأحد 02-10-2005 واتفقوا على جملة أمور للتصدي لهذه الشرسة الشرسة التي تال خاتم المدعوة الشمسية في الوجود (رسول الله صلى الله عليه وسلم).

• اتفق المجتمعون على تأسيس لجنة للنصرة لرسول الله صلى الله عليه وسلم ووضعنا ونسمية الشيخ راشد خليخل رئيسا لها.

• نقد ما ورد في هذه الجريدة تمثل بيان لأحد الدعاة لترجمه للغة الدنمركية إلا أنهم لم ينشروه نقد أو بعض الفقرات المجتزأة منه.

FIGURE 3. Introductory page from the folder brought by the Danish imams and mosque activists to Cairo, December 3–10, 2005. Raed Hlayhel's introduction begins (partial translation from Arabic): "We urge you [recipient of the letter or dossier] to—on the behalf of thousands of believing Muslims—to give us the opportunity of having a constructive contact with the press and particularly with the relevant decision makers, not briefly, but with a scientific methodology and a planned and long-term program seeking to make views approach each other and remove misunderstandings between the two parties involved." The letter also says: "Even though they [the Danes] belong to the Christian faith, secularization has overcome them, and if you say that they are all infidels, then you are not wrong."

Ahmed Abu Laban was the best known of the clerics, and he received a major share of the public blame in Denmark for what followed. (Abu means "father of," and although Danes knew the man as "Abu Laban," it is strictly speaking not a proper name. His full name was Ahmed Abdel Rahman Abu Laban.) When I spoke to him in December 2006, a month before his sudden death, he accepted responsibility for taking the complaints against the cartoons to the Islamic ambassadors in Copenhagen and wistfully expressed his regret that he did not get to meet with al-Qaradawi, whom he admired greatly.[6] Abu Laban told me that Hlayhel was primarily responsible for the folder but acknowledged that it was a collective endeavor. He conceded that it was a mistake to have made Akkari and Hlayhel the leaders of the delegation to the Middle East. I find Abu Laban's account of the internal divisions in the groups and his account of Hlayhel's role plausible for a number of reasons. Some of the mistakes and misrepresentations in the folder suggest that Hlayhel and Akkari were the authors, because they reiterated the same fallacies and viewpoints in other contexts. Both now live in Lebanon, and I have not been able to question them directly.

Carsten Juste, the chief editor of *Jyllands-Posten,* also took a dim view of Hlayhel's role in the cartoon controversy. "The important person in the claque was Raed Hlayhel. He had been very angry at us since we wrote about a sermon he gave in Copenhagen, where he described women as the devil's work. With his departure from Århus, things have gotten much quieter, thank God."[7] Ahmed Abu Laban was someone you could talk with, in Juste's view.

The dossier itself warrants a detailed description. It consists of Danish material in Arabic translation and Hlayhel's interpretive essay in Arabic. Some outrageous statements about Muslims made by members of the far-right Danish People's Party were also included and translated into Arabic. The twelve cartoons were reproduced one by one, with the captions translated, as were *Jyllands-Posten*'s editorials. In addition, the dossier carried copies of other cartoons from other Danish publications also purporting to show the Prophet, including one from a conservative paper, *Berlingske Tidende,* which showed the Prophet as a woman with a beard. Then there were the three false cartoons.

One was a blurry photograph of a man wearing pig ears and a snout. In the context it was assumed to be a cartoon depicting a Muslim as a pig, an animal that observant Muslims are not allowed to eat and consequently could only be interpreted as a particularly lowly insult. The image was subsequently identified as a picture of a contestant in a French pig-squealing contest and had no relation to attacks on Muslims in Europe. The origin of the other two drawings is uncertain, but one (anonymous) report is that they originally appeared on a right-wing U.S. web site.[8] One shows the Prophet as a pedophile rapist. Another depicts a prostrate praying Muslim being mounted from behind by a dog. The folder has a note to the effect that these pictures were not published by *Jyllands-Posten,* but if one leafs through the folder and just looks at the pictures, this is not obvious.

Akkari and other of the activists later explained to Danish journalists that the additional materials were examples of hate mail they and other Danish Muslims had received. The consequence, however, was that *Jyllands-Posten* was blamed for cartoons that the newspaper had never published.

When asked by the newspaper *Politiken,* Danish experts judged the translations of the Danish material in the dossier from Danish into Arabic to be largely accurate, if unprofessional. The impression conveyed by the dossier was nonetheless misleading and on some points plainly false.

UNLIKELY ALLIANCES

News about the delegation's visits to Cairo and Beirut with the dossier created a furor in Denmark. When the Muslim countries started a trade boycott and violent protests broke out at the end of January 2006, the members of the Cairo delegation and their folder were blamed for the international protests and accused of treason.

However, the international divisions between Sunni radicalism and the more moderate versions of Islamism were played out on a small scale among the activists and clerics from the four mosques at the center of the protests. All four mosques had a reputation for the Wahhabi-style of preaching. They were built around the charismatic clerics, who joined forces in the cartoon protests. Theological similarities notwithstanding, rivalry and theological disagreements drove the clerics apart and eventually also the mosques. All four mosques have also had members who have espoused extremist views and had been linked to jihadist conspiracies plotting murder and terrorist mayhem. Two of the clerics clearly distanced themselves from the extremist movements but the others had closer association with such groups.

There are 115 mosques in Denmark.[9] Most are housed in converted storefronts or old factory buildings, and they are usually identified by the name of their street address rather than the Arabic names that Danes find complicated.

When Ahmed Abu Laban died after a brief illness in January 2007, the outpouring of grief from his congregation at the Islamic Faith Community in a working-class neighborhood in Copenhagen showed Danes a different picture of a man they had blamed for the cartoon debacle. Much has been made of Abu Laban's political past and international connections. He was born to a Palestinian family in Jaffa and gained refugee status in Denmark in 1984 after his expulsion from Egypt and the United Arab Emirates for political activities. Lene Kühle, an expert on Danish mosque communities, notes that Abu Laban once worked as a missionary in Nigeria and credits him with having founded a network of small mosques

FIGURE 4. The four imams—Raed Hlayhel, Ahmed Akkari, Abu Bashar, and Abu Laban—arrive back in Copenhagen after meeting of the Union of Muslim Scholars in Bahrain, March 22–24, 2006. Photo: Getty/AFP.

of Somali and Arab congregants across Denmark and, in 1996, the Copenhagen mosque, which encompassed at the time of his death about seven thousand families.[10] He belonged to an earlier generation of Muslim Brotherhood exiles in Europe but had acclimated himself to Denmark. His theology was uncompromising—the Prophet cannot be depicted, he said—but his politics had become accommodating, and he advocated Muslim participation in Danish society and political institutions. He advocated that Muslims had to understand and accept Danish political culture, even though he himself sometimes had trouble doing so. In the contemporary panoply of Islamist sectarian divisions, Abu Laban should be counted as a moderate.

The other clerics were less well known. Mahmoud Fouad Albarazi is originally Syrian and has acted as imam for a mosque in Copenhagen that he started in 1998. He became a Danish citizen in 2002. He disdains "rabble-rousing clerics" and claims both to have trained with scholars belonging to an unbroken chain of intergenerationally transmitted learning dating back to the Prophet and also to have memorized more than a hundred thousand hadiths (oral or written histories of the Prophet's actions and statements). He has a degree from Al-Azhar University, the premier institution of religious learning in Islam, and is reportedly the best educated of the clerics.[11]

Albarazi was a member of al-Qaradawi's European Council for Fatwa and Research until 2004, when he was replaced (reportedly because he is difficult to get along with). He has since claimed membership in a North American fatwa council, which nonetheless does not list him as a member.[12] Abu Laban and Albarazi were not on good terms despite their joint origin in the Muslim Brotherhood in the 1980s.

Abu Bashar was associated with a mosque in the Vollsmose neighborhood in Odense, the third largest city in the country. Abu Bashar's actual name is Muhammad al-Khaled Samha. He is a Palestinian born in Syria and became a Danish citizen in 2004.

Akkari and Hlayhel both came from a mosque at Grimshøjvej in Århus. The mosque is located in a high-rise housing development, Gellerup, with about twenty thousand inhabitants, some 50 percent of immigrant origin. Hlayhel's reasons for coming to Denmark are unknown. It is possible that someone at the mosque recruited him to come as the imam, but the family was granted a visa for humanitarian reasons because of an ill child. He was fired and expelled from his mosque in October 2006. The congregants objected to his position on that summer's war in Lebanon. Danish Muslims are overwhelmingly Sunni, but many admired Hezbollah, a Shia party, for engaging the Israel Defense Forces during the invasion of Lebanon in July 2006, which began when Hezbollah started firing rockets at towns in northern Israel. Following the radical Sunni line on such issues, Hlayhel reportedly condemned Hezbollah and all Shias as infidels and targets for violent jihad.[13] He now lives in Tripoli in northern Lebanon and has been linked to radical Sunni groups in the area that are active among Palestinian refugees.

Hlayhel belongs to the orbit of Fatah-al-Islam, which was implicated in the Cologne train bombing and is a splinter group of an older organization, Fatah al-Intifada. The Syrian government is accused of backing both groups as a counterweight to the Shia Muslim Hezbollah, and Sunni radicals have engaged in combat with Hezbollah militants. Fatah-al-Islam is considered to be aligned with Al-Qaeda. The Council of Foreign Relations describes Fatah-al-Islam as a fringe group with little direct backing from Lebanese Muslims and Palestinians but as ideologically influential. Whatever Hlayhel's involvement, his views reflect the radical Sunni view of Shia Muslims as apostates.[14]

Ahmed Akkari, who became the spokesman for the activists, also lives in Lebanon today. Akkari was born in 1978 in Lebanon. He came to Denmark with his family in 1985 as a political refugeee from the Lebanese civil war and became a Danish citizen in 2005. Of the four imams, he is the only one who speaks good Danish.

Akkari was subject to a police investigation after he and Hlayhel were captured on a hidden camera joking about what could only be understood as a death threat against Naser Khader, a member of parliament from a liberal center party who became the clerical coalition's strongest opponent in the final stages of the protests. In March 2006, a French television crew recorded the two sitting in a car, and Akkari said: "If Khader becomes minister of integration, shouldn't someone dispatch two guys to blow up him and his ministry?" The exact tone of the remark is unclear, since the comment was made in Arabic and translated from Arabic to French and from French into Danish and English. Given that death threats were arriving by the thousands at various addresses in Denmark at the time, the remark was not a joking matter. Khader was at the time already under constant police protection. The day after the program was aired on French television, the coalition of imams dismissed Akkari as its spokesman.

"DEMOCRATIC MUSLIMS" AGAINST THE CLERICAL PROTESTERS

As the international protests spread, the momentum in Denmark shifted from the mosque activists. New umbrella groups emerged that took a different view of the political requirements for how Muslims properly should live in Denmark. Two imams, Fatih Alev, a young man of Turkish origin who has grown up in Denmark, and Abdul Wahid Pedersen, a Danish convert, called a demonstration in February 2006. Speaking in the gray winter weather before a subdued crowd, Alev explained that the issue was not the cartoons themselves—the "depiction" of the Prophet—but their message. Some of them—though not all—maligned Islam and described Muslims as inclined to violence because of their faith, said Alev and Pedersen. The two imams tried repeatedly to present a picture of the status of Muslims' lives in Denmark that was much more positive than the one broadcast by Hlayhel and Akkari.[15]

In February 2006, a new organization, Demokratiske Muslimer (Democratic Muslims), was organized by the member of parliament Naser Khader. The organization's name was taken by some critics to imply that Muslims who were not with Khader were undemocratic. Several thousand Danish Muslims sent in their membership subscription within the first few weeks, as did fifteen thousand other people who joined a separate support group for non-Muslims. The coalition of the four imams and their mosques fell apart when Abu Laban distanced himself from Akkari and Hlayhel.

It is tricky to carry out public surveys of Muslim opinion in Denmark because neither the census nor the population registry records religious affiliation. (The same problems exist in other countries.) Random sampling does not work in the case of small minorities—Muslims are about 4 percent of the population—particularly if residential segregation is a significant factor. Survey organizations instead cull samples of respondents from public registries for refugees and immigrants coming from predominantly Islamic countries. This means that immigrants who have become citizens or have married and changed their names are less likely to be included in the samples. In Denmark, the bias may be slight, since half the Muslims immigrated to Denmark after the mid-1980s and are therefore less likely to have disappeared from the registries of legal foreigners, but the sampling method is nevertheless a source of extra uncertainty beyond the usual ones associated with public opinion polling.

A survey carried out by a Danish research institute in March 2006 showed that 81 percent of Danish Muslims said that they found the cartoons offensive, and 49 percent testified they were "very offended." Sixty-nine percent also agreed with the clerics that the prime minister owed Muslims an apology. When the pollsters asked Muslims whether during the conflict they felt "mostly Muslim" or "mostly Danish," only 2 percent said that they felt "mostly Danish."[16]

The survey's findings provoked outrage. Several politicians complained that Muslims lacked national feeling and disrespected freedom of speech and Danish values. It was pointed out that when the Danish flag was being burned abroad and Danish property attacked, it was only proper that they should have set aside feelings of Muslim solidarity and sided with their country. The minister of integration, Rikke Hvilshøj, commented that the 10 percent of respondents who said that they were in sympathy with the demonstrators in the Middle East should "consider if Denmark was the right place for them to live."[17]

In the heat of debate it was forgotten that the surveys and the politicians in effect asked Muslims to choose between their God and country, a choice that many religious people, Christians and Jews, might feel that no person should have to make.

A week later, the same polling organization asked Danish Muslims which Muslim spokesman best represented their views. Only 40 percent thought that anybody qualified. For the remainder, the most popular representative was Naser Khader, supported by 13 percent. The second most popular was a left-wing doctor of Pakistani origin who, like Khader, is a secularist and a supporter of gay rights. Khader's nonpartisan organization, Democratic Muslims, formed in opposition to the clerics' coalition, was supported by nearly 20 percent of respondents. (After the cartoon controversy abated, Khader defected from his old party and formed a new one, Ny Alliance [New Alliance]. The new party started out with a bang but quickly lost ground because of bickering between Khader and the other party founders. It has since collapsed.)

The number of people who nominated Abu Laban or Akkari as their first choice of spokesmen for Danish Muslims is a reasonable proxy for measuring the two imams' support during the cartoon strife. Abu Laban was nominated only by 6 percent of the respondents, and Akkari, the young cleric from Århus, by 4 percent. Using the common estimate that there are two hundred thousand Muslims in Denmark and the poll's finding regarding support for the imams, the two radical clerics spoke for at most about 10 percent of Danish Muslims, or twenty thousand people. Twice as many people opposed them. And among the imams, the most popular were the relatively moderate figures.

Of the religious spokesmen the most popular was Fatih Alev, one of the imams who opposed Abu Laban and the coalition of mosques and imams. Clearly Danish Muslims were not keen to back religious spokesmen. Yet when the pollsters asked Muslims if "religious voices" were too dominant, one-third agreed while one-third did not. The rest said they did not know.[18]

SALAFISM AND JIHADISM IN DENMARK

Were the activist imams up to serious mischief? They knew people who engaged in violence or knew people who knew such people, but such association is not evidence of collusion.

In 1998, the Grimshøjvej mosque in Århus was implicated in a bank

robbery carried about by operatives from the Algerian terrorist organization the GSPC (Salafist Group for Preaching and Combat). The same network also produced Denmark's only Guantanamo Bay prisoner, Slimane
Hadj Abderrahmane. In February 2008, three young men—one with Danish citizenship and two of Tunisian nationality—were arrested for a plot to
strangle Kurt Westergaard, one of the cartoonists. The co-conspirators all
belonged to Hlayhel's circle in Århus.

Abu Bashar's political leanings are obscure. A train ticket to Odense
and Bashar's phone number were found in the possession of one of two
young men responsible for placing suitcases containing time-release
bombs on trains leaving Cologne on July 31, 2006. The plot has been
associated with the Lebanese extremist group Fatah-al-Islam, the same
group Hlayhel has been linked to by a Danish journalist visiting him in
Tripoli.[19] The bombs failed to detonate, and it was not until the suitcases
were turned in as lost luggage that their contents were discovered. Both
bombers and a helper were arrested. During interrogations, the bomber
with Bashar's phone number claimed that his anger over the cartoons had
inspired him to his act.[20] No charges have been made against Bashar in
connection with the train plot, and it could be a matter of his knowing the
wrong people. No explanation was provided when Bashar was laid off in
July 2006 from his job as prison chaplain. In 2007, a group from Odense
was arrested for plotting to blow up targets in Copenhagen. Three men
were later convicted on terrorism charges. All claimed that they were
angry about the cartoons. The men belonged to Bashar's mosque. Neither
the mosque nor Bashar himself were directly implicated.

Abu Laban, too, had problems in his congregation. The families of
some of the young men belonging to the Glostrup group, whose members were convicted in a bomb plot in Sarajevo and later for unspecified
plans to blow up targets in Copenhagen, belonged to his mosque. Again,
neither Abu Laban nor the mosque has been accused of tolerating terrorists. The young men left Abu Laban's mosque because the preaching
there was not to their taste, and the families of the young men were
entirely opposed to their enterprise. One father stopped his son from
joining the cell that was later rounded up in Bosnia.

It is hard to know what to make of the links between religious orthodoxy and political extremism. Gilles Kepel links Abu Laban to Gamaat
Islamiya, the Egyptian organization of Ayman al-Zawahiri, Al-Qaeda's

number two, and to the Gamaat's "emir," Omar Abdel-Rahman, the so-called blind sheikh convicted in the 1993 World Trade Center bombing, whom Kepel claims was "hosted" at Abu Laban's mosque.[21] Kepel cites no sources, but a report on "Jihad in Denmark" by Michael Taarnby Jensen, a Danish researcher, is likely the source for Kepel's assessment of Abu Laban's political inclinations.[22] Taarnby Jensen links Abu Laban to Abu Talal (also known as Talat Fouad Qassem), a confirmed jihadist who was arrested in Croatia in 1995 and handed over by the Central Intelligence Agency to Egypt, where he reportedly was executed.[23] Taarnby Jensen's source is a single Danish newspaper article from 2006, which noted that in the early 1990s Abu Talal used to preach at a mosque where Abu Laban also preached before he founded his own congregation.

Lorenzo Vidino, an American terrorism expert, has linked Abu Laban and the cartoon crisis to the global jihadi movement. His argument is based on Abu Laban's presumed association with Said Mansour, a convicted preacher of jihad, who has been living in Copenhagen since the 1980s. Mansour is Moroccan-born and became a Danish citizen in 1988.[24] He is currently serving a prison sentence for proselytizing for jihad. This is his second sentence on terrorism charges. Vidino also claims that Abu Laban can be connected—through Mansour—to Musab al-Zarqawi, the deceased leader of Al-Qaeda's operations in Iraq and the Gamaat Islamiya.

Vidino praises the Danes for being awake to these nefarious connections when they refused to appease the cartoon protesters: "While much of Europe has been asleep at the wheel, oblivious to the monumental threat radical Islam poses to its future, at least one country is increasing[ly] awake. Denmark's first battle is domestic, unmasking the enemy's fifth column inside its borders. As embassies burn, the rest might want to catch on, too."[25]

I take a different view. Most families have both bad apples and rags-to-riches success stories. Knowing someone who gets into trouble with the law is not evidence of one's own guilt but rather of the closeness of the crisscrossing networks of family, religion, and ethnicity, as well as of the political ferment that affects Muslim communities throughout Europe. The head of the Danish police's security service between 1997 and 2006, Hans Jørgen Bonnichsen, is unequivocal in his judgment: Abu Laban was not part of "the enemy within" and not involved with the Egyptian network and its activities in Denmark.[26]

Vidino's account exaggerates Mansour's importance and homogenizes the complex political landscape of the expellees and that of the international terrorist networks. Mansour and Abu Laban knew each other in the small circles of Copenhagen radical politics, but they were not friends and had no ideological affinity. Mansour ran a jihadi publishing house out of a storefront in Copenhagen, and translated and distributed al-Zarqawi's speeches in Denmark. He was in contact with Mullah Krekar, the leader of Ansar al-Islam, which subsequently became al-Zarqawi's organization. But Mansour saw Krekar in Oslo, where Krekar has lived since 1991, when he was given political refugee status in Norway.[27] The Danish police investigated Mansour's activities after the 1993 World Trade Center bombing. His most illustrious jihadi contact was Omar Abdel-Rahman, the Blind Sheikh from Brooklyn convicted in the 1993 attack.

Omar Abdel-Rahman visited Copenhagen in December 1990 and May 1991 and stayed in Mansour's home during his visit.[28] The two men's activities were entirely legal at the time. A picture of Mansour with Abdel-Rahman sitting in what appears to be Mansour's home was reprinted in the Danish press. Mansour also had close contacts with Abu Hamza al-Masri, the former cleric at the Finsbury Park Mosque in London and founder of the radical group Al-Muhajiroun, who is currently being held in Belmarsh prison and has been indicted on terrorism charges in the United States in connection with the formation of a terrorist training camp in Bly, Oregon.

Abu Laban's vision of the good society was not the new caliphate. He wanted recognition for Islam and for Muslims, and he wanted Muslims to live by religious law. His political objective was to enable the adjudication of personal law issues under religious law and make it possible for Danish Muslims to live fully religious lives. He regarded the depiction of the Prophet as the core problem of the cartoons and worried little about Islamophobia and the slander of Muslims. What concerned him was the violation of a religious prohibition. He thought Danish democracy fully capable of accommodating religious Muslims.

THE IMPORTANCE OF MISINFORMATION

Danes thought that the sheikhs deliberately provoked the cartoon crisis by persuading Islamic countries to campaign against Denmark. The timing of the second eruption of demonstrations and protests in late January 2006, six weeks after the delegations visited Cairo and Beirut, reinforced the impression of cause and effect. Bragging that they had mobilized the mighty ummah, the global Muslim nation, the activist clerics fueled Danish anger. Many international newspapers also credited their claims.[29]

The sentiment in Denmark was that the imams had succeeded only by lying about the things Danes do. It could be argued, however, that the dossier had little effect on events, certainly on the actions of the Muslim governments. The visit to Cairo was arranged after the Egyptians had complained to the United Nations. The idea about a trade boycott was also well under way by the time the delegation handed out their homemade dossier in Cairo. Arguably, at most the folder with cartoons stoked an already angry conflict. Raed Hlayhel and the other delegates to Cairo and Beirut—who also met in Damascus with Ahmed Badr-Eddine Hassoun, the Syrian grand mufti—would never have obtained access to religious authorities, journalists, and high-ranking diplomats had a high-level decision not already been made to make the cartoons a matter of international relations.

My view is that the dossier and the false cartoons made a significant difference but not an essential one. Few of the Middle Eastern leaders I interviewed knew the difference between the false cartoons and the real ones until I handed them the folder and explained which ones had been published by *Jyllands-Posten* and which had not. I also discovered an information divide between Internet users and those who rely on others to keep them informed. Ministers and diplomats, secretaries-general, and presidents of national associations generally rely on assistants and secretaries to mind their email. As a rule, they had only a secondhand acquaintance with the cartoons unless they had seen the dossier. Surprisingly, many had not actually seen the cartoons until they were shown or told about the folder. And everyone who had seen the dossier, in Mecca or Cairo, in December 2005 or at some other later occasion—the meeting in Bahrain of al-Qaradawi's Union of Muslim Scholars in March 2006 was the first time many of the Muslin Brotherhood had seen the cartoons—thought that the ugly, sexually explicit cartoons had been published by *Jyllands-Posten*. Evidently the dossier was the primary source of information for Middle Eastern religious authorities, and it shaped their view about the treatment of Muslims in Denmark.

The trip to Cairo gave the activists a platform and lent them a legitimacy they would not otherwise have enjoyed. Albarazi, Hlayhel, and Akkari were allowed significant airtime on Al Jazeera and other Arab-language television stations. Their folder traveled far and wide in pan-Arabic political circles. The BBC World News showed footage of Bashar displaying the pig-snout caricature during one of the delegation's meetings in Cairo. It was a particularly embarrassing faux pas because the BBC had officially declined to show the cartoons. The BBC quickly issued a correction, but the original story stuck in people's mind. People who told me that the BBC was their primary source of knowledge about the cartoons also thought that the pig-snout picture had been published by *Jyllands-Posten*.

The cartoons were the lead item on the largely state-controlled Middle Eastern news programs at the end of January 2006. News stations showed footage of protesters in front of the Danish embassies and Danish goods being removed from the shelves of supermarkets. The dossier also featured in the broadcasts. News stories showed the cartoons indirectly by using footage from meetings where officials were passing the folder around and pointing with disgusted looks on their faces to the enlarged pictures of the cartoons. The offending pictures were blotted out, but the outlines were visible. The image of the man wearing the pig snout was regularly given particular prominence.[30]

An editorial writer in the Egyptian *Al-Ahram Weekly*, a widely read English-language paper, wrote: "What sort of input to humor or intellect is it to portray a man who has contributed to the spiritual composition of a large portion of humanity as a pig?"[31] Indeed.

The European branches of the Muslim Brotherhood were no wiser about the false cartoons. Lhaj Thami Brèze, secretary-general of the Union of Islamic Organizations of France (UOIF), did not know that the dossier included cartoons that had never been published in *Jyllands-Posten* when I spoke to him. Ahmed Sheikh, the president of the Muslim Association of Britain (MAB), another Muslim Brotherhood affiliate, who said he had first seen the cartoons at a meeting in Bahrain in March 2006 (long after the MAB had cosponsored a demonstration at Trafalgar Square in London against the cartoons), was no wiser. Most of the media coverage neglected to mention specifics about the cartoons, but occasional references to the false cartoons can be found.

THE MUSLIM BROTHERHOOD

The importance of the dossier was demonstrated later. Three weeks after Akkari and Hlayhel met with Sheikh Faysal Mawlawi, the deputy head of the European Council for Fatwa and Research, in Beirut, the Muslim Brotherhood was drawn into the conflict. Abu Laban had earlier sought in vain to meet with Sheikh Yusuf al-Qaradawi, who is of Egyptian origin but resides in Qatar. The unfortunate dossier reached the elderly man nonetheless. On January 29, 2006, the Muslim Brotherhood clerics who belonged to the International Union of Muslim Scholars issued a statement condemning the cartoons. Al-Qaradawi not only founded the union but continues to serve as president and theological principal. Although he had tried to stay out of the conflict, al-Qaradawi was drawn in.

The union's statement expressed disappointment that diplomatic channels had failed to elicit an apology from the Danish government. It appealed to all Arab and Muslim governments to support "Muslim people's anger at this direct insult of the Prophet (peace and blessings be upon him) by the publishing of these offensive cartoons. Arab and Muslim governments should also exercise all possible political and diplomatic pressure on the Danish and Norwegian governments so as to halt all such organized anti-Islam campaigns that aim at spreading hatred of and contempt for Islam, its sanctities, and its believers." It concluded by recommending a trade boycott.

The first Friday in February 2006 al-Qaradawi delivered a fiery sermon on Qatar TV, a satellite station, and told Muslims across the world to stage a "day of rage" against the scurrilous cartoons: "The *Ummah* [nation] must rage in anger. It is told that Imam Al-Shafi'i said: 'Whoever was angered and did not rage is a jackass.' We are not a nation of jackasses. We are not jackasses for riding, but lions that roar. We are lions that zealously protect their dens, and avenge affronts to their sanctities. We are not a nation of jackasses. We are a nation that should rage for the sake of Allah, His Prophet, and His book. We are the nation of Muhammad, and we must never accept the degradation of our religion."[32]

The sermon was transmitted by Al Jazeera and transcribed on the web site IslamOnline, which al-Qaradawi created in 1997. Although *ummah* can be translated into English as "the community of believers," the web site always uses the more eloquent and political term "the nation." Al-Qaradawi turned the cartoon protests against "our feeble governments," as he described the governments of Islamic countries, which he accused of toeing the American line, and warned them not to "split from their peoples." He also warned Western governments against being silent about "crimes" offending the Prophet. The actions of the editors and the inactions of government would cause terrorism because Muslims feel they must take the defense of the Prophet in their own hands.

It quickly became clear that the European branches and the younger generation of the Egyptian Brotherhood were not in agreement with al-Qaradawi's incitement to rage and his policy recommendations. Ibrahim El-Houdaiby is a young Egyptian Brotherhood activist who lives in the Untied Arab Emirates. He is a fourth-generation Brotherhood member and is close to Yusuf al-Qaradawi, whom he professes to love.[33] The Egyptian Brotherhood was founded in 1928 by Hassan al-Banna, a twenty-one-year-old Egyptian nationalist and religious reformer. Hassan El-Hodeiby, Ibrahim El-Houdaiby's great-grandfather, took over the leadership in 1948 after al-Banna was assassinated. His grandfather, Mamoun El-Hodeiby, was supreme guide from November 2001 until his death in 2004. Tariq Ramadan, another inspirational young Islamist reformer, is a grandson of al-Banna.

El-Houdaiby recalled first getting text messages about the cartoons in October 2005 from various religious sources. (These may also have been postings on web sites, which most people in the Middle East read on their cell phones.) We spoke over the phone.[34] El-Houdaiby railed against the Salafists—a term he used to indicate the Wahhabi-associated organizations in the Middle East—and their "narrow and shallow understanding of Islam" and described the Egyptian government's decision to whip up protests against the cartoons as a plot directed against the Muslim Brotherhood. The cartoons were the wrong issue for Muslims to get worked up about, he stated. They were offensive, but not worth the fuss. "I revere the Sheikh [al-Qaradawi], but on this issue he was wrong."

It became apparent during our conversation that El-Houdaiby did not know that the most insulting cartoons had been taken from the Internet and added to the folder by activists and had never been published by *Jyllands-Posten* or any other newspaper. El-Houdaiby assured me that al-Qaradawi also had no idea about this and promised to pass the information on to him. The sheikh, however, is ill, and my request for an interview was not granted. Would knowledge about the false cartoons have changed his views? Unlikely.

Between al-Qaradawi, the statement from the International Union of Muslim Scholars, and the condemnations from the established religious authorities in Saudi Arabia and Egypt, there was hardly an imam in the Middle East who had missed the message. The cartoons were condemned in mosques across the Middle East starting on January 27 and the following two Fridays in early February. (The statement circulated before its official release on January 29.)

When Danish embassies and offices in Beirut, Damascus, and Tehran were attacked and burned, the self-same religious authorities and clerics tried to damp down the fires they themselves had started. Three weeks after al-Qaradawi's speech and the statement's release, a group of forty Muslim scholars—some in al-Qaradawi's camp and others not—issued the first fatwa on the cartoons emanating from recognized and respected scholars and professors. They declared the cartoons "an unacceptable crime" and called on "the Danish government and the Danish people" to apologize, including a vague threat that an apology was required "to ensure that Denmark is not isolated from the international community." This was presented as a religious edict on the cartoons, but the statement allocated more space to Koranic directives to be courteous in disagreement and not to react violently to a provocation.[35]

The list of signatories included Deobandi, Shiite, and Sunni authorities, as well as grand muftis and professors from Egypt and Saudi Arabia. It also included the American Hamza Yusuf Hansson and the Egyptian televangelist Amr Khaled. Missing from the list were only the Turkish religious establishment, which as a state institution generally prefers to issue its own declarations. Amr Khaled later accepted an invitation to an event intended to promote reconciliation organized by the Danish foreign ministry in Copenhagen. The gesture and Khaled's willingness to work with other Western governments earned him criticism in Egypt.[36]

Once the extremists started to call for murder, the moderates started to triangulate on the appropriateness of "forgiveness" and how to calm matters down. The Muslim Brotherhood posted a menu of appropriate actions on IslamOnline: "However, this does not justify violence in responding to this ridicule of Prophet Muhammad (peace and blessings be upon him). We all know the teaching of Prophet Muhammad (peace and blessings be upon him) where he said: "Whoever hurts a dhimi (non-Muslim), it is as if he has hurt me." The statement listed the actions permitted to Muslims according to scripture:

> The right course to be followed, however, is as follows:
>
> 1. Express anger and protest in a polite way through rallies and peaceful demonstration.
>
> 2. Send e-mails to relevant authorities to inform them about our stance.
>
> 3. Boycott the products of the countries that did not apologize for the defamation of the Prophet Muhammad (peace and blessings be upon him).
>
> 4. Launch a campaign to educate the people about Prophet Muhammad (peace and blessings be upon him).

There is no way to test if the clerical endorsement of peaceful political actions had a restraining effect. In any event, the crisis continued to escalate.

THE PROTESTS ENTER THE EXTREMIST CYCLE

During February 2006, clerics and political leaders from the radical opposition in Muslim countries—people we may call "radical Islamists," as compared to the democratic Islamists governing Turkey—joined the campaign. Demonstrations spread across the world and violence erupted. Casualties tallied from local newspaper accounts of these demonstrations amount to two hundred dead and as many as eight hundred injured (table 2). Although the casualties and injuries were reported as occurring during demonstrations against the cartoons, in fact the cartoons now became intertwined with local political grievances.[37]

In this novel phase of the spiraling cycle of protest, the new actors pushed radicalization. The claims changed from the narrow focus on the religious insult committed by a Danish newspaper and the recalcitrance of the Danish government to atone for that act, which had preoccupied Middle Eastern religious authorities and governments in the second stage of the protests. The cartoons became yoked to the radical Sunni movement's larger complaint against the West, "the Zionist-Crusader nations" in jihadi parlance, and the radicals' long-running protests against national governments.

Table 2.

Number of victims associated with demonstrations against the Danish cartoons (estimates based on local newspaper reports)

DATE (2006)	COUNTRY	DEAD	INJURED
February 5	Lebanon	1	50+
	Turkey	1	—
February 6	Afghanistan	5	6
	Somalia	1	7+
	United Arab Emirates	1	—
February 7	Afghanistan	4	20–30
February 8	Afghanistan	4	20
February 10	Kenya	1	1
February 14	Pakistan	2	?
February 15	Pakistan	3	85
February 17	Libya	11	50+
February 18	Nigeria	45	185
	Pakistan	—	4+
February 19	Pakistan	—	50
February 21	Nigeria	60	300+
February 22	Nigeria	20–27	?
February 23–24	Nigeria	80+	?
April 14	Egypt	1	12+
May 13	Germany	1 (suicide)	—
	Total	241–248+	790–800+

Demonstrations were often triggered when a local newspaper decided to reprint one or more of the cartoons. In those cases the resulting violence was against surrogates and often did not affect Danes. In Benghazi, Libya, the protests, which turned violent, were directed against the Italian minister Roberto Calderoli, a member of the far-right Northern League, who wore a T-shirt with one of the cartoons printed on its front when he appeared on a television program. Calderoli was forced to resign after the deadly Benghazi demonstrations. Libya has few ties to Denmark but has a long-established relationship with Italy, its former colonial ruler. Italian and Egyptian papers attributed the demonstrations to Calderoli's shirt and the cartoons, but the demonstrators were also described as shouting antigovernment slogans.[38]

In Nigeria, where the highest casualties were reported, several waves of demonstrations took place. In the Muslim-dominated northern cities of Maiduguri and Katsina, the demonstrations developed into attacks on businesses owned by Christians. More than thirty Christians were killed and many more injured, including members of the police force. The toll on this one day was reported to be forty-five dead and 185 injured.[39]

In some cases the street protests and attacks on Danish diplomatic missions and aid workers were the result of government direction or had powerful political sponsorship. The Syrian government was blamed for attacks on the Danish embassy in Damascus and the Danish embassy in Beirut on February 4 and 5. In Beirut, a Sunni group that is regarded as "Syrian-backed" sponsored the demonstration that preceded the attack.

In Egypt, the English-language *Al-Ahram Weekly* reported that the attack on the Danish embassy in Beirut resulted from complicated machinations involving the al-Hariri clan's effort to counter the Shiite Hezbollah in the battle for control of Lebanon's fractious politics. The publication cites Hilal Khashan, a professor of political science at the American University of Beirut, as stating that in February 2006 "the Hariri group bussed many groups in from Akkar" for the demonstration against the cartoons, "but they went on the rampage, burning the Danish Embassy, a Christian church and a number of stores."[40]

The demonstration that led to the torching of the embassy took place on a Saturday, after the end of prayers, and had been organized by text messages. The absence of police suggested that the authorities had been taken by surprise. The religious authorities in Damascus did not condone the violent demonstrations. Ahmed Badr-Eddine Hassoun, the Syrian grand mufti, who had met with one of the protesting Danish imams and been given their dossier, condemned the cartoons on Syrian television and in other contexts but also condemned demonstrations. Afterward, he reassured the Danes that the government would take responsibility for rebuilding the damaged embassy building. The Syrian government eventually did accept liability for failing to protect the embassy in Damascus and offered restitution. One day later, on Sunday, the embassy in Beirut was attacked. A Danish friend (who wishes to remain anonymous) had been evacuated from Damascus only to arrive in Beirut for another day of

FIGURE 5. Rioters set fire to the building housing the Danish embassy in Damascus, Syria, February 4, 2005. Photo: Getty/AFP.

anti-Danish demonstrations. He described the attackers in Beirut as "a Syrian rent-a-mob," which illustrates how the cartoon protests by this time were entangled with the local struggles between Sunni movements in the region.

The Beirut and Damascus demonstrations proved typical of many demonstrations against the cartoons in Africa, Europe, and South Asia: thousands of people summoned by text messages and mobile phone calls, the messages anonymous and organizers unknown, the demonstrations held without permission of the authorities. This method mimics those used by flash mobs and rave parties, large-scale gatherings of individuals in locations announced on short notice by text messages. The attendees do not know one another but are linked by a Boolean chain of forwarded messages created when each recipient of a text message forwards it to everyone in his or her mobile phone book. Demonstrations can quickly balloon. In the case of flash mobs, the participants are usually instructed to carry out a particular act—dance, empty everything off a store's shelves of a store, or have a pillow fight—and then disperse. The events appear spontaneous but are in fact organized. Aside from deciding the location and the act, the organizers also often ensure that the mob is filmed and that video clips are posted on YouTube afterward.[41] In the cartoon demonstrations, the slogans and the violence—attacks on property, frenzied denunciations of the cartoonists and the West—were afterward usually attributed to the presence of a small number of individuals who led the way, as in the case of my friend's "rent-a-mob" observation. Political responsibility was difficult to ascertain, which led to rumors about the involvement of the Syrian secret police and other dark forces.

Email spam and death threats to *Jyllands-Posten*'s editorial offices in Århus and Copenhagen increased in late February 2006. The threatening mail and calls came from everywhere, and often it was difficult to pinpoint locations. Reports of bounties circulated, but their source was hard to trace. One sheikh promised a reward in gold and another in dollars. Inflation set in, and an Indian minister from Uttar Pradesh, Yaqoob Qureshi, offered a million dollars and the killer's own weight in gold for beheading one of the cartoonists. One has to presume that the minister's offer was not to be taken literally, and the real risk to the editors' and cartoonists' lives is difficult to assess.

One bounty offer in particular was felt keenly on the Internet. In February 2006, Maulana Mohammed Yousaf Qureshi, the chief cleric at the Mohabat Khan mosque in Peshawar, located in the North-West Frontier Province of Pakistan, announced that he would give a $25,000 reward and a car for killing "the cartoonist." Apparently, he thought that one person was responsible for all the cartoons. The reward inspired a chain-email campaign that flooded the inboxes at *Jyllands-Posten* and the Danish prime minister's office. The email is reproduced here (see boxed text). The senders' email addresses are redacted, but the rest of the content of the letter, including the advertisement for using Yahoo, is a faithful copy.

In February, demonstrations in Pakistan spread from Karachi, Lahore, and Islamabad to the North-West Frontier Province. Maulana Fazl ur Rahman, leader of a faction within the Jamiat Ulema-e-Islam Party, based in the North-West Frontier Province, and a chief enemy of Pervez Musharraf, Pakistan's president from 1999 to 2008, declared on February 6 that he and his allies would start a movement to oust the president. The cartoons, he said, were part of an American scheme to bring Muslim countries to their knees. Musharraf's reaction had been feeble, and resolutions were not enough. Diplomatic relations should be severed with all countries

Box 3. Death threat offering a bounty for killing Flemming Rose and the cartoonists sent as an emailed chain letter on February 1, 2006, copied to Jyllands-Posten's office.

From: Gul Badshah Khan [mailto:gul—badshah@yahoo.com]
Date: 4. februar 2006 07:21
[redacted]
Emne: Golden Mail (US$25106) from Holy Makkah.
Dear Reader (Muslim or Non-Muslim),
"Any one who will Properly Punish, Mr.Flemming Rose, the culture editor of the "Jyllands-Posten" a Denmark newspaper who came up with the idea of soliciting illustrators to draw their interpretations of Prophet Mohammed (Sallal-laho Alaehe Wasallum) will receive a reward of US $25,106. (No time limit)"
1. Gul Badshah Khan US $10,000 Holy Makkah
2. Afzal Zeeshan US $15,000 Holy Madinah
3. Sayed Khalid Pasha US $53.26 Al Khobar
4. Mr. Wajid US $53.26
[add your name]
Following are the Denmark Cartoonists, who participated in the competition will soon receive their rewards from slaves of Prophet Muhammad (Sallal-laho Alaehe Wasallum)
1. Kurt Westergaard
2. Jens Julius Hansen
3. Franz Fuúchsel
4. Arne Sørensen
5. Annette Carlsen
6. Erik Abild Sørensen
7. Rasmus Sand Høyer
8. Claus Seidel
9. Poul Erik Poulsen
10. Peder Bundgaard
11. Bob Katzennelson
12. Lars Refn
Contact:
Gul Badshah Khan
IT Engineer, Holy Makkah
Mobile: 00966–504630407
Please forward this mail, so it reaches to the right person.
Note: You can add your share, even if it is $1 by adding your name and genuine contact number then CC it to gul—badshah@yahoo .com & jp@jp.dk (offending news paper)
Send instant messages to your online friends http://uk.messenger .yahoo.com

FIGURE 6. Demonstrators protest the cartoons in Peshawar, Pakistan, February 14, 2006. The printer's copyright listing on placards carried by the demonstrators in the photo traces the origin to the North-West Frontier Province, a stronghold of extremist groups. Photo: Getty/AFP.

that had republished the cartoons. Fazl ur Rahman's statement "main-streamed" the complaint against the cartoons into Pakistani electoral politics. A week later, fifty thousand turned out in demonstrations in Peshawar, where mobs over several days of demonstrations set fire to motels, busses, and American franchise restaurants. By the end of February, preventive house arrests for opposition leaders, emergency orders, and clashes between the police and demonstrators had turned into what reporters described as "fierce running battles" on the streets of Lahore.[42] Slogans blamed the cartoons on the United States. The printer's copyright statement on a picture from a Pakistani demonstration traces the origin of the poster linking Anders Fogh Rasmussen to George W. Bush's war on terror to the North-West Frontier Province (fig. 6).

The portrayal of the street as an Arab or Muslim form of political expression, the stage for "rent-a-mobs" or extremists with anti-Western agendas, became routine in the Western press. Occasional reports, however, described the demonstrators as legitimately angry, ordinary Muslims who have been deprived of proper representation by their government. At different times both characterizations may apply.

In February, the protests turned against the governments that had originally started them. They had less to do with outrage at the cartoons than with a broader strategy of collective mobilization and agitation.[43] Political mob violence may involve accidental death and mayhem, but these were not spontaneous outbursts. The cartoons became a medium for the radical Sunni and, to a lesser extent Shiite, groups across the Middle East and in Pakistan to mobilize popular anger against local governments for purposes that had nothing to do with the feelings of observant Muslims or the human rights of Danish Muslims.

CHAPTER 5

Seeking the Third Way

IN APRIL 2006, not long after the worldwide protests had peaked, the Pew Global Attitudes Project surveyed public opinion in a number of predominantly Muslim countries and the opinions of both Muslims and non-Muslims in Europe. Pew asked respondents whether they had heard of the cartoons, and if so, how they had heard of them. The survey revealed the cartoons' extraordinary global news market saturation (table 3). More than 90 percent of Muslims in the United Kingdom, France, and Germany—and in Egypt, Jordan, and Nigeria—had heard about the cartoons. Muslims and Christians were polled separately in Europe and Nigeria, and non-Muslims were only slightly less cognizant of the cartoons. In Turkey and Pakistan, 89 and 87 percent of respondents, respectively, had heard of the cartoons. In the United States, in contrast, the cartoons were less known.

Most people had heard about the cartoons via television. Few people gained their information about them from the Internet. A sizeable minority of European Muslims had heard of the cartoons from friends and family or in the mosque—presumably through their imam's sermons. In Spain, 24 percent of Muslims heard about the cartoons via a friend, a family member, or in the mosque. Sixteen percent of British Muslims and 11 percent of French Muslims reported that they had learned about the cartoon through personal contacts.

Table 3.

Survey questions: Have you heard of the Muhammad cartoons and how did you hear (percent)?

COUNTRY	Q: HAVE YOU HEARD OF THE MUHAMMAD CARTOONS?	Q: HOW DID YOU FIRST HEAR OF THE CARTOONS?			
		TELEVISION	RADIO OR NEWSPAPER	INTERNET	FAMILY/FRIENDS OR MOSQUE
Egypt	98	64	14	2	19
France (GP)	86	59	35	2	3
France (M)	93	65	19	5	11
Germany (GP)	91	59	32	4	3
Germany (M)	96	73	14	4	8
Indonesia	75	89	4	—	7
Jordan	99	57	16	2	23
Nigeria (GP)	79	21	37	1	41
Nigeria (M)	91	10	45	—	45
Pakistan	87	43	25	—	31
Spain (GP)	84	57	32	3	8
Spain (M)	80	54	18	3	24
Turkey	89	96	3	1	1
United Kingdom (GP)	88	55	40	1	5
United Kingdom (M)	96	56	21	4	16
United States	65	63	23	7	5

Note: GP = general population; M = Muslims

Source: The Pew Global Attitudes Project, *Muslims in Europe: Economic Worries Top Concerns about Religious and Cultural Identity.* Released July 6, 2006. Research carried out April 2006. Telephone interviews. Muslim oversample, margin of error 5–6 percent in Europe; 3 percent elsewhere.

The cartoons were something Muslims talked about when they met—but in fact most Muslims first learned about the cartoons from the television. Only a minority of Muslims in Europe regularly pray at mosques, although the number varies greatly from France to the United Kingdom and within subcommunities. The imams' role as broadcasters of news and views is accordingly limited. Yet although Muslims and non-Muslims heard about the cartoons from the same news sources, they interpreted the news differently.

There was excited talk during the cartoon controversy about the formation of a global virtual political village.[1] The Pew survey suggests, however, that it is easy to exaggerate the role of the Internet in the conflict. Muslims got the news about the cartoons the same way most of the rest of the world's population: sitting in front of the TV.

The survey draws a picture of how public opinion was manufactured and, in particular, how global Muslim populations obtained knowledge about the cartoons. Over a three-week period, the cartoons and the protests against them linked Europe, the Middle East, Africa, and many parts of Asia in a shared news cycle. The media created its own stories, and demonstrations begot counterdemonstrations from continent to continent. The Middle Eastern religious authorities' condemnations of the cartoons in late January 2006 were disseminated through mosques and the media, and as the news spread, the demonstrations grew.

It is nonetheless false to say that the media created the cartoon protests. In the absence of a political organization in the form of existing networks and movements—Hezbollah in Lebanon and Jamaat-i-Islami in Pakistan—mass demonstrations were rare. In Egypt, the only sizable demonstration took place at Al-Azhar University and with the blessing of religious authorities. Demonstrations in Iran were held with the approval of the government or, perhaps more accurately, parts of the government. The Pakistani demonstrations were organized by radical sheikhs and Islamist fringe parties. In Indonesia, Libya, Kenya, and elsewhere, the protests remained confined to sit-ins at Danish foreign missions and were small in scope. There is little support for the assertion that Muslims reacted with spontaneous rage.

The media in the Middle East is largely state-controlled, but in recent years satellite television stations have challenged the dominance of state-owned networks. Al Jazeera, based in Qatar, was created as an Arab news and current affairs network but added an English-language channel in November 2006 and is now widely watched in Europe. The network claims to reach forty million Arabic-speaking viewers, most in the Middle East, and about a million in the United States.[2] The use of satellite dishes has made it difficult for governments to control access to the channel, should they wish to do so. Al Jazeera carried constant news about the cartoons and the protests. In other ways the cartoons also illustrated in other ways how radical movements exploited the new media technologies for the purpose of political mobilization. The Internet played an important role in spreading propaganda, both in coordinating actions between the fringe groups and as a vehicle of intimidation and radicalization.

Cyber attacks and viral email—so-called denial of service attacks intended to shut the recipient's computers down—followed late in the protest cycle in late February and March 2006. More than two thousand Danish computers were hacked. Most of the victims were randomly selected and had no relationship to *Jyllands-Posten*. Girl scout troops, school districts, private companies, and nursery schools were among the victims according to H-Zone, a watchdog site that tracks hackers.[3] Danish ministry web sites were vandalized with the equivalent of Internet graffiti. *Jyllands-Posten's* Internet site and its internal computer system were briefly incapacitated. One morning, the chief editor, Carsten Juste, turned on his computer and found nine thousand new messages in his inbox. If there was anything important in the tsunami, he never saw it. The avalanche of threatening emails to the newspaper in Denmark and the cyber attacks on Danish web sites originated in North Africa, Saudi Arabia, or Pakistan.

The international media coverage facilitated mobilization, but the large demonstrations in Europe are best understood in local terms. Muslim associations were pulled into the conflict in reaction to government actions or as republication of the cartoons in local media made them a domestic issue. We need to consider once again the old-fashioned and poorly understood politics of parties, states, and Muslim civic groups.

STANDING UP FOR EUROPEAN MUSLIMS

The European protests in February 2006 were sparked by the republication of the cartoons in European newspapers. Few people had seen the cartoons when they were originally published in Denmark.

The very public denunciation of the cartoons by Middle Eastern religious authorities in late January 2006 placed European Muslim associations and opinion leaders in an awkward position. Although they were generally reluctant to allow Middle Eastern governments and clerics to speak for them, they nevertheless considered that the cartoons were an offense to religious people and an insult to all Muslims, religious or secular. The same divisions between radicals and moderates that charac-terized the reactions in the Middle East quickly emerged also in Europe, though here the moderates prevailed. On February 3, a few thousand men, mostly young but also graybeards and little boys, demonstrated in London against the cartoons. The demonstration was among the ugliest seen in Europe in recent years. The protesters chanted: "Denmark, Den-mark watch your back; bin Laden is coming back" and "We want Danish blood." Invocations to the greatness of God—"Allah Akhbar"—were inter-spersed with shouts of "Bomb, bomb, bomb—Denmark" and other coun-tries, where the cartoons had been reprinted.[4] The London demonstration was organized jointly by Hizb ut-Tahrir and Al-Muhajiroun, an offshoot of Hizb ut-Tahrir created by the radical cleric Omar Bakri Muhammad and now disbanded. Four participants in the demonstration were later arrested on charges of incitement of violence, and each was sentenced to six years in prison.[5]

A week later, on February 11, many more people, thousands of women, old and young men, and children carrying the British flag, demonstrated at Trafalgar Square. They denounced both the cartoons and the previous week's demonstrators and wore "proud to be British and Muslim" buttons. This time only approved placards and posters were allowed.[6] An amusing account was posted on a British blog.

> When I arrived Azam Tamimi was in full-swing. He seemed to have little to say about what positive actions should be taken by Muslims in Britain—it reminded me of Disraeli's retort to Gladstone (or is it the other way round?): "Sir, your are carried away by the exhuberence of your own verbosity." Anyway the crowd loved it, specially when Azam said, "Let it be understood —don't mess with our Prophet." The suggestions for positive ac-tions were best made by the veteran Ikhwan [Muslim Brother-hood] leader Dr Kamal Helbawi, who called for pamphlets on the life of the Prophet to be made available on a large scale.
>
>   Baroness Kishwer Falkner followed Azam—it was a bit like Elgar after the Rolling Stones. A donnish [that is, academic] Lib Dem peer, it was courageous of her to come even though she was booed by the crowd when suggesting that there was no ben-efit in Muslims insisting on further apologies from the Danes.

She clearly was not in tune with the anger and outrage amongst Muslims."[7]

Azzam Tamimi is a member of the Palestinian organization Hamas and lives in London, where he is the director of the Institute of Islamic Political Thought, an Islamist think tank. Kishwer Falkner is a member of the House of Lords from the Liberal Democrats. The probability that these two would agree on anything is small. I asked Falkner, who is a friend, why she decided to participate. She replied that she was offended by what the cartoons implied about her identity and views as a Muslim and wanted to help give balance to the demonstration, and then she switched the topic to the terrible weather.

Policy Exchange, a conservative British think tank, pursued the cartoon issue in a survey supplemented by in-depth interviews with forty young Muslims. The survey took place a few months after the cartoon protests had subsided but while the cartoons and the protests were still fresh in people's minds. It found that 37 percent of Muslims agreed with the proposition that "one of the benefits of modern society is the freedom to criticize other people's religious or political views, even when it causes offense." Fifty-seven percent disagreed.[8] The figures seem to suggest that the accusation that Muslims are not so keen on free speech has factual support. But it is complicated. In contrast to many other surveys, which ask Muslims only about controversial issues, expecting to find bad news, Policy Exchange also tracked the views of non-Muslims by asking comparable questions of both groups. Non-Muslims were less supportive but also less opposed to the idea that free speech involves a right to cause offense. Among non-Muslim respondents, 29 percent agreed with the proposition, while 43 percent disagreed.

One interpretation is that the cartoons crystallized opinion among Muslims and that Muslim respondents felt compelled in much larger numbers to make up their minds about the limits of freedom of speech. Just 5 percent of Muslims had no opinion. The majority population, meanwhile, was less sure what to think: 28 percent had no view on the matter. In in-depth interviews conducted by Policy Exchange, several Muslims judged that the cartoon protests had been "excessive" and thought that Muslims behaved "badly."

THE MUSLIM BROTHERHOOD IN EUROPE

The Muslim Brotherhood was founded in Egypt by Hassan al-Banna in 1928. Today it is a transnational political organization. The national branches vary greatly with respect to their outlook on core issues, such as women's rights and the relationship between faith and state. Often the divisions exist within the associations. Part political party and part social movement, the Muslim Brotherhood has spawned sectarian splinter groups and dissenting national branches across the Middle East. The ideological orientations of the national groups range from Hamas to the small Algerian Movement for a Peaceful Society, which is to be distinguished from the outlawed Islamic Salvation Front (FIS). Emigrants and political exiles spread the Muslim Brotherhood to Europe and North America, where national organizations advocate political participation and embrace increasingly reformist positions. The Egyptian Muslim Brotherhood is the "mother organization" and retains a special status within the broader movement. In fall 2005, the Egyptian Brotherhood was attempting to field candidates in national parliamentary elections in the face of harassment by the Egyptian authorities. The European Brotherhood organizations were attuned to the reverberations of actions taken in Egypt, and vice versa.

Experts cannot agree on the Muslim Brotherhood's democratic credentials. Sometimes it is hard to tell if they are talking about the same organization. In testimony to the U.S. House of Representatives Permanent Select Committee on Intelligence, Steven Emerson, a former CNN commentator and now an independent terrorism investigator and consultant, argued that the Muslim Brotherhood is the mainspring of all Sunni radicalism and that the United States should stop focusing on Al-Qaeda and fight Islamist ideology at the source. Meanwhile, Robert Leiken of the Nixon Center has argued strongly in favor of recognizing the Brotherhood's credentials as an "opportunity" when the United States goes looking for moderate interlocutors in the Muslim world.[9] In a history of the Brotherhood, Carrie Rosefsky Wickham observes that the repressive actions directed against the organization in recent years are not due to its radicalization or its antidemocratic values but came about because the movement has become a viable political competitor to the Mubarak regime in Egypt. The more moderate the Brotherhood becomes, the more it threatens the government.[10]

Europeans have recently edged closer to accepting the Muslim Brotherhood as a legitimate political opposition in Egypt, and in January 2008, the European Parliament condemned human rights abuses in Egypt, imprisonment of members of the opposition parties, and the government's creation of special military tribunals to prosecute election candidates from the Brotherhood.[11]

The popularity of electoral Islamism has grown in the wake of the electoral success of Turkey's AK (Justice and Development) Party. The AK Party, which has governed Turkey since winning nearly 50 percent of the national vote in the 2007 general elections, came into being as a replacement for the banned and more radical Refah (Welfare) Party and other Islamist parties.

Tarek Masoud, a political scientist, argues that we should be concerned less with what the Brotherhood says than with what it does.[12] The critical issue is whether the organization goes along with participatory democracy and free elections. Masoud draws a parallel between the Brotherhood's development and the moderation of European socialism, which was brought about by the social democratic parties' decision to embrace elections as the legitimate road to power. The ballot box is a tool for turning revolutionaries into moderates as long as access to participation is open. It would be naive to expect that all the former revolutionaries will be converted to democratic engagement and compromise, but clearly this is what has happened to many in the new generation of Brotherhood leaders.

Al-Qaradawi's "Muslims are not jackasses" speech caused discomfort in Muslim Brotherhood organizations in Europe and among the OIC diplomats. Lhaj Thami Brèze, the president of the UOIF (Union of Islamic Organizations of France), which is aligned with al-Qaradawi's council, dismissed the call for Muslims to "rage." The cartoons were blasphemous, he stated, and were a matter for the courts: "It is not a problem of representation. It is fine with me if they want to draw the Prophet, but they have to show he is very beautiful."[13]

Brèze elaborated the association's position in May 2006 at the UOIF's annual meeting at the exposition center in Le Bourget. More a fair than a political congress, the meeting attracts huge crowds. The UOIF, he said, "judged that [the cartoons] went beyond the freedom of expression and constituted an aggression." It was, however, a matter "for the law to sort out." He asked French Muslims to "take a responsible attitude" and leave it to the lawyers. Brèze never cited the Koran, the hadiths, or Muslim beliefs. Instead he cited Olivier Roy, a political scientist who has supported Muslim complaints of a double standard in the treatment of Christians and Muslims, and thanked President Jacques Chirac and Prime Minister Dominique de Villepin for "condemning the caricatures and for appealing to a sense of responsibility."[14]

The blasphemy argument was a direct response to the Islamist radicals' attempt to link the protests to their anti-Western agenda. In a curious way, the cartoons replayed within the ranks of contemporary Islamism the old split between revolutionary Marxism and reformist socialism over what to do with the institutions of liberal democracy.[15] When socialists made the decision to work within the "institutions," claims became parsed as matters of piecemeal reform and the pursuit of recognition. Revolutionary Islamists called for the end to democracy and free speech. Reformist Islamists saw an opportunity for Muslims' recognition as equal to other religious groups by demanding protection under existing blasphemy laws. Using the courts to seek equality was an option only in countries where blasphemy laws are written in a way that makes the charge applicable to all faiths, as is the case in Denmark and France. In the United Kingdom, the blasphemy complaint was not appropriate because the existing law protected only the Church of England. (The law was subsequently abolished in March 2008.)

The UOIF was intent on avoiding a repetition of the Salman Rushdie affair and wanted no street demonstrations. Together with other French Muslim associations, the UOIF filed a legal complaint on the grounds of blasphemy against France Soir and Charlie Hebdo, the two French publications that republished the cartoons. The rector of the Paris Grand Mosque, Dalil Boubakeur, joined the suit. The French court agreed to hear the case but dismissed the charges against the editors of Charlie Hebdo.[16]

The European Brotherhood organizations belong to an umbrella organization known as the Federation of Islamic Organisations in Europe (FIOE). In 2008, it published a new twenty-six-point charter that affirms Muslims' commitment to strengthening the European Union and to promoting better relations between Europe and "the Muslim World." The charter is in essence a platform for reformist Islamist policy advocacy within the European political framework. It sensibly refrains from using the old Muslim Brotherhood slogan, "The Koran is our constitution," and recognizes that Muslims will remain a permanent minority in Europe. The charter's only invocation of the Koran is the famous affirmation of the inherent multitude of humankind (49:13): "O Mankind, indeed we created you from a male and female and have made you different nations and tribes so that you may get to know one another."

The casual reader may get the impression that Scripture is invoked in the charter to justify gender inequality. It is not. The purpose is to provide Koranic support for multicultural toleration. The FIOE supports what is usually described as "difference feminism"—the inherent equality and practical difference of the male and female genders—but that is not the message here. As the charter says, "Islam affirms the diversity and differences that exists between people and is not discomforted by this multicultural reality."

Like other European political groups, the FIOE has set up shop in Brussels, and it maintains a presence as a lobby group.[17] Its charter produced a measure of rapprochement between established European political institutions and the Muslim Brotherhood. Risking an overestimation of the Brotherhood's influence among European Muslims, the vice president of the European Parliament described it as "a code of good conduct for Muslims in Europe which commits them to taking part in building a united society."[18]

The FIOE charter postdates the cartoon crisis, but the process of creating the charter began in 2002, after the 9/11 attacks and the associated political convulsions among Western Muslim political organizations, and the political shift toward a "Euro-Muslim" position traceable to the late 1990s. The cartoon controversy presented European Muslim associations with a potentially toxic mixture of political opportunity and risk. Filing suits on grounds of blasphemy held the promise of an official judicial recognition that Muslims had the same rights as Christians to court protection. Politically, Muslims would benefit from demonstrating their adherence to the laws and the expectations that religious Christians comply with. The risks were that the lawsuits would be seen as confirming accusations that Muslims favor press censorship.

The Muslim Association of Britain, a Brotherhood organization, co-sponsored the Trafalgar Square demonstration. It, too, preferred to frame the cartoon issue as a matter of Muslims' right to equal treatment in European law and civic life, but because British legal discourse on these matters is framed as a question of "Islamophobia," the gist of the complaint was about discriminatory treatment and racialism rather than matters of faith.

The strategy proved unworkable. None of the blasphemy lawsuits filed in France and Denmark was upheld. The final judicial venue available is the European Court of Human Rights in Strasbourg, where Danish Muslim associations have filed a claim. The blasphemy debates and attendant questions about a double standard for how European courts and permissible speech provisions treat Christians, Jews, and Muslims are discussed further in chapter 6.

WHEN PERCEPTIONS FRAME REALITY

The cartoons set in motion a political process that, much like a gathering storm, sucked up energy from existing tensions in the air and released them in a downpour. Forty to 50 percent of Muslims in Germany, Great Britain, and France think that many or most Europeans are hostile to Muslims, according to a Pew survey.[19] Twenty to 25 percent of Muslims also report having had a bad experience because of their religion.

Interestingly, in Europe the general (non-Muslim) population was just as likely to say that most or many Europeans are hostile to Muslims, an answer that may suggest both empathy with Muslims or reflect a ready acknowledgment of the respondent's own prejudices. Sociologists find that many people cite general opinion in order to justify their own anti-Muslim bias.[20] Turks, Pakistanis, and Egyptians had an even more negative view of how Europeans treat Muslims. Fifty-seven percent of Turks, 61 percent of Pakistanis, and 63 percent of Egyptians agreed that most or many Europeans are hostile toward Muslims.

In the wake of the 9/11 Commission a number of high-ranking current and former members of Congress created Terror Free Tomorrow to gain a better understanding of popular opinion in Muslim countries. This organization carried out a face-to-face survey (considered more reliable than telephone interviews) in April and May 2006 that asked about the cartoons (table 4). The survey revealed that two-thirds of Saudis, Turks, and Pakistanis—and majorities in the United Arab Emirates and Palestinian Territories—felt that the Danish cartoons reflected Western antagonism against Islam itself.

The farther they live from the West, the more convinced Muslims are

Table 4.

Survey question: Which of the following statements are the closest to your opinion concerning the Danish cartoons of the Prophet Muhammad (percent agree)?

	PAKISTAN	PALESTINE	SAUDI ARABIA	TURKEY	UNITED ARAB EMIRATES
They are an isolated example that does not reflect the overall views of the West toward Islam	6	20	23	11	25
They reflect the increasing secular attitudes of the West toward all religions	18	26	12	9	12
They reflect Western antagonism against Islam itself	67	52	65	67	56
Don't know	9	1	1	14	0

Source: Terror Free Tomorrow, "New Polls throughout Muslim World: Humanitarian Leadership by US Remains Positive Results from Polls in Saudi Arabia, the United Arab Emirates, Pakistan, Turkey, the Palestinian Territories and Indonesia," http://www.terrorfreetomorrow.org.

that the West hates Islam and Muslims and that the cartoons were evidence of the problem. A Palestinian survey organization, Near East Consulting, based in the West Bank city of Ramallah, demonstrated the problem of opinion-making in the absence of knowledge. Conducting a survey in the second week of February 2006, Near East Consulting found that 99.7 percent of the respondents had heard about the cartoons, but only 31 percent had seen them.[21] Seventy percent said that they had heard about the cartoons within the preceding one or two weeks.

On February 2, 2006, gunmen took over the European Union's office in Gaza City and a German teacher was taken hostage in Nablus. (The teacher was released when the kidnappers discovered his national identity. They wanted to capture a Frenchman or a Dane in retribution for the reprinting of the cartoons that occurred in France and Denmark. In fact, German papers reprinted the cartoons too, but the kidnappers apparently did not know that.) On February 10, about two thousand children and women (adult men had been banned from attending Friday prayers) demonstrated before the Al-Aqsa Mosque in Jerusalem, chanting, "bin Laden —strike again," according to the Associated Press. On the same day, seven thousand people marched in a demonstration in Gaza City organized by the extremist organization Islamic Jihad.[22]

The high level of knowledge about the cartoons undoubtedly owed much to media coverage of the violent demonstrations. Knowing about the cartoons stimulated negative assessments of the West. Eighty-eight percent of respondents to Near East Consulting's survey said that the reactions against Denmark were justified, but few condoned violence or kidnapping. Nearly 60 percent believed that Denmark was an enemy to Islam, and although 53 percent thought the issue would soon calm down again, 47 percent thought it would cause additional rifts between the Muslim world and the West.

The Palestinian reactions, as they emerged from this detailed survey, revealed many of the ironies of the cartoon protests. The news media covered the violent demonstrations and the kidnappings and in the process disseminated news about the cartoons. Palestinians learned about the cartoons through the framing created by the demonstrations. Even if they disapproved of the means used by the demonstrators, they generally thought that protests against the Danes were justified. In other words, people knew of the cartoons but knew little about them. They further believed that the cartoons evidenced Danish—and Western—hostility to Islam. The Palestinians had little regard for the claims that the cartoons were expressions of core democratic values. Ninety-three percent did not think that they had anything to do with freedom of speech. Two-thirds also believed that the cartoons reflected an official Danish position and that it was an insufficient solution to the crisis to take *Jyllands-Posten* to court. The cartoon story clearly contributed to a widening of the perception gap between East and West and was taken as evidence for the existence of the gap.

European Muslims were more appreciative of the free speech dilemma. A British poll carried out by Ipsos MORI in February 2006 found that although 58 percent of British respondents thought the cartoons would not cause offense to the ordinary person, 62 percent accepted that

Muslims were right to be offended, and 72 percent agreed that British publications were right not to print the cartoons.[23]

The Program on International Policy Attitudes at the University of Maryland pooled a large number of national public opinion surveys to analyze the gap between Muslims and non-Muslims over the cartoon issue. The pooled surveys reveal a higher level of support among western Europeans for the Muslim complaint against the cartoons than one would expect from the polarized news coverage.[24] In France and Norway, two countries singled out by Muslim protesters after *France Soir* and *Magazinet* reprinted the cartoons, 54 and 57 percent of respondents, respectively, thought it was "wrong" to publish the cartoons. In Denmark, it all depended on how you asked the question. If asked whether the prime minster or *Jyllands-Posten* should apologize to Muslims, two-thirds of respondents said no. Asked if they had sympathy with Muslims' complaints even if the newspaper had "a right" to publish the cartoons, 60 percent agreed. Only 20 percent said the newspaper was in the wrong to do it, and 20 percent said the newspaper was "right" and they had "no sympathy" for the complaining Muslims.[25] Over time public sympathy shifted against the newspaper.[26]

American and European Muslim public intellectuals published a flurry of manifestos. The best known was published by Ayaan Hirsi Ali and Salman Rushdie along with many other intellectuals, including Bernard-Henri Lévy, the noted French author and activist. The manifesto decried the Muslim protests and called for unrelenting resistance against Islamism: "The recent events, which occurred after the publication of drawings of Muhammed [sic] in European newspapers, have revealed the necessity of the struggle for these universal values. This struggle will not be won by arms but in the ideological field. It is not a clash of civilizations nor an antagonism of West and East that we are witnessing, but a global struggle that confronts democrats and theocrats."

Western Muslim intellectuals were divided over what to say about the cartoons but not along the usual left-right spectrum. A group of American conservatives, who described themselves as "we, the moderate Muslims," condemned the cartoons as disrespectful and expressed understanding for the feeling of coreligionists. Yet they also called on Muslims to observe the Koran's injunction that "there can be no compulsion in religion" and to act with restraint: "We support and cherish democracy—not because we reject the sovereignty of the Almighty over people, but because we believe that this sovereignty is manifested in the general will of the people in a democratic and pluralistic society."[27] Tariq Ramadan, a Swiss-educated scholar living in London, whose political views are generally described as left-leaning, similarly condemned the cartoons but described them as an instance of racism and called for everyone to slow down to stop the madness. "This is not a matter of additional laws restraining free speech; it is simply one of calling upon everybody's conscience to exercise what is right in the eyes of others."[28]

Western Muslim intellectuals were utterly divided, as usual, about the nature of the crime—racism, blasphemy, or violation of Scripture—and even whether a crime had been committed. Most nonetheless agreed that they did not want the governments of Muslim countries and official Islamic organizations to tell them what to do.

CULTURAL POLITICS AS INTERNATIONAL RELATIONS

Globalization has changed our political environment every bit as much as it has changed how business works. Our cognitive adjustment—to say nothing of institutional adjustments—has taken longer because politics remains firmly embedded in national constitutions that channel representation and political debate.

Islam returned to western Europe after a centuries-long absence as the result of immigration only four or five decades ago. (Some European countries experienced mass immigration earlier than others.) The efforts of Muslim immigrants to maintain mosques and religious schools have been strictly regulated since the 1980s. The initial impulse on the part of European governments was to devolve responsibility for pastoral services for Muslim immigrants to the countries from which they came—Turkey, Morocco, Algeria, and Pakistan. But many migrants were uninterested in the theologies favored by Islamic states. They made use of Europe's freedom to pick and choose among alternatives. The believers developed faith communities in their own image, and as a result Europe became home to a bewildering mix of Islamic sects and denominations.

Much of what is thought of as fundamentalism among Europe's Muslims is a benign example of the creation of transnational religious communities among immigrant groups.[29] Similar developments may be found among "born-again" evangelical Christians from South America living in Spain, Hindus in Britain, and many other groups who never make headlines. It is in many respects a welcome phenomenon. As Tariq Ramadan has tirelessly noted, Europe's Muslims have a unique opportunity to modernize Islam precisely because they are free to make choices.

Fatima Mernissi, a Moroccan feminist and professor of sociology, writes that the progress of Islamicism (her translator's choice of word) has obscured the secularization of Muslim societies promoted by Arab nationalism in the 1930s and 1940s.[30] Arab nationalism was "proudly modernistic" and pushed an intellectual renaissance that was linked to rather than separate from Western political thought. So it is today. "We do not live in separate worlds, but in highly interconnected ones," she writes with reference to the decline of Arab modernism and the ascendancy of fundamentalism, which she defines as a political project that "sacralizes hierarchy and denies pluralism."

But it is naive to think that openness produces only good things. Anna Tsing, a cultural anthropologist, suggests that we pay more attention to the implications of new "ideologies of scale," by which she means the ways in which the projects of different actors may "rub up against each other awkwardly, creating messiness and new possibilities."[31] She points out that scale also affects the capacity to mobilize. And the very reach of global projects is subject to change and new contestation. Domestic quarrels may spill over into global arenas.

The claim that the cartoons and the protests against them were an episode in the "clash of civilizations" implied an inaccurate dualism. Danish Muslims by no means agreed with the claims made by the mosque activists with respect to the cartoons. In Muslim countries, disarray and conflict grew as the protests escalated. Some Muslim journalists and intellectuals proclaimed their support for *Jyllands-Posten*'s project. Newspapers based in Muslim countries reprinted the cartoons. Even if some publications did so in order to mobilize opinion against the immorality of the West, as was apparently the case with two Algerian newspapers, the fact that the cartoons were published conflicts with the argument that depiction was forbidden.

Amartya Sen, a distinguished Nobel Prize–winning economist, condemned the stereotyping involved in the cartoons but argued that a presumption of mutual adjustment is required in pluralist societies and that Muslims were victims of reductionism as well as perpetrators in claiming that the cartoons were a religious offense.[32] But cutting the blame both ways does not eliminate the practical problem. Who is required to make the adjustments? Should Danes stop drawing pictures, which is what Danish right-wingers say Muslims are demanding (and as a few Muslims did say), or should Muslims learn to accept "ridicule, mockery, and sarcasm"?

In fact, for the most part, European Muslims were not making religious claims. What was at stake was not what Islam forbids but what the West allows. Putting aside for the moment the claims and motives of various sectarian religious and political groups, the Muslim point was not that the Danes could not make pictures of the Prophet but that the pictures said inflammatory things about Muslims. They concluded that the Danish state and the newspaper did not extend the same protection against prejudice and defamation to Muslims as to Christians. It was not an antiliberal argument but an argument about the entitlements Muslims have in liberal democracies.

CHAPTER 6

Muslim Iconoclasm and Christian Blasphemy

"DARKBLOOD," ONE OF THE many hackers who attacked and defaced thousands of Danish web sites in February 2006, announced, "On Sept 29th, 2005 issue of Jyllands-Posten, I saw and read dreadful news and cartoons." The cartoons were not published on September 29 but on the next day. Evidently DarkblooD had deliberately looked up the cartoons on the paper's Internet site, where the posting date was the day earlier. And the date of the email indicates that he (or she) went to the newspaper's web site six months after publication, presumably in the full knowledge that the sought-after pictures were *haram*, forbidden by God. Who, then, is the sinner? A Muslim who deliberately looks up forbidden images or the non-Muslim newspaper that prints them?

The answer was obvious to the editors of *Jyllands-Posten*, and probably to most Danes. Islamic theological strictures are irrelevant to nonbelievers. And if Muslims don't like what they see, they can avert their eyes. Yet Denmark has laws that may be relevant. Like many other countries in Europe, Denmark recognizes blasphemy as a punishable offense. The meaning of such laws has changed over time, and in recent decades they have been broadened in some countries to encompass insults to non-Christian religious beliefs. Many Danish Muslims assumed that although *Jyllands-Posten* could not be expected to uphold Islamic law, the paper was nevertheless guilty of insulting religious believers, punishable under Danish law.

Non-Muslim Danes tended to stereotype the Muslim reaction to the cartoons as simple zealotry. In fact, however, Muslim views were divided, and political arguments were as common as religious opinions. Some Muslim spokesmen did indeed assert that there was an absolute Koranic ban on the portrayal of the Prophet and that this proscription applied to non-Muslims as well as to Muslims. More common was the view that the cartoons defamed Muslims, a claim that does not involve religious law at all. Some Muslims felt that Muslims living in the diaspora simply had to get used to distasteful aspersions on their faith and leave matters alone. A minority cheered the newspaper on and sided with the newspaper's editors. But Muslims in Europe generally complained about a double standard in the treatment of Muslims compared to that of Christians and Jews, and appealed for protection from blasphemy or hate speech. The difficulty with blasphemy laws, it turned out, is that enforcement of the statutes is rare, and unequivocal evidence that the community of believers have a scriptural basis for feeling offended is required.

As the controversy spread beyond Denmark, the issues were often stated in more general and cruder terms. Members of the Western press typically complained that Muslims were iconoclasts who wished to censor the use of images by Westerners. This criticism emphasized a view of Islam as backward-looking, even medieval. In addition, some media outlets depicted Muslims not only as prisoners in a theological dark age but as hypocrites, because Muslim artists have also produced images of the Prophet.

This chapter investigates the charges of double standards and hypocrisy that were leveled against the editors of *Jyllands-Posten,* the protesting Muslims, and courts unwilling to enforce blasphemy protection in the case of the cartoons.

FAITH, LAW, AND THE CARTOONS

Muslim critics of the cartoons tended to espouse one of three positions. The first was that representation of the Prophet is forbidden in Islam and that this prohibition must be universally respected. The second was that religious law is specific to Muslims, so if Christians wish to draw respectful pictures of Muhammad, that is of no concern to Muslims. However, the cartoons in *Jyllands-Posten* defamed Islam and Muslims. Where European law recognizes blasphemy as a punishable offense, Muslims had a right to protection under the law. *Jyllands-Posten* and its many supporters behaved hypocritically when they told Muslims to put up with the cartoons while they treat Christians and Jews with special regard. The third position was that most of the cartoons were of no real consequence and that religious prohibitions were irrelevant. But one cartoon—Kurt Westergaard's drawing of the Prophet with the bomb in the turban—clearly suggested that Islam is a violent faith. This defamatory stereotyping of Muslims and their faith constituted incitement to hatred of Muslims, which was against Danish law. Other claims were also made, but these are of interest because they raise broader questions about the accommodation of religious Muslims in Western democracies and the capacity of civil law to afford equal protection to Christians and Muslims.

Leaders of European Muslim associations were reluctant to demand that Danes—and the European media in general—should observe a prohibition against representations that derived from Islamic religious law. They did not want to make the argument against the cartoons based on Scripture. There is in any case disagreement as to what religious law prescribes and even more controversy about the role of Muslim law in historically and sometimes constitutionally Christian Europe. Many European Muslims adamantly oppose the view that Islamic law should be incorporated in the civil code, arguing that they have left theocratic states and have no desire to reempower Islamic law. Alternatively, some observant Muslims sometimes argue that they are better served by a secular state that does not get involved with faith matters. The Muslim political elite is also keenly aware that arguments about the religious foundation of the civil code are likely to backfire in countries that have yet to eliminate the vestiges of Christian dominion. Even those who regard the prohibition against representation as a tenet of their faith usually shied away from asserting the supremacy of religious over civil law in societies where Muslims are a minority.

When I last saw Ahmed Abu Laban, he regretted the violent turn the cartoon protests had taken but stuck to his original mission, which was to ensure that the Prophet would never again be pictured in Denmark. If this could be accomplished by statute that would be best, he thought, but otherwise a voluntary agreement with the media would be fine. When I expressed doubts about the realism of his goal, he said: "It has been done before," and gave me videos of two films from the 1970s. Both were

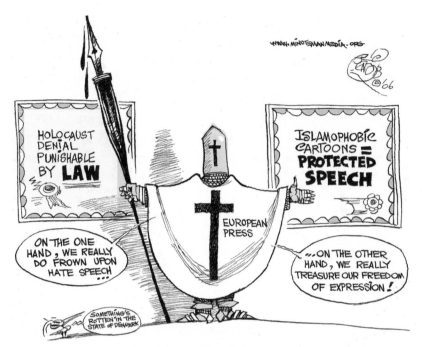

FIGURE 7. Berkeley-based cartoonist Khalil Bendib lampoons European double standards on free and not-so-free speech. The accusation of a double standard was the most common complaint Muslims made in the cartoon controversy. Reprinted with permission from Studio Bendib.

Hollywood productions and both featured the Prophet Muhammad as an off-camera lead actor. Abu Laban used them to show that he was not crazy to think that Westerners could learn to live with such a rule.

MUHAMMAD IN THE WESTERN IMAGINATION

Abu Laban's use of the two films to underpin his argument that Europeans should not be permitted to make pictures of the Prophet was curiously anachronistic. Christians have drawn images and made sculptures of Muhammad for centuries. Medieval paintings, often found in churches, routinely depict crusaders at war with Islamic armies and the triumphant expulsion of Muslims from Spain. Renaissance artists continued the tradition, which remained significant well into the twentieth century. In *The Divine Comedy*, Dante Alighieri confined Muhammad to the Eighth Circle of Hell. An illustrated version from 1491 features a picture of the tormented Muhammad.[1] *The Divine Comedy* is one of Europe's most popular illustrated works. Artists from William Blake to Salvador Dalí reworked the illustration of Muhammad's torment. The nineteenth-century French artist Gustave Doré's illustrations of Dante's work were reprinted and sold as commercial prints, and one can still come across copies in antiquarian bookstores. There is also an Orientalist artistic tradition in which the Prophet is represented as a "Mohammedan" wearing Turkish-style clothing. Finally, there is a somewhat ecumenical modern Christian tradition of books and instructional material for Bible study in which Muhammad is typically portrayed as an imposing if exotic-looking Prophet, in the style of popular illustrated journals. (Mormons have produced many illustrations in the respectful vain, because Joseph Smith, the founder of the religion, presented himself as a prophet in the tradition of Muhammad.)[2]

This Christian illustrative tradition more or less disappeared, however, in secular modern art, and the mass media was largely indifferent to Islam before a wave of anti-Muslim sentiment began to wash over us after the Salman Rushdie affair in 1988. When Muslims appeared in films they were generally depicted as heroic freedom fighters, as in the epic *Lawrence of Arabia* (1962), or as anticolonialists in the style of Frantz Fanon's Third Worldist views. One such movie is *The Battle of Algiers* (1966), which was recently rereleased on DVD. This Italian film excoriated French colonialism in Algeria. In *The Battle of Algiers*, the Islamists hang out with pretty women who wear burqas before they go out to bomb the French. Islam and Marxism here blend seamlessly into liberation theology.

The first of the two films Abu Laban gave me to watch is a Hollywood production originally entitled *Mohammed: Messenger of God*. Financed by the government of Libya, the movie was produced and directed in 1976 by Moustapha Akkad, who went to film school in California and worked and lived in Hollywood. The film stars Anthony Quinn as the Prophet.[3] Al-Azhar University and the High Islamic Congress of the Shiat in Lebanon were involved in approving its accuracy. Still, the movie was initially banned in a number of Arab countries; to appease the censors, its title was changed to *The Message*.

The Message was conceived as following in the line of the religious "greats" movies, which started with *The Ten Commandments* and *Ben Hur.* This may explain why its fighting Muslims dress and act like the Jews and early Christians of those films. It opens with spectacular footage of pilgrims circling the Kaaba on the Hajj but goes downhill from there. The film's focus is on the struggle between Muhammad's early followers and the tribe and traders controlling the Kaaba.[4] The iconoclastic prohibition is explained when one of Muhammad's followers says, "Real God is unseen and is not made of clay." One young man breaks with his family, smashes the little religious figures in the households, and inveighs against poverty and injustice. No man should starve, the rich should not defraud the poor, the strong should not oppress the weak, and girls should not be forced into marriage but should be allowed to choose their husbands. Tariq Ramadan argues that this is still Muhammad's message, but most movie audiences would not credit it today.[5]

The second film Abu Laban handed me was *Lion of the Desert* (1981), also directed by Akkad, but set in World War II. This movie portrays the real-life Libyan tribal leader Omar Mukhtar (again played by Quinn) as a brave jihadi fighting the evil Nazis. That Mukhtar is now a jihadi role model may prove only that the jihadis are as concerned about popular culture as is Hollywood. Moustapha Akkad himself died on November 11, 2005, of injuries sustained from a car bomb attack on the Grand Hyatt hotel in Amman, Jordan, carried out by Musab al-Zarqawi's branch of Al Qaeda. His daughter also died in the attack.

The contrast of these movies to post-9/11 Hollywood fare is stark. In *The Grid*, a television miniseries, the good guys arrest an Arab would-be terrorist who has killed an FBI agent. The plot is an illustration of the "ticking bomb" scenario that has made the rounds among legal philosophers debating the legitimacy of using torture: The terrorist has information that will enable us to save many lives. What may we do to get it out of him?[6]

Another series, Fox's *24*, has been described by its producers as "a heightened drama about anti-terrorism." In one season's episodes, a Muslim terrorist (who conveniently for the cast lives in Los Angeles) steals a nuclear missile, intending to deploy it at a local mall.[7]

In the United States, for understandable reasons, Muslim associations have been more upset about the routine representation of American Muslims in television productions as mass murderers than with the Danish cartoons.

WHAT MUSLIMS DO AND DO NOT DO WITH RESPECT TO FIGURATIVE REPRESENTATION

How do devout Muslims explain the existence of miniatures in Islamic art collections that represent the Prophet? (Reproductions of these artworks proliferated on the Internet as the debate over the cartoons took off.)[8]

An early manuscript that portrays Muhammad is a history of the Prophet's life, *Jami' al-tawarikh* (Compendium of Histories), by Rashid al-Din, from around 1300, created by a workshop of artists in what is today western Iran for a Tartar khan in the Persian part of the Mongol Empire. Today, it resides in the Khalili Collection in London. Another manuscript with images of the Prophet is the *Miraj-Nama* (Journey of the Prophet Muhammad), a fifteenth-century illustrated history from the Timurid dynasty in what is today Iran and Azerbaijan. Today it is housed in the Bibliothèque Nationale in Paris. Two other important manuscript sources of miniature paintings of the Prophet are *Siyer-i Nebi* (The Life of the Prophet) and *Khamseh of Nizami*.[9] *Siyer-i Nebi* is a fourteenth-century poem. Two hundred years later, the Ottoman ruler Murad III commissioned illustrations for the poem, and the work was completed in 1595. Three of the six volumes are housed in Istanbul's Topkapi Palace. In this work, Muhammad's face is obscured, but it is otherwise a full-figure representation. The *Khamseh of Nizami* is a work from the Safavid dynasty also dating from the sixteenth century, with seventeenth-century embellishment. It is housed in the British Museum.

The earliest of these illustrated manuscripts are primarily historical chronicles showing scenes from the Prophet's life. Rashid al-Din's *Jami' al-tawarikh* has a picture showing the Prophet in full-frontal figure rededicating the black stone at the Kaaba in Mecca. Later it became common practice to obscure the Prophet's face with a white veil or simply blot out his face. And in still later manuscripts, the Prophet became endowed with an aura, or flaming nimbus. Battle scenes and picnics featuring Muhammad and his family have contemporary clothing, food, and weapons, which creates an oddly anachronistic effect. In Ottoman gilded manuscripts Muhammad is depicted as a sultan. In depicting the Prophet's exploits, the miniatures show off the splendor of the courts and showcase the artists' talents and the richness of the material. The Prophet is drawn in multiple guises: as a statesman, a warrior, and a family man. Some themes in Muhammad's life are clearly favorites for depiction, among them the baby Muhammad being presented to the elders after his birth; Muhammad having a picnic with his sons; and Muhammad going to war with Ali at his side.

The Persian manuscript *Miraj-Nama* contains scenes of religious significance.[10] Among the more common depictions are those of Muhammad riding between heaven and earth on the back of the Angel Gabriel or on his horse, al-Burqa. Another miniature, from the same period but of unknown origin, shows the Prophet flying over the Kaaba in Mecca and the rock of the Dome in Jerusalem, two significant places in the origin of Islam.

These manuscripts are clearly "religious" even if, like most European religious art until recent times, they were commissioned not by religious leaders but by secular courts and rulers. Yet although these manuscripts and miniatures contradict the notion that Muslims do not draw pictures of the Prophet, these images are not caricatures. They are idealized representations that extol the virtue or the bravery of the Prophet and his close associates.

What, then, can we say about the posters and wall hangings for sale today in the bazaars of Tehran and Istanbul? Shiites, it is agreed, are avid consumers of sacred memorabilia of the Imam Ali, Fatima, and other members of the Prophet's family.[11] Today's mass-produced objects are very different from what one might find in Islamic art collections housing Ottoman and Persian miniatures. Shia popular art takes great pains to stress the physical beauty of God's Messenger and his family. The style resembles Catholic folk art and Protestant Bible study illustration. Vivid colors or pastels dominate. Fatima's beauty evokes piety. Imam Ali, too, is handsome, with a groomed beard and a firm hand clasping a menacing sword, telling of courage and strength. An aura can sometimes be seen illuminating the body from behind.

We need not go far to find such things for sale. I have found such posters and wall hangings in Istanbul's bazaars. They are favored by Alevis, members of a separate religious community in Turkey that is neither Sunni not Shia. An American web site, catering, one imagines, to students, has a poster for sale showing Muhammad being escorted to paradise by the Angel Gabriel. A different poster uses a full facial depiction without the veil covering that usually obscures the face of Muhammad and therefore probably portrays Ali.[12]

Shia and Sunni differences are evident, yet it will not do to say that only Shiites "do it." Many Ottoman (Sunni) manuscripts speak against that claim, but this is also misleading because there is no "schism" in Islam comparable to the creation of the separate "churches" of Christianity. Sunni and Shia Muslims share the same living space, intermarry, and have generally coexisted across swathes of the Middle East and the Caucasus. In European cities where migration has put them in the same poorly served neighborhoods, Shias and Sunnis mingle in mosques.

Let us also be clear about one thing: The Taliban's absolutist injunction against film, music, family snapshots, and paintings and sculptures, even against non-Islamic art, is the mad iconoclasm of a reform movement with political ambitions. Eighth-century Umayyad caliphs, fourteenth- and fifteenth-century Persian, Mongol, Indian, and Uzbek rulers, and sixteenth-century Ottoman sultans all commissioned great paintings and illustrated books. The Umayyads and Abbasids built palaces, and occasionally even sculptures, populated by people and animals, and sometimes even including Muhammad and his family. Written sources dating to the tenth century contain reports of portraits of the Prophet.[13]

Aniconism (the prohibition of the use of icons or images of humans or animals) has been preached at certain times and by certain groups, but there are plenty of images of people, animals, and the Prophet to be found. Religious injunctions are applied strictly in mosques, but popular practices are another matter. "It is often said," write historians Sheila Blair and Jonathan Bloom, "that the depiction of living things is forbidden in Islamic art, but this is simply not true."[14] When it comes to the image of the Prophet, practices were traditionally more restricted, but it was "done."

The Persian and Ottoman miniatures were not well known. All exist in unique manuscripts. They are expensive, precious works of art and have never been subjected to the printing press and made for sale, the way Gustave Doré's prints of *The Divine Comedy* were commercialized.

Was it hypocritical for Muslims to expect a Danish newspaper to observe a taboo that is not recognized even by all observant Muslims? The hypocrisy charge is unfair; some people, but not all Muslims, thought that the mere fact of depiction was the problem. The question of an unobserved taboo is still interesting because many Sunni Muslims *did* believe (and say) that a taboo—or a close equivalent—exists. In any case, it seems clear that the Danish caricatures did not violate a generalized Islamic prohibition on figurative representation but rather insulted Muslims by portraying the Prophet in a disrespectful manner.

"NOTHING CAN BE COMPARED WITH HIM"

Iconoclasm prohibits the display of icons and derives from prohibitions against the worship of false gods or idols, a doctrine common to Judaism, Christianity, and Islam. The extent to which this doctrine applies to representations of saints and prophets varies, but the Protestant Reformation spawned iconoclastic movements throughout Europe. Danish Lutherans, for example, painted over the rich decorations of pre-Reformation village churches.

The Koran is ambiguous on the question of the permissibility of figurative representation and contains only a few relevant passages. One verse that is sometimes interpreted as containing an injunction reads, "Creator of the Heavens and the earth, he has given you spouses from among yourselves, and cattle male and female; by this means He multiplies His creatures. Nothing can be compared with Him. He alone hears and sees all" (42:11; trans. N. J. Dawood). This verse and another that prohibits worship of false gods (21:52–54) are similar to the Christian prohibition of idol worship in the Ten Commandments: "Thou shalt not make unto thee any graven image, or any likeness of any thing that is in heaven above, or that is in the earth beneath, or that is in the water under the earth."

Believers regard the Koran as the revealed word of God. In theory, they need only read the Holy Book to understand God's plan. Yet the meaning of Scripture is not self-evident. Interpretation cannot be avoided. Islamic jurisprudence, *fiqh*, draws on the wisdom of religious scholars as it has accumulated over the centuries about the meaning of the Koran and the Prophet's sayings and exemplary life. The scholars (*ulema*) apply this body of knowledge and interpretation to contemporary issues. Their decisions may be published as edicts, or fatwas (religious statements explicating religious law). Over the centuries the opinions of the ulema have allowed the development of Islamic pluralism and facilitated adaptation to modern life.

Islam has many centers of religious authority, and individuals usually regard some as more reliable than others. Inevitably, disagreements occur, despite periodic attempts to purify the faith and unify believers. Global migration has turned sects and denominations into transnational networks, and with the advent of televangelists and modernizing movements, the competition for the hearts and minds of believers has increased. Globalization has made the ummah more tangible, but at the same time, fragmentation and division are manifest in the mixed neighborhoods and divided families of cosmopolitan cities.

The point is that Islam is not a church, and no unified religious authority exists to tell the believers what to think. Moreover, while the cartoons elicited strong feelings, the recognized religious authorities in Egypt or Saudi Arabia did not issue fatwas, which would have given Muslims theological grounds for condemnation. Scholars condemned the cartoons and even prescribed a religious duty to boycott Danish goods, but they did not clarify the basis in Islamic law for how Muslims should approach images produced by unbelievers.[15]

The one relevant recent fatwa on the permissibility of depicting the Prophet was in fact produced in the United States, in 2000, and it concluded that a sixty-year-old frieze depicting Muhammad in the Supreme Court building *was* permissible.

The author is Taha Jaber al-Alwani, a professor at al-Azhar University and member of the OIC's Fiqh Council and Chairman of the Fiqh Council of North America, and a highly respected authority on Islamic law.[16] The edict notes that the concrete problem at hand is a sculpture praising the Prophet for his contribution to humanity, and it is placed in a location of great authority outside the Islamic realm. Al-Alwani observes that the Koran is ambiguous on the issue of figurative depiction in general, and it is necessary to turn for guidance to the ahadith, the prophetic sayings of Muhammad as narrated by his followers. There are several such hadiths, thirteen in all. One relates the story of Aisha, the Prophet's wife, who told of how the Prophet one day tore a curtain she had put up, which she then made into pillows. Another says, "Angels do not enter the house in which there are portrayals or pictures." A hadith that says, "The people who will receive the severest punishment from Allah will be the picture makers," has been used by the Taliban and other groups to support an absolute prohibition—even on movies and cameras—but it is generally regarded as referring to the tribal idol-worshippers that Muhammad combated and as not pertinent to the question of representation.

The interpretation of legal propriety is, al-Alwani argues, invariably tied to the intention of image-making. Figurative representation that aims to depict God is disallowed when it aims to emulate divine power or God directly or, alternatively, is done in the pursuit of worship of other gods.

Islam looks askance at lavish decoration, but figurative representation for ordinary decorative purposes, such as Aisha's cushions, are a different matter and not relevant to questions about the permissibility of the Supreme Court frieze (nor to the cartoons). The question of angels entering into houses with pictures is also not relevant, because angels would in any case not enter into the Supreme Court because it is not a house of revelation. Worship aims to contemplate the abstractness of God, and the interference of images with worship is clearly prohibited. The frieze does not attempt to emulate divine power but praises Muhammad as a statesman.

To be sure, caricatures, or cartoons, are not hagiography. Al-Alwani notes that Islam has revered the Prophet for his physical beauty, and some of these descriptions have inspired Persian and Ottoman artists, whose societies have a long tradition of visual representation. The hagiographic tradition is alive and well in popular culture, evident in the popularity of posters and wall hangings depicting the Prophet, Fatima, and Imam Ali as supernaturally beautiful. The Prophet's personal biography is a model for all Muslims. Al-Alwani argues that reflection on the life of the Prophet helps "believers achieve a balance between his Prophethood and message, which belongs to the transcendental, and his humanity and human-ness, which belongs to this world."[17]

Al-Alwani concludes that Muslims should be proud to have their Prophet pictured on the walls of the Supreme Court among other lawmakers. For Muslims, Muhammad is not just one lawmaker among others, but in an age "replete with disdainful images of the Prophet Muhammad (SAAS), it is comforting to note that those in the highest Court in the United States were able to surmount these prejudices."[18]

The statement preceded the cartoon crisis by five years but speaks clearly to the problem of the cartoons. They did not intend to honor the Prophet's contribution to humanity, as did the Supreme Court frieze. They did not extol the Prophet's magnificence, as did the Ottoman artists and the contemporary posters for sale in bazaars. They aimed instead to make the abstract concrete and likened the message to petty—or violent—politics. They made ugly what is to Muslims beautiful. The reason the Supreme Court frieze is a matter to be proud of is exactly the reason so many Muslims reacted angrily to the cartoons. The cartoons violated a specific prohibition against depicting the transcendental source of Islam—in the form of Muhammad, the carrier of God's message—and made matters worse by depicting the belief as violent and the messenger as ugly.

BLASPHEMY IN CIVIL LAW

Can Muslims and their faith be legally protected against insult and religious defamation by the same laws that historically have applied to Christians? Many European countries have laws against blasphemy and racialist speech—often referred to as "hate speech" laws—which in theory should be applicable to all faiths. We may think (as I do) that blasphemy laws are not a good idea, but it is hardly contestable that in countries that have such laws an obligation exists to treat Muslims and Christians equitably. An attendant duty exists on the part of courts and legal experts to develop enforcement criteria encompassing *different* traditions and beliefs.

The absence of a clear doctrinal prohibition against figurative representation may not preclude claims to protection under blasphemy statutes. Civil law protects not the belief but the *believers,* and it would probably be sufficient to establish that the cartoons were injurious to believing Muslims.

Blasphemy laws are secular expressions of the New Testament prohibition in Mark 3:29: "But whoever blasphemes against the Holy Spirit never has forgiveness, but is guilty of an eternal sin." Prohibition against blasphemy remains entrenched in the penal code in many European countries, but the laws are now rarely enforced, and when efforts have been made to have the laws enforced, the courts have found it difficult to decide which forms of expression are punishable under the law.

The First Amendment to the U.S. Constitution, which protects free speech, is widely interpreted to inhibit protection against blasphemy. However, some states do have laws against blasphemy.[19] Among the European countries with laws against blasphemy are Austria, Denmark, Finland, Germany, Ireland, the Netherlands, Poland, Spain, Switzerland, and the United Kingdom.

The British government abolished blasphemy protection—which applied only to the Anglican Church, and then only in England and Wales, where it is the established faith—in March 2008, when the House of Lords passed an amendment to a criminal justice bill eliminating the offenses of blasphemy and blasphemy libel. (The Church of England was

divided on the bill, with two lord bishops supporting it and three oppos-
ing.) Most European countries have in recent years amended the blasphemy laws to include Judaism. Local governments also have the authority to ban performances. Monty Python's *Life of Brian* was banned in
several cities in the United Kingdom and was banned for some years in
Ireland, Norway, and Italy. Prosecutions for blasphemy are brought from
time to time in these countries, but they generally fail.

Christian publications in Europe generally concluded that publishing
the cartoons was a bad idea. The French newspaper *La Croix* defended the
rights of religious people and criticized the decision of other publications
to reprint the cartoons. During the cartoon crisis, the British philosopher
Roger Scruton complained that nothing was sacred any more and articu-
lated the religious argument: "If we mock the religious taboos of Muslims
we pour scorn on the icons of Christianity." He viewed the cartoons as
emblematic of Europe's excessive secularism. "The condition of the public discussion that we need is respect," Scruton wrote in a commentary.
"That means that we must respect the icons of the Muslim faith, even if
we think them ridiculous, indeed especially if we think them ridiculous.
The cartoons that have precipitated the current crisis were worse than a
mistake: they were an act of sacrilege, like trampling on the crucifix or
spitting on the Torah. This is not a contribution to free speech but an
obstacle to it."[20]

Abdul Haqq Baker, the manager of a Salafist mosque in London,
agreed with Scruton. "Secularization has gone too far, when the doors are
broken down to insult people's faith and nothing is sacred any more."[21]
Blasphemy laws should be resurrected, he argued, and broadened to include all the Abrahamic faiths. (He was in principle prepared to include
other faiths but admitted that he did not know what constituted blasphemy in Buddhism and Hinduism.)

Section 140 of the Danish criminal code allows for fines and up to four
months in prison for someone who publicly mocks or scorns the beliefs of
a recognized Danish religious community or their faith. The law was last
applied successfully in 1938, when a Nazi group distributed leaflets claiming that Talmudic law sanctioned the rape of non-Jewish women.

In 1973 a complaint was brought against Jens Jørgen Thorsen, who
had a history of insulting Christianity. He had depicted Jesus on the cross
with an erection, and so when he received public funding to make a film

about the sex life of Jesus, a predictable uproar ensued. The prosecutor declined to file a suit, but the government withdrew financial support from the production. Fifteen years later, Thorsen finally had his funding restored and was allowed to produce his movie. It was a flop. (At the time, *Jyllands-Posten* took the side of the Christian protesters, but the paper would probably be on Thorsen's side today.)

In the Danish system, complaints are submitted to the public prosecutor, who rules on the merit of the claim before deciding to go to court. When Muslim litigants filed a complaint against the cartoons, it was initially rejected. On appeal, the national prosecutor also decided that a conviction was unlikely and declined to take the case to court. This seems a reasonable conclusion given the history of failed prosecutions, but the prosecutor's reasoning on the substantive issue reveals the difficulties of applying historically Christian code and jurisprudence to other religions. The hadiths prohibit the depiction of humans, he noted, a prohibition that includes the Prophet. But, he continued, there are many ancient as well as recent depictions of the Prophet made by Muslims themselves, which shows that Muslims do not observe the prohibition. Therefore, drawing the Prophet does not constitute a violation of Danish civil code's prohibition on mockery of central tenets of recognized faiths. This was, in my view, a misreading of art history. The valuable miniatures now in the possession of Islamic art collections do not constitute a precedent in the manner the prosecutor deduced.

It is a pity that the argument was not taken to court, in which case undoubtedly everyone would have been educated in the difference between depicting the divine and the human Prophet and between caricatures and idealized portrayals. The prosecutor nonetheless rebuked *Jyllands-Posten* for incorrectly asserting that free speech principles do not allow for consideration of religious feelings and for their claim that Muslims—or members of any other religious group—must put up with "mockery, ridicule, and sarcasm."[22] Muslims nonetheless also lost a libel suit against the newspaper.

Section 140 has been invoked with some regularity in recent years, but with little success. Catholics complained about a supermarket that was selling sandals with pictures of Jesus printed on the soles. Muslims complained when the public television station broadcast *Submission*, a controversial twelve-minute film produced by Ayaan Hirsi Ali and Theo van Gogh, the murdered Dutch filmmaker. Evangelical Christians complained about a television program with a rock band that features graffiti saying, "Death to Christians." It is fair to conclude that although the charge of double standards may appropriately be flung at European newspapers, which freely insult Muslims while pulling their punches against Christians, the Danish prosecutor and the courts have been consistent in dismissing suits.

Attempts by Europe's Muslims to use blasphemy laws against Rushdie's *Satanic Verses* and the Danish cartoons have been unsuccessful. Muslims, it could be argued, are victims less of double standards than changing legal norms. Courts and lawmakers have increasingly refused to subordinate free speech to religious prohibitions. In fact, the laws are in flux, and judicial practice is in a state of confusion. In Germany in 1994, there was a successful prosecution of a musical comedy in which pigs were crucified and the doctrine of the Immaculate Conception was ridiculed. An Italian court sentenced a sociologist, Stefano Allievi, in March 2007 to six months in prison and a fine of three thousand Euros in response to a blasphemy claim made by Adel Smith, a convert who achieved notoriety in Italy for successfully filing suit to get crucifixes removed from classrooms. Allievi is a well-known expert on European Muslim affairs. He has appealed against the conviction, which concerned remarks made about Smith in an academic book, and has so far avoided prison.[23]

In contrast to the United States, Europe has a copious catalogue of hate speech laws, prohibitions on Holocaust denial, bans on incitement to political violence or hatred, and the old blasphemy laws. Arguably Europe is already overly committed to the regulation of speech, and more regulation is not the way to go. The Council of Europe recommended in 2007 that blasphemy should not be regarded as a criminal offense out of consideration for religious freedom and stressed instead the importance of penalizing expressions about religious matters that intentionally aim to disturb the public peace.[24] Europe's Muslims increasingly agree that more restrictions are not desirable and point out that it is ironic that four cartoon demonstrators in London were sentenced to six years in prison while all the blasphemy suits against newspapers were dismissed.

CHAPTER 7

Danish Intolerance and Foreign Relations

WHY DID PRIME MINISTER Anders Fogh Rasmussen stubbornly refuse to recognize the Muslim diplomats' complaint and insist, for months, under building pressure, that there was nothing he could do? The escalation in February and March 2006, nearly six months after the cartoons were published in *Jyllands-Posten,* came as a surprise in no small part because the extensive diplomatic activity that started in October 2005 and lasted through autumn was kept from the public. This became clear in early March 2006 when journalists from *Politiken,* a newspaper that had been critical of the government's actions throughout the affair, obtained OIC secretary-general Ekmeleddin İhsanoğlu's letter from the foreign ministry's files after a freedom of information request.[1]

The OIC's letter was nearly identical to the one mailed by the eleven envoys (reproduced in chapter 2) but left out the request that the responsible parties be held accountable "under law of the land." The letter was forwarded to a parliamentary committee on March 3, 2006. Members of the committee protested that they had been kept in the dark. The existence of a previously undisclosed letter from an important actor that, contrary to the prime minister's assertion, contained no demand that the government prosecute *Jyllands-Posten,* put things in a new perspective. Danish law requires the government to inform the parliament about "threats to the country's national interests," and committee members made noises about starting a constitutional inquiry into the government's handling of the crisis. Nothing came of it.

Fogh Rasmussen defended himself by describing the letters from the eleven ambassadors and the letter from the OIC as "the same thing" and not separate incidents. He stressed his fundamental principle: "Danish society is based upon respect for free speech, religious toleration, and all religions are treated equitably. Free speech is the basis of our democracy. Free speech is far-reaching, and the Danish government has no influence on what the press writes."[2] He agreed that dialogue between cultures and religions is essential and invited the diplomats, their governments, and İhsanoğlu to participate in the Danish government's partnership program, Det Arabiske Initiativ (The Arab Initiative).

The tone grinds. The letter was written by the foreign ministry but issued in the prime minister's name. (The foreign ministry normally handles international correspondence, but in this case the original letter was sent to the prime minister, and the response went out in his name.) Does the ministry not know how to write a diplomatic letter in English? I asked an old friend who is a diplomat in the Danish foreign ministry and therefore must remain anonymous. We do, he answered, but the letter was "made to order" from the prime minister's office.

On January 30, 2006, Rasmussen said in an interview on Danish television that the controversy was all about free speech and insisted that "a Danish government cannot say 'sorry' for a Danish newspaper." He added that he personally would never publish anything that offends people's religious beliefs. Three days later, on February 2, he apologized (or at least, the speech was widely taken to be an apology), but Rasmussen also insisted that the media are independent in Denmark, and "there was nothing he could do about it." He could not resist lecturing his critics. "I myself am very often criticized and I have to accept that because that's part of our society that we have freedom of expression." The remark implied that Muslim governments should learn to live with freedom of expression in the Danish way.

MEANWHILE, BACK HOME

Like most small European countries, Denmark has a system of proportional representation, and the bar is set low to qualify for a seat in parliament. In February 2005, half a year before the cartoons were published, ten parties contested the parliamentary elections, and just three failed to gain enough votes to qualify for representation. With seven parties in parliament, the math of forming a government becomes complicated. The election was a narrow victory for Anders Fogh Rasmussen and his party, the Liberals. The party lost four seats but, with 29 percent of the votes, remained the largest party in parliament and was able for a second time to form a government together with the Conservative Party. However, the Conservatives, with just over 10 percent of the national vote, are only the fourth largest party, and even combined the two parties do not have a majority. Fogh Rasmussen consequently also depended in parliament on the votes of a far-right party, the Danish People's Party (described below).

The absence of a parliamentary majority is normally a critical liability —and in many countries unconstitutional—but in Denmark a government can be formed if there is not a majority against it. The opposition was too divided to produce an alternative and chose to allow the prime minister to form a minority government. A center-left coalition government was in theory possible in 2005 between the second largest party, the Social Democrats, and two smaller parties, but leadership problems and disagreements over immigration policy stood in the way.

Usually, minority coalition government creates a compulsion to negotiate across the center and encourages consensus-building.[3] When Fogh Rasmussen formed his first cabinet in 2001, however, he remodeled the premiership and ditched consensus politics. Fogh Rasmussen borrowed a great deal from George Bush. In 2003, he sided with the Bush administration on war in Iraq. Denmark was one of the five original countries to participate in the invasion. (The others, aside from the United States and the United Kingdom, were Spain and Poland.) "Iraq has weapons of mass destruction," Fogh Rasmussen told the country. "It is not something we think. We know it." He has yet to admit that the evidence proves him wrong. Only the three parties supporting Fogh Rasmussen's government voted in favor of sending troops to Iraq. Denmark has a tradition of pacifism and had never before gone to war with such a divided parliament. It was even more unusual for Denmark to participate in a war that the United Nations had condemned. (The Danish troops were deployed under British command and were withdrawn in coordination with the wind-down of the British military presence around Basra in 2007.)[4]

Fogh Rasmussen was able to form his third cabinet in 2007 after parliamentary elections in November 2006, again in coalition with the Conservatives and with the support of the Danish People's Party in parliament. In April 2009, Fogh Rasmussen was appointed secretary-general of NATO and stepped down as prime minister. No election was held, and the government continued under the leadership of Fogh Rasmussen's successor, Lars Løkke Rasmussen.

The cartoon crisis cost Denmark international reputation and trade. The boycott cut sales of Danish goods by 50 percent in Iran and Saudi Arabia. Six months after the start of the boycott, Danish Industry, the national trade association, estimated losses at $180 million. Arla, the beleaguered dairy maker, incurred half of that loss.[5]

Fogh Rasmussen's foreign policy was not a liability for the Mærsk Group, a family-owned Danish company and one of the world's largest shipping companies. The company obtained a six-year contract with the U.S. government for shipment—ships, crew, and command—of material to Iraq in 2002. Reports vary as to the benefit to the company's balance sheet of the contracts, but they are presumed to be significant. Mærsk provided assistance to the United States during the Gulf War in 1991, and the collaboration with the U.S. Navy's military sealift command began in 2001.[6] The contract predated the Iraq invasion by many months and probably signed before Fogh Rasmussen's decision to commit troops to the war.[7] Irrespective of Mærsk's role, the facts do not support the theory that business interests drove Danish foreign policy.

Then there is the matter of "soft power." This now ubiquitous term was coined by Joseph Nye to describe American self-interest in being regarded as the international arbitrator of universal values: If people believe that your intentions are generally good, the transaction costs of getting what you want are lighter.[8] Fogh Rasmussen showed little interest in maintaining Denmark's international reputation as both a liberal-minded member of international organizations and a fair and reliable business partner—two things that Danish business leaders regard as assets for trade and that the diplomatic corps regards as leverage for influence beyond the normal expectations of a small nation.

In Denmark, three explanations are given for Fogh Rasmussen's costly refusal to enter into dialogue with Egypt and the Islamic intergovernmental organizations over the cartoons. The first is that Fogh Rasmussen and his foreign minister, Per Stig Møller, underestimated the anger and the resolve of the Muslim diplomats. Misjudgment goes a long way toward explaining *Jylland-Posten*'s actions, but there is little evidence to support the view that Fogh Rasmussen and Stig Møller were uninformed about the probable consequences of their policy. Danish diplomats in the Middle East and Danish representatives to the Organization for Security and Co-operation in Europe, various UN and Council of Europe committees, and other international organizations fully recognized the seriousness of the matter. Interdepartmental notes released to a Danish newspaper indicate that there was a high degree of coordination between the foreign ministry and Fogh Rasmussen's ministry. The prime minister would not have been kept in the dark.[9] And the extensive diplomatic contacts between Muslim diplomats and the governments (see chapter 3, table 1) gave no reason to doubt that there would be serious repercussions.

THE DANISH PEOPLE'S PARTY

The second explanation is that Pia Kjærsgaard, leader of the Danish People's Party, told Fogh Rasmussen that if he conceded to Muslim pressure, she would withdraw her support for his government. (We shall get to the third explanation in time.)

The popularity of the Dansk Folkeparti, or Danish People's Party (DPP), sustains the harsh tenor of Danish public debates on immigration and Muslims. In 1995, the party split off from an older far-right and anti-tax party, the Progress Party. (The first DPP was formed in 1941–1943 by Danish sympathizers with the NSDAP, the German Nazi Party.) Today the DPP has eclipsed other far-right parties with its combination of a pro-welfare state platform and refusal to accept immigration.

The growth of the DPP was part of a European trend. Parties that targeted Muslim immigrants scored gains in many countries in the 1990s. Some of these anti-immigrant parties were new arrivals on the political scene. Others were old parties that adopted anti-immigrant and anti-Muslim rhetoric and attracted new voters to a populist agenda. The Belgian Vlaam's Blok burst on the scene in 1999, the same year Jörg Haider's Freedom Party got 27 percent of the Austrian vote and came neck-to-neck with the governing conservative party. In September 2001, Carl Hagen's Progress Party became the third largest party in Norway with 15 percent of the vote. Anger against Muslims fueled the successes in

2002 of the Lijst Pim Fortuyn, which with 17 percent became the second-largest Dutch party, and later of the VVD, Ayaan Hirsi Ali's party. Jean-Marie Le Pen's National Front was propelled to second place in the 2002 presidential race in France.

One survey, now a decade old, found that 48 percent of Danes believed that Muslims currently living in the country are "a threat to Danish culture and religion."[10] Only 9 percent thought that Muslims were a source of cultural and religious renewal. The coalition between the DPP and Fogh Rasmussen's government has been held together by successive measures to control immigration—measures so strict that Denmark has been reprimanded by international courts and human rights agencies. It was this climate of opinion that produced the cartoons and explains the heated reaction to Muslim protests.

In the 1998 parliamentary elections, the first that the DPP contested, the party captured thirteen seats. Four years later, it became the third largest party in parliament. In 2005, the DPP received 13 percent of the national vote and gained twenty-four members in parliament, becoming an essential parliamentary support of the government. In the first election held after the cartoon controversy had broken, the DPP gained another seat. This matters. In multiparty democracies with a system of proportional representation, elections are won and lost by margins of a few percentage points. The DPP's unbroken streak of election gains sent a powerful message to other parties: resistance to immigrants and multiculturalism matters more to voters than the economy and taxes.

Today, nearly 4 percent of Danish residents are Muslim. Nearly half of Danish Muslims are recent immigrants to Denmark or have been born to immigrant parents since 1980.[11] In the 1990s the DPP opposed immigration in blanket terms, but in the past decade it has focused almost entirely on Muslim migration. As was the case in other European countries, the influx of non-Western immigrants—including political refugees, who in legal terms are not immigrants but in political reality are seen as such—peaked in 1995, when about 46,000 individuals entered the country. The number of entrants has since held steady at about 31,000 annually. In the meantime emigration has picked up as Danes leave (and immigrants remigrate) to live elsewhere in Europe, and in 2003 and 2004, net immigration was only 5,500–6,500.[12] (These are the most recent figures available.) Clearly, Denmark successfully shut the door on further immigration.

Integration policy is in theory intended to encourage immigrants to assimilate, but the DPP argues that making sure prospective immigrants know what is expected of them if they come to Denmark is the best way to deter new immigration. Immigrants who are in Denmark are put under pressure to adapt to Danish norms and values. The threshold for integration is set high, and the DPP works hard to ratchet it upward.

Most European countries have recently removed barriers to the acquisition of citizenship, a notable instance being the new German nationality law passed in 2000. Fogh Rasmussen's governments have taken the opposite line: they have made it harder to acquire citizenship. Legal residents are eligible for citizenship after nine years' residency, provided they prove fluency in Danish, have a clean criminal record, and can support themselves financially. Dual citizenship is prohibited. The Danish constitution requires that naturalization—the acquisition of citizenship by non-nationals—takes place by act of parliament. The list of applicants for naturalization is voted on by parliament twice annually. For years, between 2,000 and 5,000 individuals were naturalized annually but in 1998 the numbers started to creep up. In 2000 nearly 20,000 people were naturalized, about half from Islamic nations.

The Danish People's Party campaigned to reduce the number and started to find ways to whittle away at the list. The message was that being Danish is a very special privilege. When asked by a journalist about the 4,500 adults and 2,700 children granted citizenship in 2006, Søren Krarup, a member of the DPP, said, "That is far more than we will accept." He thought the right number might be 2,000, including children. He acknowledged that the purpose of the citizenship reform was to reduce the number of new citizens.[13]

In December 2005, just before the cartoon controversy reemerged as an international crisis, an agreement was reached to redesign the naturalization rules and to introduce a formal examination requirement. Officially, anyone with nine years of schooling in Denmark should be able to pass the test. In reality this means that only highly educated foreign-born immigrants or second-generation immigrants who have completed their education in Denmark can cope with it.

Ministers argued that anyone can pass the test by studying a manual that provides the correct answers to the test questions. One question on the sample list is: "When did Iceland break away from Denmark?" Correct answer: 1944. Another asks: "What is the name of the prime minister who led the four-party government in the 1980s?" This is a trick question. The correct answer is a politician who has not been active in Danish politics since 1993, and the two false answers provided on the multiple-choice test are the names of politicians who are still active and well known. Some questions evoke Denmark's brief glorious past, such as "What was the name of the Scandinavian union forged by a Danish king?" and "When did the Danish women's handball team win the World Championship?" The correct answers here are the Kalmar Union, which lasted from 1397 to the 1430s, when the Swedes broke up the pact, and 1997. Danes with a taste for board games might know the answers.

The government insists that these are the things you need to learn to know how to be Danish. The test consists of forty questions drawn from a pool of two hundred. An applicant who gets more than twelve wrong answers out of forty is disqualified. Statistics are not yet available to show how successfully immigrants have been prevented from becoming Danish citizens.

The DPP has also been unusually resistant to the sectarianism that plagues the far right. The Dutch Lijst Pim Fortuyn and the Austrian Freedom Party imploded after internal strife. The DPP has also escaped the legal sanctions applied to other far-right groups. The Vlaams Blok was outlawed in Belgium and reemerged under a new name. (The name change is minimal: Flemish "tendency" as opposed to the Flemish "bloc.") Parties of the German far right, the Republikaner Party and the German People's Party, are courting legal trouble for violation of constitutional provisions against extremism. Kjærsgaard's careful and strict leadership has steered the DPP clear of the rocks.

Kjærsgaard has successfully taken to court critics who have implied that she is racist, and I choose my words carefully.[14] The Danish People's Party is a nativist party. Nativism seeks to limit—or outright halt—immigration. It appeals to popular prejudice and stereotyping and describes immigrants as a threat to the ethno-national community. The DPP's 2002 platform stated, "Foreigners should be absorbed in Danish society, but only under the condition that they do not pose a threat to social security and democracy."[15] Nativism differs from legitimate debates of immigration policy by seeking to deprive legal residents of immigrant origin of rights routinely extended to natives.

In her speeches and weekly newsletters Kjærsgaard seamlessly weaves praise for Danish traditions of gender equality with demographic fear-mongering about the excessive fertility of immigrants, criticisms of their family practices, and condemnations of crime, rape, and vandalism that are attributed to immigrant youth gangs. All sustain an argument for reducing benefits for immigrants. And then she skips directly from speaking about immigrants to speaking about Muslims. The elision is rarely contradicted, and when it is challenged, it makes no difference to the speakers or the listeners. Here is a sample: "The Social Security Act is passé, because it was tailored to a Danish family tradition and work ethic and not to Muslims, for whom it is fair to be provided for by others, while the wife gives birth to a lot of children. The child benefit grant is being taken advantage of, as an immigrant achieves a record income due to a dozen children. New punishment limits must be introduced for gang rapes, because the problem only arrived with the vandalism of the many antisocial second-generation immigrants." These remarks were posted in Kjærsgaard's weekly newsletter.[16]

Over time, Kjærsgaard and her party colleagues have moved the boundaries for what can be said without inviting official or public censure. Mogens Camre, a former social democrat who was a DPP representative in the European Parliament until the 2007 election, set a temporary record for racialist rhetoric in a speech at the party's annual meeting in 2004. "Let me say it clearly: Muslims live in Muslimland—and that is not here."

When the eleven diplomats from Muslim nations complained in their October 2005 letter to Fogh Rasmussen about a "smear campaign" in Danish public debate, they were thinking not just of cartoons. They had more egregious examples in mind.

BRIAN, HOLGER, AND LOUISE

Few people outside Denmark knew the targets of the complaints made by the Muslim ambassadors in their letter to the prime minister. In Denmark everyone knows them. One is a minister, the second a radio station, and the third a member of parliament and former porn star. The minister survived the criticism, but the others were in fact punished under the "law of the land," as the Muslim ambassadors desired, but without the government's involvement.

Brian Mikkelsen, the minister for cultural affairs in Fogh Rasmussen's cabinet, a member of the Conservative Party, became a subject of heated newspaper debate the week before *Jyllands-Posten* published the cartoons. This was prompted by a speech he delivered at the Conservative Party's annual congress.

Mikkelsen, who is thirty-nine and has a graduate degree in political science, boasted at the convention about his government's accomplishments: "We have gone to war against the multicultural ideology that says that everything is equally valid." Then he switched from war to a sporting metaphor: "The culture war has now been raging for some years. And I think we can conclude that the first round has been won." The Danish cultural heritage is a source of strength in an age of globalization and immigration, Mikkelsen continued, but he warned Danes not to let up, citing the same examples of appeasement of Muslim norms that Flemming Rose was to use in *Jyllands-Posten*—illustrators who are afraid to sign their drawings of Muhammad and the stand-up comedian who dared not make fun of the Koran. He concluded by urging his party to fight for the restoration of the Danish canon of literary tradition and national artistic expression.

Rose quoted Mikkelsen almost verbatim in his essay in *Jyllands-Posten*, and it was suggested that they had collaborated, which both Rose and Mikkelsen denied. Rose wrote his essay *after* Mikkelsen's speech, but the cartoons were commissioned before it. More likely Mikkelsen and Rose were both echoing ideas that were current among commentators in the summer of 2005.

Mikkelsen's speech was not well received in the Danish press. Commentators pointed out that Muslims were not the only "foreigners" and that Danes generally enjoy foreign films, music, and food. Others pointed out that "Danish" did not mean "better" and that most Danish authors and artists had got started by importing foreign styles and genres.

One conservative commentator, Ulrik Høy, applauded Mikkelsen for "getting the ball rolling" on the culture war. The Danish word is "kulturkampen." (Older Danes would not use the word because it resonates too closely with the Nazis' invocation of "Kulturkampf" to purify Aryan culture, but Mikkelsen is perhaps too young to share such sensitivities.) "There is a need for a culture war and a need for people who will take extreme measures," Høy said. "When the police, the military, and the secret service have dealt with the holy war in Londonistan and its affiliates, people in Brande can probably relax."[17] Brande, readers should know, is a town in Jylland long considered the epicenter of righteous Christian piety.

The provocative use of language combined with incantations of reverence for traditional Danish values is disingenuous. The political outlook and style of the neoconservatives owe a great deal more to the radicalism of the 1960s than to the nineteenth-century "golden age" in Danish literature and painting that they like to invoke.

Radio Holger is a self-described "Danish nationalist" radio station in Copenhagen. During the summer of 2005 the station called for the preventive extermination of Muslims. In one of many offensive statements, Radio Holger declared: "There are only two possible reactions if you want to stop this bomb terrorism—either you expel all Muslims from Western Europe so they cannot plant bombs, or you exterminate the fanatical Muslims, which would mean killing a substantial part of Muslim immigrants."[18] The station was sanctioned, and a court removed its license to broadcast. It now carries on as an Internet radio station.

Another person on the ambassadors' list was Louise Frevert, who at the time was the spokeswoman on culture and education for the DPP. She is a colorful figure: an openly lesbian porn star and an ambitious legislator who wanted to be mayor of Copenhagen. A week before the 2005 local government elections, Copenhagen residents were startled to view an election poster carrying DPP's familiar logo and depicting a blond woman about to perform oral sex on an unseen man.[19] It was an original photo of Frevert, who had a career in the 1970s as "Miss Lulu." When told of the posters, Frevert commented, "I do not see what the big deal is." Neither did the party leadership.

Just two months earlier, Frevert had compared Muslims to a cancer on society that had to "be cut out." Criminal charges were brought against her for racist speech, and she retracted, blaming her web master, a retired navy officer. Her web site was cleaned up and filled with small talk about the weather and gardening. The link to "articles no one dares print" ended in a statement about the importance of observing the law.[20] Frevert later left the DPP after personal conflicts with Kjærsgaard and joined a small centrist party that was not sure it wanted her.

Danes are firmly supportive of the state of Israel, and the DPP is no exception. Yet the party includes individuals who have past and present

links to the neo-Nazi community or long records of anti-Semitic statements. The best-known exponents of anti-Semitism are two pastors,
Søren Krarup and Jesper Langballe, who belong to a pietistic movement
in the national Lutheran Church. (They have now left the clergy, which
has civil service status in Denmark.)

In recent years both Krarup and Langballe have warned of dangers
that Muslims pose to Danish identity, but Krarup's anti-Semitism reemerged in 2004 in a public confrontation with Arne Melchior, a former
member of parliament whose father and brother were both chief rabbis in
Copenhagen. Melchior objected to Krarup's statement in a book published in 1960 about George Brandes, a Danish Jew who is regarded as a
key national liberal figure. "Because of his Jewish blood," Krarup had
written, "he was incapable of piety and devoid of understanding of the
country's history." Krarup also accused Brandes of participating in the
"rape" of Danish culture. Confronted by Melchior forty years later, Krarup
once again said that to be fully Danish, you had to be a Christian.[21]

The DPP used the cartoon protests and the "Muslim threat" to Denmark in its 2007 election propaganda. Election posters showing a hand
drawing a picture of Muhammad with the slogan "Danish values" printed
at the bottom went up on streetlamps across the country. A three-minute
election ad ran two minutes of beautiful pictures of the Danish coun-
tryside and ethnic Danes going about their business and then cut to
pictures of the airplanes flying into the World Trade Center, women in
burqas on the streets of Copenhagen, and a blond woman being raped as
a voiceover intoned: "Denmark is under threat."[22] Hardly a day goes by
without someone saying or writing that a believing Muslim cannot be
"fully" Danish.

THE FAR EXTREME

Far-right extremism poses a challenge for the Danish People's Party. Pia
Kjærsgaard strictly polices the ranks to keep the party free of far-right extremists. Members of DPP's youth organization have been kicked out for also
belonging to Dansk Front (the Danish Front), the largest such group.

In August 2006, journalists from a tabloid called a number of DPP's
local leaders and pretended to be members of Dansk Front or the neo-
Nazi party Danmarks Nationalsocialistiske Bevægelse (the Danish National Socialist Movement, or DNSB).[23] They wanted to join the DPP, said

the journalists. But given their background, would they be allowed to join and hold dual memberships? Nine of the thirteen local DPP leaders agreed to let the callers join even though party rules disallow such dual membership. According to the tabloid, the local leaders saw no problem in working with the neo-Nazis but cautioned the callers against talking about it. Several of the district leaders warned of trouble if Kjærsgaard "found out."

Kjærsgaard did find out, and trouble duly followed. When the story was published, the offending local leaders were immediately expelled. Dansk Front is assumed to be the largest far-right extremist group in Denmark. The group captured headlines when members were arrested in May 2006 on charges that they conspired to firebomb the homes of two government ministers. Dansk Front is openly racist and advocates a ban on Islam. It is known to collaborate with the international neo-Nazi and racist groups Blood & Honor and Combat 18.[24] Both the Danish and the Dutch security services have issued public warnings about growing recruitment of young people and radicalization among youth connected to these groups.

Dansk Front itself refrains from using the usual Nazi insignia and relies instead on graffiti and tags that are popular with young people. Nonetheless, members have used the Nazi salute, "Sieg Heil," at demonstrations. In October 2006, I observed about a hundred young men at an unannounced gathering on Copenhagen's main pedestrian street using a modified version of the Nazi salute, a steady pumping of the right arm with the hand closed in a fist, while they sang rousing battle songs.

It is not known how many Danes are involved with neo-Nazi groups, but as in other northern European countries, support for these groups has apparently grown in recent years. Jonni Hansen, the leader of the DNSB, received 611 votes in the 2005 regional election. The votes fell far short of getting him elected, but Hansen's presence always spells trouble. He has twice been convicted on assault charges. Another group is the Danish Union (Dansk Forening), which split with Hansen's organization on the question of the Holocaust. Hansen claims that the British and American invasion forces starved the Jews to death.

The extreme-right groups played a curious role in the escalation of the cartoon conflict. On February 4, 2006, the police arrested 179 people from a demonstration organized by Dansk Front and from a counter-

demonstration in Hillerød, north of Copenhagen. Dansk Front had announced plans to burn a copy of the Koran at the demonstration. The
police action prevented the demonstrators from burning the Koran as
promised, but a team of French neo-Nazis who had come up for the event
filmed themselves acting out the "pissing" metaphor attributed to a Danish comedian and retold by Rose in *Jyllands-Posten*.[25]

During the cartoon crisis a common comment was that Muslims
could protest as much as they wanted but that they "behaved badly."
Clearly ethnic Danes are also capable of acting outside the legitimate
space allocated for protests in a democracy.

THE DISSENTERS

The Danish establishment did not take a kindly view of the populist
rhetoric prevailing in the country. Uffe Ellemann-Jensen, a popular retired politician from the Liberal Party and a former foreign minister and
European Union commissioner, was among the first to describe *Jyllands-
Posten*'s decision as a juvenile gag.

He suggested to the American network CBS (and on Danish television) that "a little self-censorship is not a bad thing" and lamented in the
Economist that Danes thought free speech meant they had an obligation to
say everything that came into their minds. A group of well-known authors
issued a statement lamenting the harsh tone and obviously discriminatory
intent of the government's policy. They accused the Danish People's Party
of picking on the weakest in society and compared the treatment of Muslims in Denmark to what happened to Jews in Germany in the 1930s.[26]

Herbert Pundik, a former newspaper editor who was among the
7,200 Danish Jews transported to Sweden in October 1943, pointed out
that *Jyllands-Posten* had hurt Muslims' feelings and warned the Danish
government against adding insult to injury by lecturing the Muslim ambassadors on free speech and "Danish principles."

The harshest criticism came from twenty-two former Danish ambassadors, who in early December wrote an open letter to the government
criticizing the prime minister's decision not to meet with representatives
of the Muslim countries' governments and with the Danish Muslim activists, who by that time had collected sixteen thousand signatures protesting the publication of the caricatures. The ambassadors also expressed
their dismay over the sharp tone of Danish public debates about Muslims,

reminding everyone that "Danish values first and foremost call for toleration of those who think differently."[27] High-ranking civil servants, even
former ones, rarely criticize the government. One of the signatories to the
letter later told me that the ambassadors had rationed their moral capital
for some time, because they all knew it meant that they could never again
protest against anything. In late January 2006, the Confederation of Danish Industries finally spoke up and demanded that *Jyllands-Posten* explain
itself and address the consequences of its actions.[28] The press was not
kind to the critics, and the prominent Danes who criticized the government were ridiculed and accused of disloyalty.

The Danish government's inaction during the conflict left the country's diplomats scrambling to control the damage. Inevitably, the diplomats contradicted the government. On January 28, 2008, Hans Klingenberg, the Danish ambassador to Saudi Arabia and the Gulf states, chose to
put the blame on *Jyllands-Posten*. In an interview with the Associated
Press, broadcast in several Arab countries, he said, "It is quite obvious for
me that what this private newspaper has done has hurt tremendously. Not
only Muslims in Denmark, but millions of Muslims around the world."[29]
At home, the Danish People's Party proposed that Klingenberg be cen-
sured for stepping out of line.

Tøger Seidenfaden, the chief editor of *Politiken,* Denmark's second
largest newspaper and a critic of *Jyllands-Posten,* observed acerbically that
the violent protests saved the Danish government from the consequences
of its stubbornness. The Danish claim that Muslims were the bullies and
the paper and the government the victims of intimidation gained belated
credibility.

With time, public opinion in Denmark shifted. An opinion poll taken
before the outbreak of international demonstrations and the initiation of a
boycott against Danish products in January 2006 showed that 57 percent
of Danes thought the newspaper did the right thing by publishing the
cartoons. Four months later, when the protests had subsided but feelings
were still raw in Denmark, 47 percent thought the paper did the right
thing and only 46 percent that free speech comes before respect for
religious traditions and rules. Forty-two percent thought it depended on
the context and 9 percent that respect for faith should come before free
speech.[30]

CONVERTING DANES TO NEOCONSERVATISM

Belatedly we come to the third hypothesis regarding Fogh Rasmussen's motives, which was that he was acting from principle—that is, that he genuinely believes that there is a "clash of civilization" between the freedom-loving West and authoritarian Muslim regimes and that Denmark had become a front-line state in a global struggle. This is certainly the position of his ally, the DPP. "It has been said that September 11 marks the beginning of a fight between civilizations," Pia Kjærsgaard told parliament immediately after the 9/11 attacks. "I don't agree, because a fight between civilizations would imply that there were two civilizations, and that is not the case. There is only one civilization, and that is ours."[31]

Without the support of the DPP, Fogh Rasmussen's three premierships would not have been possible, and without the premierships, Fogh Rasmussen's well-known hopes for a future at the helm of the European Union or NATO would have been illusory.[32] In abstract terms those considerations are sufficient explanations of Fogh Rasmussen's actions during the cartoon crisis. But this is probably not enough to explain the prime minister's stubbornness. His government was never in danger from the opposition during the cartoon crisis. The Social Democrats declared early on that they supported him on the cartoon issue, and he need not have worried about Kjærsgaard. "It is much worse," a dissident party colleague told me. "He believes the stuff."[33]

Anders Fogh Rasmussen began his political career in the Liberal Party's youth organization, of which he became national chairman in 1974. He was born in 1953 in a small provincial town in Jylland and was educated as an economist at the University of Århus. I do not remember meeting him in the canteen shared by economists and political scientists, but I might well have done. I started studying political science in 1973 in the same buildings. Fogh Rasmussen certainly did not participate in the left-wing demonstrations and occupations that were so common in those years. It was he, however, who turned out to be the real revolutionary.

First elected to parliament in 1978, Fogh Rasmussen worked his way up to the leadership of his party. In 2001 the Liberals came to power on a platform of welfare reform and privatization. The DPP's influence was felt in the arena of domestic politics rather than in foreign policy. Years later, the welfare state had not been scaled back and taxes have not been cut. The neoliberal agenda was in shambles. In consequence, foreign policy was the one arena in which Rasmussen could make his mark. He became an early convert to the American neoconservative agenda under the administration of George W. Bush.

The United States undertook a fundamental shift in foreign policy with respect to Arab nations in 2002 in connection with the president's so-called War on Terror, launching what became known as the American Middle East Partnership Initiative and later as the Freedom Agenda. The promotion of democracy, a free press, and elections in the Middle East was made a high priority. Democratization was regarded as a necessary adjunct to the War on Terror. Danish participation was launched under the slogan "Det Arabiske Initiative" (the Arab Initiative), rendered in English more grandly as Partnership for Progress and Reform. This policy reverberated with the neocons' objectives associated with the so-called Project for the New American Century, a blueprint for using democratization in the Middle East as a "forward strategy" for protecting American security interests.[34]

In 2003, Foreign Minister Per Stig Møller described the new policy as "development aid as an instrument for the prevention of terrorism." As he stated, "This is the philosophy behind the reorientation of the Danish government's policy towards the Arab world: To develop closer cooperation with the positive energies in the Arab world supporting reform and development, modernisation and democratisation. Also the EU's efforts in the area must be enhanced. Already during the Danish EU-Presidency we [sic] started the preparation for the new Partnership for Progress and Reform."[35]

A glossy pamphlet from the Danish foreign ministry stated the purpose for reform: "We all remember precisely where we were on 11 September 2001 when we got the news of the terrorist attacks on the World Trade Center in New York and the Pentagon in Washington. Very few of us could have had the ability to imagine the nature of the blind hatred of the West, and against the USA in particular, lying behind this terror."[36]

The government's grammar is fuzzy; the logic is no better. There are many good reasons to establish links and support for prodemocracy groups. Hosni Mubarak's regime in Egypt has governed by means of selective use of emergency laws since 1981, and the opposition—Islamist or liberal—is routinely imprisoned. But from the Egyptian viewpoint, the language smacked of blaming the victim. How could the Danish ministry

cite the crimes of Osama bin Laden and Ayman al-Zawahiri—whose suicide bombers attacked the Egyptian embassy in Islamabad in November
1995 and at Sharm al-Sheikh in July 2005—as the reason to fund NGOs
in Egypt?[37]

For all the bombast, the Danish program does what an Egyptian
diplomat described as "nice things." It funds women's and children's
rights groups, election monitoring, and the exportation of a Danish in-
vention, the "Ombudsmand" institution. (An Ombudsman—in English
spelling—is an independent civil monitoring agency with the capacity to
adjudicate conflicts between government officials and citizens.)

In March 2005, Fogh Rasmussen traveled on state visits to Israel and
Egypt. The trip was described in the Danish press as a highlight of the new
"activist foreign policy" and a triumphant conclusion to Fogh Rasmussen's support for the "roadmap to peace" and the "Arab Initiative," together with Denmark's military contribution in Iraq. Unexpectedly, however, the second leg of the trip, the visit to Cairo, was abruptly canceled
with twenty-four hours' notice. After a visit to Ramallah that left Palestinians gaping when Fogh Rasmussen endorsed Israel's right to defend itself
by building walls on Palestinian territory, the prime minister returned
home without visiting Cairo, where he had been slated to open the new
Danish Dialogue Institute at the Al-Ahram Center for Political and Strategic Studies. The reason for the cancellation was ostensibly that President
Mubarak did not have time in his schedule, but the real reason probably
was that Fogh Rasmussen undiplomatically had asked to meet with leaders of the opposition.[38]

At the opening speech for the 2006–2007 parliamentary session, six
months after the cartoon crisis, Fogh Rasmussen stated more clearly than
before his adherence to the neoconservative agenda of preventive democratization. "On September 11, 2001, nineteen terrorists hijacked four
planes in the United States. Thousands of innocent people were killed.
And since then the world has not been the same. During the last five years
it has become clear that we are in the midst of a global war of values. It is
not a struggle between cultures or religions. It is a war of values between
rational enlightenment and fundamentalist darkness. Between democracy and dictatorship. Between freedom and tyranny. You cannot be neutral in that struggle. We must actively support freedom and government
by the people. . . . We must promote the Freedom Agenda. We do that

through the Arab Initiative, which has as its goal the strengthening of the organizations and movements that work for democratic reform, women's rights, and better education."[39]

Fogh Rasmussen acted entirely in accordance with previous policy when he refused to acknowledge the diplomatic protests by referring to high principle. He also never encountered serious parliamentary criticism of his handling of the cartoon crisis.

The prime minister never acknowledged that Denmark's Arab Initiative suffered a setback in the wake of the cartoon crisis. A festival planned for summer 2006 in Copenhagen, "Images of the Middle East," which was supposed to have taken place in collaboration with the OIC and its cultural and educational affiliate, the ISESCO, was boycotted. The Danish foreign ministry later noted that twelve of twenty-one planned projects with Islamic nations were completed despite the cartoon affair and that eventually seventeen were expected to be completed after a delay or in a reduced fashion. The report adopted an optimistic tone and remarked that the fallout had been expected to be greater, but it spoke darkly of Denmark's "image-shift."[40]

INTERNATIONAL CRITICISM

It came as a shock to the Danish authorities that European and American allies and friends were less than forthcoming with their support. Suggestions from foreign leaders that the conflict was a silly spat and that the government should smooth things over were greeted with incomprehension.

On February 3, 2006, the day that demonstrations spread throughout the Islamic world, a spokesman from the U.S. State Department said about the cartoons, "We find them offensive. And we certainly understand why Muslims would find those images offensive."[41] Louise Arbour, the United Nations commissioner on human rights, already unpopular with Fogh Rasmussen's government for her previous criticism of Danish policy toward refugees, wrote in a public letter to the OIC that she was "alarmed" by such an "unacceptable disregard for the beliefs of others."

Officials from the European Union were also unsupportive. The British EU trade commissioner, Peter Mandelson, described the cartoons as crude and juvenile, and accused the newspapers that reprinted the cartoons of throwing fuel on the flames.[42]

A week later, UN secretary-general Kofi Annan, OIC secretary-general Ekmeleddin İhsanoğlu, and the high representative for common foreign and security policy of the EU, Javier Solana, issued a joint statement condemning the publication of the caricatures.

After the attacks on the Danish diplomatic missions in Beirut and Damascus in early February 2006, the diplomatic community balanced criticism of the caricatures as abuses of free speech with condemnation of the violent protests against them. The UN statement read, "We are deeply alarmed at the repercussions of the publication in Denmark several months ago of insulting caricatures of the Prophet Mohammed and their subsequent republication by some other European newspapers and at the violent acts that have occurred in reaction to them. The anguish in the Muslim world at the publication of these offensive caricatures is shared by all individuals and communities who recognize the sensitivity of deeply held religious belief. In all societies there is a need to show sensitivity and responsibility in treating issues of special significance for the adherents of any particular faith, even by those who do not share the belief in question. We fully uphold the right of free speech. But we understand the deep hurt and widespread indignation felt in the Muslim world. We believe freedom of the press entails responsibility and discretion, and should respect the beliefs and tenets of all religions."[43]

In the world of international diplomacy, this was a serious reproach, but many people thought the Danes got off lightly.

CHAPTER 8

The Freedom Agenda Rebound

WHY DID THE EGYPTIAN foreign ministry invite the Danish clerics to Cairo in early December 2005? And why did Egypt decide to ratchet up the diplomatic protest movement and declare the cartoons depicting the Prophet a violation of a not previously existing human right, a right to be protected against the denigration of "religious figures"? Egypt cannot be held accountable for the whole chapter of demonstrations, riots, and threats that flowed from the cartoon controversy. Nor can the Arab League and the Organization of the Islamic Conference. But they had a role in the story.

The Danish imams had begun to agitate on their own initiative to whip up a response from Muslims, and they had succeeded in arousing some segments of the global Islamist movement. Fatwas and promises of rewards for murder were published by radical clerics in Pakistan and India in October and November 2005, well before the visit of the Danish mosque delegation to Cairo in December. Even without prompting from the Egyptian government, Sheikh al-Qaradawi and his council of Muslim scholars may still have become involved and summoned Muslims to "rage" against the defamation of the Prophet.

The escalation of the crisis owed much also to the global media movement to reprint the cartoons, and by February and March 2006, events were clearly out of control. Even if we accept that Egypt's invitation to the Danish clerics to visit Cairo gave them a platform and access they would

not otherwise have had, the state-sponsored riots in Damascus and Tehran—and in Beirut, where credible sources placed responsibility on Syria
—were prompted by the governments of Syria and Iran. However, the
Egyptian government certainly played a large part in internationalizing
the cartoon affair.

The reason may be in part that it is easy to forgo Danish butter and much
harder to improve social conditions or to resolve divisions over Palestinian
statehood. A cost-benefit calculation of the gains and losses places the costs
almost exclusively on the Danes, but the benefits are hard to see unless we
place the cartoon protests in a bigger picture. They were a reaction against a
Western push for Arab democratization and social liberalization. In the end
we are back to the question of motives and causes. The cartoons infuriated
Muslims, but what is written in newspapers in small countries is not
normally the source of intergovernmental protests and high-level mediation. "Why worry about cartoons when there is Palestine and Abu Ghraib
to worry about?" one Muslim Brotherhood activist in Cairo asked sarcas-
tically. In his view—and that of many others—Hosni Mubarak's government whipped up anger about the cartoons to discredit the Brotherhood.

Leery of conspiracy theories, I asked a member of the Egyptian foreign ministry why Egypt had decided to make an issue of the cartoons. I
met with Fatma El-Zahraa Etman, the assistant foreign minister for European relations, who managed the ministry's involvement in the cartoon
affair. The meeting was organized at short notice. Weeks earlier, I had
asked to meet with the foreign minister, Ahmed Aboul Gheit, but the
request was apparently not received. I was grateful to El-Zahraa for her
time. "Every country in this region is facing enough problems from the
inside and outside," she told me. "Eighty-nine percent of the Egyptian
people hate the United States. Some times we can go against the will of
the people, but we cannot do it one hundred percent of the time." Responding to my evident puzzlement, she reassured me. "Of course, we
will never do something like this to the United States. We are allies." And
then she blurted out, "But who cares about the Danes?!"[1]

The minister was exaggerating slightly. According to the Pew survey
she was citing, only 78 percent of Egyptians hate the United States.[2] She
was accurately reflecting the opinion of many Middle Eastern diplomats
when she showed her disdain for the Danes. But her statement puzzled
me for another reason. The president of the United States, the State

Department, and leading American newspapers had criticized the Danes and the cartoons. The Anti-Defamation League, an arm of American Jewry's political machinery, criticized them. What did the United States have to do with it? And if nobody cares what Danes do or do not do, why make a fuss about cartoons published in a provincial paper written in a language nobody reads—and in a country you profess not to care about?

THE CLASH OF CIVILIZATIONS

The cartoon affair was the "perfect post 9-11 crisis," I was told by Abdel Monem Said Aly, director of the Al-Ahram Center in Cairo (and my colleague at Brandeis University in Boston). It symbolized the new division of the world, much as the Cuban Missile Crisis had redefined the Cold War for Americans.

Has the "clash of civilizations" instituted a permanent state of tension between Muslim countries and the West? Is the cartoon crisis evidence for the existence of a new Sitzkrieg, or Phoney War, dominating international relations?[3] One objection is that it involved the Europeans rather than the United States.

Amr Moussa, the powerful secretary-general of the Arab League, invoked the clash of civilization—it is real, he said, "make no mistake about it" (see chapter 3). In a long monologue about foes of Islam after 9/11, Moussa mentioned in the same breath the cartoons and Daniel Pipes, an American writer who sees the eradication of radical Islam as his mission and declared *Jyllands-Posten* a friend in that war: "If the Western governments cannot control such people how can we control our radicals?" The cartoon protests were an opportunity to educate Western governments. Hesham Youssef, Moussa's chief of staff, summed up the problem differently: "We always thought that we were closer to the Europeans because of our shared past, but the cartoons have shown us this is not the case. The Americans are much closer to our sensitivities on these issues."

How, then, did the United States get involved with the cartoons? I asked Said Aly. He responded that Muslims regarded the cartoons as evidence that the West is "out to get us." They confirmed that the West was acting on a "clash of civilizations" template. Bush had been talking about the Crusades and invoking "Judeo-Christian" values, said Said Aly. The terrorist issue was being used against Muslims despite the obvious fact that terrorism was a shared problem. Crises in Kosovo, Bosnia, and

Palestine all involved aggression against Muslims. Said Aly is well aware that the United States intervened on the side of Muslims in both Kosovo and Bosnia, but as he noted, we both also knew that you cannot argue with public perceptions. As I understood Said Ali, the people thought the cartoons were the fault of the United States, and the Egyptian government had to act on that basis.

The cartoons became a catalyst for popular feelings among Muslims the world over. And yet the cartoons were never intended as an attack on the world's Muslim population. Many Danes and most Europeans found *Jyllands-Posten's* exercise indefensible. The Danes were openly criticized by the United States and the European Union and were treated as an embarrassment by the United Nations. For their part, Muslims initially reacted to the cartoons in a variety of ways, often dismissing them as insignificant abuse by an irresponsible provincial paper in a small country. The claim that they were evidence of a global Islamophobia emerged only when the cartoons were reprinted in western European newspapers and by a few liberal publications elsewhere, all of which happened six months into the conflict. The cartoons were made into a chapter in the undeclared war between the West and Islam only as a result of the political processes that took place before the eruption of violent demonstrations, driven in no small part by the actions of Egypt and the Arab League. It was an instance of the deliberate use of the "clash of civilizations" to make a political point: Do not mess with our domestic politics.

TEACHING THE DANES A LESSON
The Danes do not generally see the crisis as an episode in a global struggle between civilizations. They take a more parochial view. One popular theory is that the Egyptians wanted to punish Anders Fogh Rasmussen for previous diplomatic missteps and a preachy foreign policy.

Said Aly acknowledged that Fogh Rasmussen had ruffled feathers. Mona Omar Attia, the Egyptian envoy in Copenhagen, was personally offended by Fogh Rasmussen's refusal to meet with the eleven ambassadors. The Danes are a small nation and easy to attack. And they were vulnerable because of the prime minister. Danes have no memory of colonialization and think they are carriers of pure values. So they were clumsy, patronizing, moralizing. Europe's big countries are more diplomatic, polished. And as Said Aly remarked, "Who cares about the Danes, anyway?" so there was no countervailing consideration to deter a confrontation.

Gehad Auda, a professor of political science and member of the general secretariat of the National Democratic Party (NDP), Egypt's ruling party, described the cartoons as a perfect issue for the Egyptians, because this was about loving the Prophet. The Saudi Arabian approach to the defense of Islam is to glorify the law and religious doctrine. Egyptians (and Turks) are pragmatic about religious law but revere the Prophet and his life as the guide to the good life. Politically speaking, the cartoons were a good opportunity to send a message to Europeans about respect and to remind the salafists—Saudi Arabia and Sheikh al-Qaradawi included—that Egypt, too, is concerned about Islam. Saudi Arabia and Egypt are in competition to be seen as the nation that represents and protects Islam. This was all circumstantial speculation about why the cartoons presented a good opportunity for the Egyptians.

At the very least, the Danes did not help themselves. But as several of my interviewees remarked, why bother with the Danes? They were not important in themselves.

BEATING THE BROTHERHOOD

Another theory popular in Denmark is that the Danes were simply scapegoats, sacrificed by an Egyptian government that was intent on burnishing its reputation as a defender of Islam in preparation for parliamentary elections that took place during the fall of 2005.[4] This is a plausible-sounding theory, but it fails on two grounds. The first is that most voters did not know about the cartoons during the electoral campaign, and the second is that the Egyptian government hardly needed to launch a campaign against the Danes to defeat the Egyptian Brotherhood.

Ahmed Aboul Gheit, Egypt's foreign minister, first mentioned the cartoons at a press conference on November 14, 2005, shortly after the first round of parliamentary elections. But the press conference was for foreign media, and it was not covered in the Egyptian press, with the exception of Al-Fagr, the small newspaper that published partial pictures of the cartoons in October 2005. The cartoons did not become a domestic political issue until early December in connection with the visit from the Danish imams and the summit meeting of the OIC. These events coincided with the last stage of the parliamentary elections, by which time the outcome had been largely decided. The largely state-controlled media did not focus on the controversy until the government wanted it to do so.

The Egyptian Brotherhood, which is the largest opposition party, had also not chosen to make the cartoons an issue in the elections. Indeed it was convinced that when a decision was made at the "highest level" to stimulate controversy over the cartoons, the government's real purpose was to discredit the Brotherhood. But the government was not addressing the Egyptian public. It was sending a message to Western powers not to undermine Hosni Mubarak's regime by supporting the opposition's right to freely contest the election.

The United States had put pressure on the Mubarak government, which has governed by means of selective emergency powers since 1981, to allow multiparty candidates in the 2005 presidential election, the fall 2005 parliamentary elections, and in local elections that had originally been scheduled for spring 2006 but were postponed to spring 2008.

The Egyptian Brotherhood is banned but tolerated. Members were allowed to stand for elections in 2005 in response to U.S. pressure, but only as independents and not on a party platform. The 2005 election took place in three stages between November 7 and December 9. In the first stage the Brotherhood won 34 out of the 164 seats contested. The result suggested that the Brotherhood would do well, but the contested seats were in known Brotherhood strongholds and may not have predicted outcomes in the next stages. Before the second stage, the government arrested eight hundred Brotherhood members, including party leaders and candidates standing in contested districts, effectively preventing the party from campaigning.

It is unclear how effective the harassment was, but the Brotherhood eventually took 87 seats, about one-fifth of the seats in the legislature. The government party, the NDP, won 311 seats, a small loss from the previous election, in which the Brotherhood was not allowed to run, but still more than the two-thirds of the parliament needed to control all legislation. The Brotherhood also contested the 2008 local elections, leading to more waves of preemptive arrests of candidates in the spring of 2008.[5] In April, twenty-five senior members of the Brotherhood were sentenced to three to ten years in prison by military tribunals, which took over the cases after the civilian courts refused to try the accused. Competing for voters on "soft" issues, such as the cartoons, is hardly necessary when imprison-ment of the opposition is a ready option.

The Egyptian Brotherhood leaders I spoke to in Cairo had different personal reactions to the cartoons. Some shrugged and said there are worse things in the press, while others described them as intolerably offensive. All agreed that this was not an issue of their choosing. Essam El-Erian, a leading member of the Brotherhood and a parliamentarian who has been described by *Time* magazine as the organization's chief political strategist, was in prison when the cartoons were published, and my impression was that he had not seen them.[6] But he had a different theory about the target of the government-inspired campaign. He be-lieved that the Egyptian authorities had made an issue of the cartoons in reaction to a resolution passed by the European Parliament that con-demned the abuse of human rights in Egypt.

The European Union had initiated a Euro-Mediterranean Partnership Dialogue—the Barcelona Process—in 1995. In 2003, the European Com-mission took a decision to "reinvigorate EU actions" on human rights and democratization targeted at those it quaintly referred to as its Mediterra-nean partners. A resolution passed in 2005 criticized the treatment of Sudanese refugees in Egypt and took up the case of two political dissi-dents, Ayman Nour, the leader of the secular El Ghad Party and a former member of parliament, and Saad Eddin Ibrahim, a professor and human rights advocate.

In January 2008, a month before I interviewed El-Erian, the Euro-pean Parliament passed a resolution condemning Egypt's human rights abuses, particularly in the area of religious toleration, and what was de-scribed as harassment of NGOs and political activists.[7] The Egyptians issued a vehement protest and summoned all twenty-seven ambassadors from the European Union member states to the foreign ministry to ex-press their displeasure.

Certainly, El-Erian said, Muslims have problems with pictorial repre-sentation, yet the main issue was not the fact that the newspaper decided to draw the Prophet but that he was depicted as a terrorist.[8] And they were also concerned with how Europe deals with its Muslim minority, he said. But they had other, more urgent priorities. The Brotherhood, he ex-plained, did not want to act on the cartoons at the time, although he hinted that their attitude might change. Later that day, February 17, 2008, two years after the first cartoon controversy peaked, the Muslim Brotherhood parliamentary bloc passed a resolution strongly condemning the cartoons and demanded that the Egyptian government break off diplomatic relations with Denmark and put its weight behind the boycott.

The ostensible reason the Brotherhood chose now to make an issue of the cartoons, two years after the cartoons first caused an uproar, was the decision by Danish newspapers to reprint one of the cartoons. The newspapers described it as an act of solidarity with Kurt Westergaard, the cartoonist, when it was revealed that he had been the target of an ongoing murder plot. But the cartoons' encore appearance had political consequences in Egypt that the Danish editors did not foresee. Moderates within the Brotherhood—and in particular Amr Khaled, a popular Egyptian tele-preacher who went to Denmark during the first crisis on a peace mission—who had argued that Muslims should educate the Danes about the harm they had done but forgive them because the problem was ignorance, were discredited. It now appeared that the Danes had acted out of malice. Politically speaking, the moment was also more opportune for the Brotherhood to stage a protest against the cartoons once the Egyptian government had officially "forgiven" the Danes.

I spoke to a young Muslim Brotherhood member, Khaled Hamza, chief editor of IkhwanWeb, the Brotherhood's English-language web site, in a Starbucks café in a shopping mall under construction in a newly built suburb of Cairo. (On the following day he was arrested by the security forces, presumably because he was trying to meet with a delegation visiting from the European parliament.)[9] Hamza told me that the cartoons were "not an issue of their choice." The Egyptian government wished to discredit the political opposition by showing the West that "this is what happens"—that is, anti-Western mobs take to the streets—when you push for democracy in the Middle East. The cartoon affair, he believed, was exploited in order to send a message to the Europeans and the United States that the Muslim masses had to be held in check by a strong, authoritarian government.[10]

Ibrahim El-Houdaiby, the young journalist and blogger from the Muslim Brotherhood introduced earlier (see chapter 4), said that "of course" he was against the cartoons, but Saudi Arabia and Egypt were making an issue of them because they wanted to arouse people against the West. The protests were a mistake because they gave expression to a narrow and reactionary interpretation of Islam and reinforced the fallacy that conflict between Occidental and Oriental values was unavoidable. Because of American policies, the Mubarak regime had been forced to allow an Egyptian "spring" (a reference to the 1968 Prague spring, a temporary flourishing of freedom) before the parliamentary elections in November 2005. In October, the press had begun to enjoy a new freedom. By November, the frost set in again. "The entire issue was manipulated at a high level," he concluded.[11] The cartoons were used to discourage the United States from pressuring the Middle Eastern governments to reform.

The United States had applied considerable pressure on the Egyptians to conduct free elections. It had also promoted a broader democratic agenda. In May 2004, Secretary of State Condoleezza Rice stated her priorities in a speech at the U.S. Institute of Peace: "First, we must work to dispel destructive myths about American society and about American policy. Second, we must expand dramatically our efforts to support and encourage the voices of moderation and tolerance and pluralism within the Muslim world."[12] George W. Bush telephoned Hosni Mubarak in spring 2005 to say that the United States expected to see free elections. The Egyptian government was also pressured to allow independent monitors to observe the vote.

The United States took up the cause of the two imprisoned critics of Mubarak's regime, Ayman Nour and Saad Eddin Ibrahim, and Condoleezza Rice postponed a trip to Egypt scheduled for February 2005 to protest Nour's imprisonment. (Anders Fogh Rasmussen's bad luck, when his state visit to Egypt was abruptly canceled, was to have scheduled his visit for March 2005, and to have made the same impossible request to see the opposition leaders.)

In June 2005, Secretary Rice visited Cairo and insisted on meeting with leading dissident political figures. None belonged to the Muslim Brotherhood, but according to the New York Times, Rice warned Mubarak's government against setting up "a false choice between his autocratic rule and the leader of Egypt's Islamic political movement, the Muslim Brotherhood."[13] She also again pressed the Egyptians to guarantee free elections in the fall and to allow the opposition to participate.[14] Although there was little official discussion about the Brotherhood, unofficially the

U.S. government acknowledged that free elections would probably benefit the Brotherhood.[15]

This was strong medicine for Mubarak's regime. Egyptian courts
attempted to uphold the election laws, but the final assessments of the
elections by international monitoring groups were nonetheless dismal.[16]
An Egyptian human rights organization listed abuses during the first
stage of the elections ranging from the locking up of polling stations to
the arrest of candidates, and yet at first declared the election good news.
Its final report was considerably more negative.[17] Ibrahim El-Houdaiby's
description of a brief political spring in October and November 2005 is
corroborated by the observations of election monitors and human rights
organizations. The timing of the cartoon crisis also fits with his assessment that the controversy was manipulated in order to send a warning to
Western governments that were pressing for more democracy in Egypt.

THE FREEDOM AGENDA AND EGYPT

Greater freedom for civil society organizations and the removal of barriers
to direct U.S. funding of such groups were important aspects of the
post-9/11 Middle East Partnership Initiative, a supplement to military
engagement in Afghanistan and later in Iraq, launched in 2002.[18] The
initiative has since been scaled back to five "pillars" promoting civil society, democracy and liberalization of the economy, and including a wom-
en's pillar for the promotion of gender equality. Early on in the Bush
presidency, Arab democratization was presented as a forward strategy for
American security, and the new policy was intricately connected to the so-
called War on Terror. It was an essential element of the Bush administration's neoconservative strategy and a complement to the military pursuit
of terrorism.

In 2003 George W. Bush gave a speech to the National Endowment
for Democracy outlining the new foreign policy.[19] The speech was written
by Michael Gerson, a former project director at Project for a New American Century (PNAC), a neoconservative think tank that counted among
its members many Bush administration officials, such as Vice President
Dick Cheney, and Secretary of Defense Donald Rumsfeld. The speech
built on a PNAC statement released in 1997.[20]

In this speech Bush reiterated core ideas of the neoconservative
movement and explicitly involved arguments advanced by such American

scholars as Samuel P. Huntington and Robert Kagan. "The lesson from the collapse of Nazism in 1945 and the cold war and the collapse of the Soviet Union in 1989," said Bush, is that "over time free nations grow stronger." We have reached a great turning point, he said, and what the United States does now will shape the next stage of "the world democratic movement." There is a "freedom deficit" in the Middle East. "These are not the failures of a culture or a religion. These are the failures of political and economic doctrines." Now was the time to apply the lesson. Military and theocratic rule in the Middle East represented "a straight, smooth highway to nowhere," but some governments still cling to old habits of central control. Therefore, said Bush, "the United States has adopted a new policy, a forward strategy of freedom in the Middle East. This strategy requires the same persistence and energy and idealism we have shown before. And it will yield the same results. As in Europe, as in Asia, as in every region of the world, the advance of freedom leads to peace."

The agenda for reform was long. It included privatization and liberalization, freedom of the press, an end to the habit of throwing the opposition in jail after hearings in kangaroo courts, the lifting of restrictions on NGOs and access to Western funding, the promotion of women's rights and the rights of minority religions, checks on corruption, and the promotion of public health, including vaccination campaigns but excluding birth control.

Bush singled the Egyptians out for special attention: "The great and proud nation of Egypt has shown the way toward peace in the Middle East, and now should show the way toward democracy in the Middle East. (Applause.) Champions of democracy in the region understand that democracy is not perfect, it is not the path to utopia, but it is the only path to national success and dignity."[21]

The speech was well received in Europe but less so in the Middle East, where newspaper columnists objected that democracy cannot be forced on people. Present practices were adapted to local realities and were "good enough."[22]

The United States made fostering an autonomous civil society a high priority, and persuaded the G8 (Group of Eight, which consists of the large Western countries plus Russia) to launch the so-called Forum for the Future. The second meeting took place on November 11–12, 2005, in Bahrain, in the middle of the Egyptian parliamentary elections and with the cartoon crisis brewing. The meeting was cohosted by Bahrain and the United Kingdom, and the agenda was to pass a new charter for "civil society and democracy" in the Middle East. The participants included foreign ministers of about thirty states, including the member states of the Arab League, and the presidents of Spain and Turkey, who jointly set up the Alliance of Civilizations, which became an agency for interreligious dialogue under UN auspices in 2005.

The United States set up a new foundation, the Foundation for the Future, to fund civil society initiatives and small business. Fogh Rasmussen signed Denmark up as a "partner" and the Danish Partnership for Progress and Reform—known in Denmark as the Arab Initiative—was copied from the American blueprint. Plans were presented in Washington before the meeting at a press conference fronted by Liz Cheney, a State Department spokeswoman (and the vice president's daughter), and Daniel Fried, the undersecretary for Euro-Asian affairs. A Kuwaiti journalist stood up to ask a question.[23]

QUESTION: [Aya Batrawy, Kuwait News Agency] Can you just explain here the breakdown of the funds that are going to this—$35 million from the U.S., I think, and other countries? And how did you get the support of Arab governments in this when you're—I don't understand the connection—like why would they support—I don't know, I mean, are they supporting this with funds—the Arab governments—because if that's the case, then why don't they just give these funds directly to the civil society? Why do they have to go through this whole thing?

MS. CHENEY: Well, I think there are two issues. The U.S. is putting $35 million into the Foundation and other governments are putting in $9 million, including I think there's about $2 million that's coming from the European Commission. The extent to which Arab governments are participating, the Government of Jordan has put $1 million into the Foundation. We expect that we'll have contributions from other governments as well. They've expressed support and they've told us that they will contribute and we expect you'll see that happen over the next week or so after the announcement of the Foundation.

With respect to the Fund, we're putting in $50 million. The Government of Egypt is putting in $20 million and the Government of Morocco is putting in $20 million.

ASSISTANT SECRETARY FRIED: And Denmark.

MS. CHENEY: And Denmark is putting in $1 million. Sorry.

The Egyptian government would have none of it. A charter statement prepared in advance of the launch of the Foundation for the Future bound the participating states to allow funding for NGOs without prior state approval. Egypt refused to sign, and when the foreign minister, Ahmed Aboul Gheit, left before the talks were concluded, the meeting collapsed. A diluted charter was signed a year later at a meeting in Sanaa, Yemen. (A smaller than anticipated foundation was set up in 2008 with headquarters in Jordan to carry out projects under the charter.)[24] In March 2008, Condoleeza Rice and Aboul Gheit announced at a press conference in Washington that the United States had waived the hold on grants to Egypt and that a $1.2-billion military aid program would go ahead.[25]

As one of the founding members of the civil society initiative, Denmark was invited to the meeting in Bahrain. The Danish foreign minister later complained to the Danish press that Amr Moussa "never said anything" when the two sat next to each other on a flight to Bahrain to the Forum for the Future in November 2005, before Egypt ratcheted up the diplomatic protests. "He could have said something," Per Stig Møller complained.[26] Why should Amr Moussa mention it? It never was about the Danes. The cartoons were surrogates for a push back against Western pressure to promote democratization in the Middle East.

A REVERSE ALLIANCE

Reverse alliances are what states do when they want to remind their allies not to take them for granted. An implicit or explicit compact with the opposition or the enemy may impress your indispensability on friends and allies. The rational balance of power politics induced the Egyptian government to roll out the full diplomatic armament against the hapless Danes. The cartoons were surrogates for a push back against the Freedom Agenda of the United States, which targeted Egypt for special attention. On the big question, the minister was surely right. No Arab government can act as an ally of the United States in Iraq and in the protracted negotiations over the "roadmap" to Palestinian statehood and then permit free elections without incurring punishment at the ballot box.

The Egyptians may have wanted to prove that elections can produce unwelcome results by orchestrating a proxy experiment in the form of the cartoon protest, but the message had already been absorbed. The U.S. government backed off from the democracy agenda at the end of 2005, but it had nothing to do with the cartoons or the spectacle of watching angry Muslims burning the Danish prime minister in effigy. Parliamentary elections in Lebanon in May and June 2005 were the first held in thirty years not to return a pro-Western majority. In fact they helped Hezbollah, the Shiite Islamist movement. The Iraqi constitutional referendum in October 2005 and the parliamentary elections in December 2005 proved that elections sometimes produce more problems than they solve. The success of Hamas in the January 2006 Palestinian elections was a yet greater shock. Advocates of the Freedom Agenda now generally accept that the United States should not rush to press for another round of elections to take place in Iraq according to the established schedule and that it was wrong to focus on free elections as the centerpiece of reform.[27]

Hosni Mubarak's regime was quick to undo the reforms carried out in 2005. The free civil society agenda has been scaled back, and the opposition is once again in prison. In April 2008, twenty-five leaders of the Muslim Brotherhood were sentenced to up to ten years in prison by military tribunals set up by the government after the civil courts refused to prosecute the men. Human Rights Watch has a list of some two to three hundred individuals held in Egyptian prisons on political charges.

The political prisoners who invited the official U.S. condemnations, Ayman Nour and Saad Eddin Ibrahim, were rearrested and sentenced again after the United States let up. Ibrahim is a sociologist and the founder of the Ibn Khaldun Center for Development Studies in Cairo. He was imprisoned in 2000 for using European Union funding to support independent election monitoring and released in 2003 after the United States withheld $130 million in extraordinary aid appropriated by Congress for Egypt. He is currently in exile but was sentenced again in August 2008 to two years in prison for "defaming" Egypt. Nour was arrested in January 2005 on charges of having falsified the paperwork for the registration of his party, the El-Ghad Party, and released later in the year after Rice canceled her planned visit. Nour ran in the presidential election, which took place in early September 2005, but was sentenced in December 2005 to five years in prison. (He was released on health grounds in February 2009.)

The cartoons were also used to scale back freedom of the press. On

February 15, 2008, the information ministers of the Arab League agreed on a new charter allowing governments to act against satellite television news broadcasters. Only Lebanon and Qatar opposed the motion. Al Jazeera (owned by the Qatari government) called the charter "a risk to the freedom of expression in the Arab world." The information ministers' meeting had been called at the request of Egypt, which hosts the Arab League and serves as a base for several Arab satellite channels. Anas al-Fiqi, the Egyptian information minister, said that his country would be the "first to implement the Cairo document." "Some satellite channels have strayed from the correct path," he said. One of the points in the document requires stations "not to offend the leaders or national and religious symbols" of Arab countries.

Al Jazeera, created in 1996, was at first hailed by the United States as a symbol of Muslim democracy, but the station's critical broadcasting from Iraq quickly earned it the enmity of the Bush administration. (Al Jazeera's English-language channels are widely available on European cable television networks and as satellite television.) The station radically changed the Middle Eastern media landscape. Its exposure of corruption and social and economic failures in Egypt and other countries has put it on a collision course with Hosni Mubarak's government, and Al Jazeera's reporters have been banned and imprisoned in Egypt and other Arab countries. The most widely publicized cases were conspiracy charges against Al Jazeera's bureau chiefs in Morocco in 2005 and in Egypt in 2006, and a six-month prison sentence to a woman journalist who reported on torture in Egypt's prisons in 2007. Al Jazeera has also been accused of favoring Al-Qaeda because it is Osama bin Laden's favorite outlet for his occasional tapes pronouncing on the sins of the regimes in the Middle East and the West.

Ironically, perhaps, Al Jazeera is the elite's preferred station because it is not state-controlled. The broadcaster's twenty-four-hour news station seems to be permanently switched on in every high-ranking official's office in Egypt. The station hummed in the background during my interview in Cairo with Amr Moussa. The televisions in the Ministry of Foreign Affairs were also set to Al Jazeera. At earlier visits to Turkish ministers' offices in Ankara, I also found the televisions tuned to Al Jazeera as well as to the twenty-four-hour Turkish news channels.

Amr Moussa dismissed my suggestion that the charter was about to kill the Arab countries' most valuable counter to Western monopoly on the dissemination of news with a wave of his hand. "Ah, that—the charter is only optional." But the Egyptian authorities have shut down several stations. Nilesat, a government-owned network that transmits other stations, took Al-Hiwar TV off the air. The station broadcast shows that included government critics. The U.S.-funded Al-Hurra station had a live show censored. And in April 2008 the Cairo News Company, which supplies footage to Al Jazeera, the BBC, and CNN, among other foreign stations, was temporarily shut down and the owner arrested and fined for broadcasting coverage of antigovernment street protests.

Few aspects of the Bush presidency's neoconservative agenda for remaking the American strategic presence in the world met with European approval. The agenda for Arab democratization was the exception. It was a source of puzzlement to observers how the "clash of civilizations" became an offensive weapon in the hands of the protesting diplomats from Muslim countries during the cartoon crisis. The complaint that the cartoons were representative of offensive denigration of Muslims and their faith—a charge that applied only in part because the actual content of the cartoons was consistently overlooked due to the newspaper's packaging of the story—effectively turned the tables on the Western alliance's use of democratization as a strategy for proactive counterterrorism.

Europe's readiness to prosecute anti-Semitic language by criminalizing Holocaust denial was contrasted to its obvious reluctance to bring prosecutions for blasphemy and hate speech in response to the denigration of Islam and Muslims. The charge of a double standard was an obvious one to make. In my view the criminalization of speech is a mistake. But the denial of the Holocaust is an effort to erase a uniquely European crime from the books and to play games with history.

The Egyptian government's quick decision to bring its complaint against the Danes to the attention of international organizations and the United Nations was an important step toward the recognition of Islamophobia as an offense against human rights. That was a goal in itself. Fearful of rising anti-Muslim sentiments in Europe and of being shut out of the European Union, Turkey has made an issue of Islamophobia in intergovernmental negotiations for some time. But a second purpose unique to Egypt's interest was to counter the Western appeal to universal values and demands for domestic change on human rights issues in Egypt and elsewhere in the Middle East. These were pragmatic and tactical decisions made for purposes other than the introduction of sanity into European debates about the integration of Muslims. The Egyptian government was pursuing self-interested objectives and acted to build international power. A teenager who feels that a friend does not properly appreciate her may briefly pretend to be best friends with the friend's enemy. In much the same way, Egypt reminded the United States and the Europeans of the risks of change. The cartoon protests are an interesting example of how a secondary power can humble a primary one. Cultural politics can be a potent weapon in international affairs.

FINALLY, A HAPPY ENDING

On April 4, 2009, Anders Fogh Rasmussen was appointed secretary-general of NATO. He took up his post on August 3, 2009. To secure the appointment, he had to overcome strenuous objections from Turkey. Turkey's prime minister Recep Tayyip Erdoğan pointedly asked if NATO's interests would be served by having a man who had earned the disdain of the Muslim world in the seat and said he was receiving many calls from heads of states in the Muslim world on the matter. Turkey drove a hard bargain and in the end refrained from vetoing Rasmussen's appointment. President Barack Obama reportedly brokered the compromise. The U.S. president stated publicly only that there had been "important efforts to make sure that everyone felt included."[28]

Turkish newspapers listed eleven concessions obtained by Erdoğan in exchange for his support of the appointment. Not all were publicly announced, but those that were significantly improved Turkey's international standing: the establishment of close contacts between NATO and the OIC; the appointment of a Turkish aide to Fogh Rasmussen and more senior appointments for Turkish generals to high posts in NATO; and the reopening of negotiations with the European Union on certain chapters related to the Turkish accession agreement.

The concessions allegedly also included promises from Fogh Rasmussen that ROJ TV, the Kurdish satellite television based in Denmark, would be closed and, according to Turkish papers, that there would be an official apology for the cartoons. If so, no apology was made when Fogh Rasmussen spoke at a meeting of the Alliance of Civilization held in Istanbul on

April 6, to which he suddenly was invited because of his new appointment. Instead, the former prime minister expressed his admiration for Islam and pledged to work for interreligious toleration. In Denmark, commentators and Fogh Rasmussen's former colleagues in parliament expressed incredulity that a police team had been dispatched to investigate ROJ TV's links to the PKK in preparation for the closure of the station after many years of inaction. In Turkey, the editors at *Hürriyet,* an influential newspaper, wrote, "In only one day, [Obama] fixed the U.S. image that Bush destroyed over eight years," but noted the Fogh Rasmussen had not actually promised to close ROJ TV when he spoke after his appointment and warned against expecting that Turkey would get everything it asked for.

Fogh Rasmussen's appointment was an unexpected outcome of the cartoon crisis. Both sides won. Turkey was reassured that the West had not closed its door to a Muslim country. And Fogh Rasmussen got the position he had long coveted. As for Danish speculations about the prime minister's motives in 2006, when he refused to concede to Muslims' demands for affirmation of their rights, is not the conclusion surely that a politician can change his or her mind when the right incentives are present?

CHRONOLOGY

2005

September 19

Flemming Rose, the culture page editor at *Jyllands-Posten*, invites forty-two Danish cartoonists and illustrators to draw the Prophet Muhammad "as they see him" for publication in the newspaper. Twelve artists respond to the challenge.

September 30

Jyllands-Posten prints the twelve cartoons under the headline "The Face of Muhammad." The cartoons are published together with an essay by Flemming Rose, the culture editor, and an editorial leader by Carsten Juste, the editor-in-chief.

October 4

A seventeen-year-old local resident calls the paper and threatens to kill the cartoonists. The police arrest the young man after his mother calls them.

October 8

A group of Danish imams and mosque leaders demands that *Jyllands-Posten* "retract" some of the cartoons and officially apologize to all Muslims.

October 11

One of the Danish imams, Sheikh Raed Hlayhel, gives an interview to Al Jazeera in which he complains about the cartoons and the treatment of Muslims in Denmark.

October 12

Ambassadors and delegates representing eleven Muslim countries in Denmark send a letter to Prime Minister Anders Fogh Rasmussen requesting a meeting.

October 14
A demonstration in Copenhagen against the paper and the treatment of Muslims in Denmark attracts 3,500 people. Two cartoonists are moved to "safe houses" after receiving death threats.

October 15
The Organization of the Islamic Conference (OIC), an intergovernmental organization of fifty-seven Islamic states and Muslim countries, sends a letter to the prime minister expressing the organization's alarm over the derogatory caricatures and other recent incidents and insults committed by Danish politicians. The Arab League sends a letter at approximately the same time.

October 16
A second seventeen-year-old man is charged with sending death threats to the cartoonists.

October 17
A small Egyptian newspaper, *Al-Fagr,* reprints six of the cartoons, one of them on the front page. Copies of the newspaper are confiscated from newsstands.

October 21
Prime Minister Fogh Rasmussen ignores the ambassadors' request for a meeting and states in a letter in response to their letter, "Free speech goes far, and the Danish government has no influence on what the press writes."

October 24
Fogh Rasmussen publicly reiterates his refusal to meet with the ambassadors. "It is so obvious what our basic principles are that there is no basis for having a meeting," he says.

October 25
The Egyptian foreign ministry informs the Danish ambassador in Cairo that Egypt expects the Danish government to condemn the mockery of the Prophet.

October 27
Eleven Muslim organizations and mosque communities in Denmark file a complaint against *Jyllands-Posten* on the grounds of blasphemy under sections 140 and 266b of the Danish criminal code.

November 3
The German newspaper *Die Welt* reprints one of the cartoons, and a Bosnian newspaper, *Slobodna Bosna,* reprints all twelve.

November 7–11
The government of Bangladesh sends an official protest to the Danish government. The Arab League and the OIC accuse Denmark of violating UN resolutions on human rights in a joint letter to the OECD and the UN high commissioners of refugees and of human rights. Egypt's foreign minister, Ahmed Aboul Gheit, sends

letters to the secretaries-general of the UN, the OSCE, and the EU's foreign policy coordinator complaining of the Danish government's violation of nondiscrimination resolutions.

November 11–12
"Forum for the Future," a summit meeting of thirty states, is held in Bahrain aiming to pass a charter on the rule of law and civil society as part of the Broader Middle East and North Africa Initiative. Egypt refuses to sign, and the meeting collapses when its foreign minister walks out.

November 16
Prime Minister Recep Tayyip Erdoğan of Turkey criticizes the Danish government during an official visit to Denmark. Fogh Rasmussen responds that he "will simply not compromise. This is about how a democracy works."

November 24
Two UN special rapporteurs responsible for monitoring religious freedom and racism, discrimination, and xenophobia request a statement about the treatment of Muslims in Denmark from the Danish mission to the United Nations.

December 2
Danish newspapers report that the country's ambassador to Pakistan has learned that a Pakistani sheikh associated with Jamaat-e-Islami, an Islamist party, has offered a reward for killing one of the cartoonists. Party leaders later say that Jamaat-e-Islami merely suggested that the Pakistani government could issue such a reward. Danes are warned by the foreign ministry not to travel to Pakistan.

December 3
A delegation of five imams from Denmark arrives in Cairo for a weeklong visit during which they meet with Amr Moussa, the secretary-general of the Arab League, and representatives from the foreign ministry and the religious authorities. The delegation brings along a dossier with *Jyllands-Posten*'s twelve cartoons and three additional drawings, which they say show how Muslims are treated in Denmark.

December 7
The OIC holds an extraordinary summit meeting in Mecca. The dossier with the twelve cartoons and the three "fake" cartoons is circulated at the meeting. The meeting passes a resolution condemning the insult to the Prophet and the use of freedom of expression as "a pretext to defame religions."

December 7
Louise Arbour, the UN high commissioner for human rights, promises an investigation and requests an official statement from the Danish government regarding human rights issues in connection with the cartoons. The first demonstrations against the cartoons take place in Pakistan.

December 10
Sheikh Muhammad Sayyid Tantawy, the leader of the Egyptian religious authorities, grand imam of Al-Azhar Mosque, and rector of Al-Azhar University in Cairo,

issues a statement that "Al-Azhar intends to protest these anti-Prophet cartoons with the UN's concerned committees and human rights groups around the world."

December 17
A second delegation of Danish imams leaves for Lebanon and Syria, bringing along the documentary dossier with cartoons.

December 20
Twenty-two former Danish diplomats write an open letter to the government chastising it for not meeting with the eleven Muslim countries' ambassadors and chargés d'affaires. A retired foreign minister and former EU commissioner, Uffe Ellemann-Jensen, supports the open letter and criticizes Fogh Rasmussen's government. A subcommittee of the Council of Europe investigating the rights of religious minorities condemns the Danish prime minister for using freedom of speech as a reason for refusing to meet with the envoys from Muslim countries.

December 27
The Islamic Educational, Scientific and Cultural Organization (ISESCO), a pan-Islamic intergovernmental association with fifty member states, passes a resolution calling for a boycott against all collaboration with Denmark.

December 29
The Arab League sends a protest to the Danish government expressing grave disappointment and surprise over the government's failure to address Muslims' concern in response to the cartoons. The league had expected more, "considering Denmark's political, economic, and cultural ties to the Islamic world."

2006

January 1
In his New Year's day speech, Prime Minister Fogh Rasmussen says that satire and antiauthoritarian speech are part of Danish democratic culture. Conceding a little to the Muslim countries, he also condemns the demonization of other religions. The speech is published in Arabic.

January 3
The OIC announces that it will boycott a Danish government initiative, a public cultural festival on "Images of the Middle East" in Copenhagen planned for August and September 2006.

January 7
The Danish district public prosecutor decides that the suit filed in October by Muslim organizations cannot proceed because no legal grounds exist for suing *Jyllands-Posten* for blasphemy. The next day the organizations appeal the decision to the national prosecutor's office.

January 10
A Norwegian Christian newspaper, *Magazinet*, reprints the twelve cartoons.

January 12
A Norwegian man of foreign descent is arrested for sending death threats to the cartoonists and the newspaper.

January 20
Emails and text messages urging people not to buy Danish goods spread in Saudi Arabia.

January 21
An influential council of clerics and Islamic scholars associated with the Muslim Brotherhood calls on Muslims all over the world to boycott Danish and Norwegian goods.

January 24
The Saudi Arabian government officially condemns the cartoons. Fogh Rasmussen says in his response to the UN high commissioner on human rights that Denmark "has nothing to be ashamed of" with respect to the human rights aspects of the cartoon crisis.

January 25
Supermarkets start to remove products from Arla Foods, a Danish dairy manufacturer with subsidiaries in Saudi Arabia, from shelves in Saudi Arabia and other Arab states. Sheikh Abdul Aziz al-Sheikh, Saudi Arabia's grand mufti, calls on the Danish government to punish *Jyllands-Posten*.

January 26
Saudi Arabia recalls its ambassador from Copenhagen. Supermarkets across the Middle East start to remove Danish goods from the shelves. The Norwegian government expresses regret that *Magazinet* did not respect Muslims' religious feelings when it reprinted the cartoons.

January 27
During Friday prayers in many mosques in the Middle East, worshippers are told to boycott Danish goods.

January 28
Hans Skov Christensen, the head of the Confederation of Danish Industries, criticizes *Jyllands-Posten* for its actions and "the harm done to third parties." An opinion poll shows that 79 percent of Danes think the government should not apologize. Twenty percent say they have no sympathy for Muslims' reaction, while 58 percent say the paper had the right to do what it did but they also have sympathy for Muslims. The crisis is discussed for the first time in the parliamentary standing foreign policy committee. Arla Foods reports that sales have come to a complete halt in the Middle East. *Jyllands-Posten* posts an open letter to Muslim citizens on its Internet site apologizing for having caused offense.

January 29
Libya closes its embassy in Denmark in protest against the cartoons. The Syrian and Bahraini governments condemn the cartoons and the Danish government's lack of

response. The Kuwaiti and Jordanian governments reprimand the Danish ambassadors. In Nablus, on the West Bank, the Danish flag is burned in angry demonstrations. Scandinavians are told to leave Gaza. Parliamentarians from the Danish People's Party and the Liberal Party, Fogh Rasmussen's party, demand that the Danish ambassador in Riyadh be reprimanded for criticizing *Jyllands-Posten* in an interview broadcast in Saudi Arabia the day before. Novo Nordisk, a pharmaceutical company, reports that Middle Eastern customers are boycotting its products.

January 30
Danes are told to avoid travel to the Middle East. Gunmen storm the European Union's office in Gaza and demand that the EU apologize for the cartoons. In a revised open letter published in English and Arabic, the editor in chief of *Jyllands-Posten* apologizes for having offended Muslims. Speaking on Danish television, Fogh Rasmussen says that "the government cannot say 'sorry' for a Danish newspaper" but adds that he personally would never portray Muhammad or Jesus in ways that may offend people's religious beliefs. Javier Solana, the EU's foreign policy coordinator, issues a statement condemning the cartoons and the violent protests. The EU foreign ministers condemn the threats against Nordic citizens.

January 31
Islamic Jihad demonstrates in Gaza. Danish troops in Iraq are threatened with reprisals. A bomb threat against *Jyllands-Posten* leads to the evacuation of the newspaper's offices in Copenhagen and Århus. Foreign Minister Per Stig Møller meets with UN Secretary-General Kofi Annan and US Secretary of State Condoleezza Rice to discuss initiatives to ease the crisis. Former US president Bill Clinton describes the cartoons as "outrageous." Russian President Vladimir Putin accuses the Danish government of abusing free speech. One of the Danish imams, Mahmoud Fouad Albarazi, appears on Al Jazeera. He cries as he tells the audience that the Danes plan to burn the Koran.

February 1
A dozen European newspapers reprint one or some of the cartoons. The owner of one of the papers, *France Soir,* fires the editor, Jacques LeFranc, for printing the cartoons. LeFranc is rehired the next day. Syria calls its ambassador in Copenhagen home. *Jyllands-Posten*'s offices are evacuated again after a bomb threat. Members of the opposition declare their support for Fogh Rasmussen's stance in the crisis. The boycott of Danish goods in the Middle East spreads.

February 2
More newspapers reprint the cartoons, also in the Middle East. Glimpses of the cartoons are telecast in Britain. Fogh Rasmussen gives an interview to the Arabic satellite station Al Arabiya. In Denmark, he says, the media is independent, and there was nothing he could do about the cartoons. Even he, he says, is often criticized, and it is something he has to accept. Gunmen force the closure of the EU office in Gaza. The Danish People's Party announces an investigation into the possibility of removing the citizenship of the protesting imams. Fogh Rasmussen's party supports the investigation.

February 3

The Pakistani legislature condemns the cartoons. The popular religious scholar and television preacher Sheikh Yusuf al-Qaradawi calls for "a day of rage" against the cartoons. The cartoons are condemned after Friday prayers in mosques across the Middle East. Text messages circulate in Britain, France, and in some Arab countries that there are plans to burn copies of the Koran at a demonstration in Copenhagen the next day. British foreign minister Jack Straw criticizes the cartoons and *Jyllands-Posten*. A spokesman for the US Department of State describes the cartoons as a provocation and an insult. The BBC receives more than twenty thousand emails in twenty-four hours to a scheduled program on the cartoon called "Have Your Say." Several hundred demonstrators storm the Danish embassy in Jakarta, Indonesia, but leave when the ambassador explains that *Jyllands-Posten* and the Danish prime minister have apologized to Muslims. Fogh Rasmussen meets in Copenhagen with diplomatic envoys from seventy-six countries to explain his government's actions. The Egyptian ambassador, Mona Omar Attia, says that the meeting is too late, because the matter is no longer under the control of the governments but in the hands of the masses.

February 4

More newspapers print the cartoons. In Damascus, demonstrators attack the Norwegian and Danish embassies. The Danish embassy is housed with the Swedish and Chilean representations, which are also set on fire. In Copenhagen, the police arrest 179 people in connection with counterdemonstrations against a demonstration organized by Dansk Front, a neo-Nazi group. The police also prevent the approximately thirty Dansk Front demonstrators from burning the Koran. At a demonstration in London, calls are made for the beheading of *Jyllands-Posten*'s editors. Three demonstrators are later arrested and charged with incitement to terrorism. Condoleezza Rice places a phone call to the Danish foreign minister. Kofi Annan calls on Muslims to accept *Jyllands-Posten*'s apology. A Danish Muslim parliamentarian, Naser Khader, starts a new organization for "Demokratiske Muslimer" (Democratic Muslims) to organize Muslims who oppose the four imams and the mosque activists.

February 5

In Beirut, demonstrators set fire to the Danish consulate. One demonstrator dies during the attack. Demonstrations spread across the Muslim world. Effigies of Fogh Rasmussen are burned in Turkey. Javier Solana, Kofi Annan, and NATO Secretary-General Jaap de Hoop Scheffer step forward to mediate between Denmark and Muslim countries. Iran recalls its ambassador from Copenhagen. The OIC, Kofi Annan, and a spokesman for the US president condemn the attacks on the Danish embassies and chastise the Syrian government for its failure to provide protection in Damascus. Danes are told not to travel in seventeen predominantly Muslim countries, and Danish residents in Syria and Lebanon are advised to leave. The Conference of European Rabbis compares the cartoons to anti-Semitic (anti-Jewish) caricatures.

February 6
The demonstrations turn deadly in Indonesia, Afghanistan, Somalia, and Kashmir. In India and Indonesia the Danish flag is burned during angry demonstrations. Tony Blair, Jacques Chirac, and Angela Merkel condemn the violence. A Catholic priest is shot in Turkey. The Danish embassy in Jakarta, Indonesia, is damaged and closed. The embassy in Tehran, Iran, is ransacked and firebombed. Sheikh Muhammad Sayyid Tantawi calls on the Egyptian government to recall its ambassadors from Denmark and Norway. In Cairo protesters demonstrate in front of the Danish embassy and at Al-Azhar University. The government of Syria apologizes for not having protected the Danish embassy in Damascus, and the grand mufti of Syria expresses regrets for the deterioration of the relationship between the two nations and promises that Syria will rebuild the embassy.

February 7
Demonstrations take place in Afghanistan, Bosnia-Herzegovina, Egypt, Finland, France, Iran, Iraq, Kashmir, Niger, Nigeria, Pakistan, the Philippines, and the West Bank. The Red Cross withdraws its Danish employees in Pakistan and Indonesia. Danish Muslim organizations file a second suit against *Jyllands-Posten*, charging the newspaper with violating prohibitions on racist speech. Fogh Rasmussen says that George W. Bush called him to express his support. The Danish imams who went to Cairo are accused of deceit and treason after it is revealed that their dossier contained drawings that were not part of *Jyllands-Posten*'s cartoon editorial.

February 8
Demonstrations continue across the world. A French satirical magazine, *Charlie Hebdo*, reprints all the cartoons together with one of their own caricatures. Danes are withdrawn from the UN office in Hebron for security reasons. Vladimir Putin describes the cartoons as a provocation and calls on Denmark to apologize for *Jyllands-Posten*'s insult to Muslims. Flemming Rose says on CNN that his paper will publish the winning entry in the Iranian Holocaust cartoon competition.

February 9
The Shiite movement Hezbollah stages massive demonstrations in Lebanon in connection with the Ashura, a religious holiday among Shia Muslims. *Jyllands-Posten* places Flemming Rose on indefinite leave.

February 10
A second weekend of demonstrations starts across the world. Three to four thousand people demonstrate against the cartoons in Paris and London, and about five hundred protesters gather in Berlin. One hundred thousand people march in a peaceful demonstration in Rabat, Morocco. Demonstrations spread to Ghana, Jordan, Kenya, Malaysia, South Africa, and Sri Lanka. Islamic Jihad threatens to kill the cartoonists. Denmark recalls its diplomats from Iran, Indonesia, and Lebanon after threats are received. The Danish embassy in Damascus has been empty since the attack the previous week. Danish tourists are evacuated from Bali and other overseas destinations deemed insecure.

February 12
Large demonstrations take place in Turkey.

February 13
Javier Solana starts a weeklong trip to various capital cities in the Muslim world to mediate between the Danes and foreign governments. His first stop is Saudi Arabia. An Iranian newspaper calls on artists to submit cartoons about the Holocaust.

February 14
The city council of Basra, Iraq, demands that Danish troops stationed there be withdrawn because of the cartoons. Demonstrators in Lahore, Pakistan, burn Pizza Hut and Kentucky Fried Chicken outlets and a Holiday Inn. In Cairo, Solana meets with Egyptian religious authorities and President Hosni Mubarak, Foreign Minister Ahmed Aboul Gheit, and Secretary-General of the Arab League Amr Moussa to discuss EU and UN initiatives to promote interfaith dialogue. An Italian minister from the far-right Lega Nord, Roberto Calderoli, is shown on television wearing a T-shirt bearing one of the Danish cartoons. Calderoli is forced to resign three days later after pressure from Libya.

February 15
Violent massive demonstrations erupt in Peshawar, northwest Pakistan. Danish companies report that orders are being cancelled because of the boycott. The religious authorities at Al-Azhar University in Cairo invite and receive a delegation from the Danish Lutheran Church.

February 16
A large demonstration takes place in Karachi, Pakistan. The European Union Parliament passes a resolution condemning both violence and abuse of free speech to insult religious figures. Danish aid workers are expelled from Chechnya and brought home for reasons of security from Pakistan and Kashmir.

February 17
The third Friday of deadly demonstrations takes place across the world. Large demonstrations are held in Bangladesh and Pakistan. Demonstrations take place for the first time in New York City and Hong Kong. A Pakistani cleric, Maulana Yousaf Qureshi, issues a reward (reportedly $25,000 and a car) to anyone who kills one of the Danish cartoonists. A Muslim minister from the Indian state of Uttar Pradesh, Yaqoob Qureshi, promises a reward of his weight in gold to assassins. The Indian police decline to take action against him in the absence of a complaint from one of the Danish cartoonists. Pakistan recalls its ambassador in Denmark.

February 18
Demonstrations occur in Nigeria. Ten thousand people participate in a peaceful demonstration in London organized by 650 mosques and religious organizations.

February 19
After an illegal demonstration attributed to extremists in Islamabad, Pakistan's capital, the Danish ambassador and his family return to Denmark.

February 20
Danish foreign minister Per Stig Møller says it is likely that Al-Qaeda will "use" the cartoons. The Danish press describes the events as the most important foreign policy crisis since World War II. The Danish newspaper *Politiken* publishes the letter from October from the eleven ambassadors revealing that Fogh Rasmussen had misrepresented the content of the letter.

February 21
Hackers shut down 450 Danish web sites, including several government sites and that of *Jyllands-Posten*. Fogh Rasmussen says at a press conference that he regrets that Muslims are so angry. The European Union asks Turkey's foreign minister, Abdullah Gül, to be a mediator between the Danish government and Muslim countries. The OIC denounces the violent demonstrations and calls on Muslims to behave.

February 23
Dissent grows in Denmark over the government's handling of the affair. The opposition parties criticize Fogh Rasmussen for having misled Parliament on January 31 and on previous occasions, when he said that the Egyptian government and the governments of other Muslim countries had demanded that the Danish government take *Jyllands-Posten* to court.

February 24
Demonstrations continue in Indonesia and Pakistan. Muslim activists in Bandung, Indonesia, are arrested after they search the hotels for Europeans and demand that the guests denounce the cartoons. About two hundred people die in clashes between Christians and Muslims in Nigeria after demonstrations against the cartoons.

February 25
The cartoons are the focus of a high-level meeting of a new UN organization, the Alliance of Civilizations, held in Doha, Qatar. Representatives from the UN, the OIC, the Arab League, and the EU, together with the hosts of the meeting, the governments of Turkey and Spain, and Qatar, agree to amend the UN Declaration of Human Rights to include respect for religious figures as a human right.

February 26
Violent demonstrations continue in Pakistan and Iran. The British embassy in Tehran is attacked. Fogh Rasmussen denounces intellectuals and industry representatives who have criticized his actions during the crisis for "lacking principles." Speaking in Doha, Kofi Annan mentions "the offensive caricatures of the Prophet Muhammad" as an example of how "misperception feeds extremism." He describes Denmark as "a country that has recently acquired a significant Muslim population, and is not yet sure how to adjust to it."

March 1
A group of twelve intellectuals including some Muslims, among them the writers Salman Rushdie and Ayaan Hirsi Ali, issues a manifesto in support of *Jyllands-*

Posten and condemning Islamic fundamentalism and totalitarianism. The UN Relief and Works Agency evacuates Scandinavian aid workers from the Palestinian territories.

March 3
A general strike in protest against the cartoons breaks out in Pakistan. French Muslim groups lose their lawsuit against *Charlie Hebdo*.

March 4
More demonstrations take place in Pakistan and Turkey. The slogans denounce the United States and President Bush. Jens Rohde, a Danish MP from the Liberal Party, is compelled to apologize for having misinformed the public when he said that twelve Muslim men had threatened the daughter of one of the cartoonists. It turned out that the exchange took place between feuding ten- and eleven-year-old girls at two schools in Copenhagen and that no adults were involved.

March 5
Al-Qaeda's number two, Ayman al-Zawahiri, calls on Muslims to boycott Denmark and Norway, France, Germany, and all other nations where newspapers printed the cartoons.

March 15
Danish attorney general Henning Fode decides that there are no legal grounds to file suit against *Jyllands-Posten* for blasphemy or hate speech. Five people who participated in a demonstration in London organized by radical groups on February 4 are arrested.

March 17
Demonstrations break out again in Pakistan. Danish Muslim groups file a complaint over the cartoons with the UN Human Rights Council.

March 18
The Indian foreign ministry asks Fogh Rasmussen to postpone indefinitely a planned state visit to India.

March 19
Arla Foods places an advertisement in twenty-five Middle Eastern newspapers criticizing the cartoons and expressing sympathy for Muslims' anger. Danish critics attack the company for appeasement.

March 20
Osama bin Laden releases an audiotape to mark the anniversary of the US-led invasion of Iraq in which he also threatens the European Union over the cartoons: "If there is no check on the freedom of your words, then let your hearts be open to the freedom of our actions."

March 22–24
Sheikh Yusuf al-Qaradawi opens a meeting of three hundred association leaders, religious scholars, and preachers associated with the Muslim Brotherhood in

Bahrain to discuss "how to defend the Prophet." Four imams from the Danish mosque coalition participate.

March 30
After the Danish public prosecutor's office refuses to file a blasphemy suit against *Jyllands-Posten*, Muslim organizations file a private suit against the editors for defamation of Muslims "in text and drawings."

April 28
Al-Qaeda's media company, Al-Sahab, posts a complete version, with English subtitles, of the fifty-two-minute audiotape released by Osama bin Laden a month earlier. On the tape, bin Laden refers to the cartoons as "a Zionist-crusader war on Islam" and pronounces the offense of publishing them "too serious for an apology."

July 31
Two suitcases containing unexploded bombs are found on trains departing from Cologne, Germany. The two Lebanese students responsible for placing the suitcases on the trains, Youssef al-Hajdib and Jihad Hama, declare when arrested that they were inspired by the cartoons, among other things, to carry out their acts.

September 12
In a lecture at the University of Regensburg, Germany, Pope Benedict XVI describes Roman Catholicism as the only true faith capable of uniting reason and revelation. In commenting on conversions, he quotes a fourteenth-century Byzantine emperor as saying that Islam is a faith "spread by the sword." The OIC calls the remarks a "smear-campaign" against the Prophet and asks the UN Human Rights Council to investigate. A perfect storm of condemnation ensues from religious authorities in Turkey, Egypt, and Iran and from the Aga Khan and the Muslim Brotherhood's Sheikh Yusuf al-Qaradawi.

September 25
Deutsche Oper in Berlin cancels a planned production of Mozart's *Idomeneo* because of a scene depicting the severed heads of Muhammad, Jesus, the Buddha, and the Greco-Roman god Neptune. The management cites fears of reprisals from Muslims as the reason. The production is reinstated after protests from German Muslim associations and Chancellor Angela Merkel.

October 26
A Danish court dismisses the private law suit against *Jyllands-Posten* filed by Danish Muslim groups. The court concedes that the cartoons offended some Muslims but argues that they were not defamatory to Muslims as a group. The Muslim groups appeal the decision.

2007

January 4
Four participants in a demonstration before the Danish embassy in London from February 4, 2006, are each sentenced to between four and six years in prison for incitement to murder the editors of *Jyllands-Posten*.

March 30
The UNHRC passes a resolution prohibiting the defamation of religious figures. The resolution mentions no specific religion.

July–August
At a rotary intersection in southern Sweden, artist Lars Vilks mounts copies of an art installation that ostensibly depicts Muhammad as a dog. A few local newspapers reprint the drawing, leading to protests from the OIC, Egypt, and other Muslim governments. The Swedish government condemns the intended insult to Muslims and apologizes in writing to the governments of several Muslim countries (including Iran, Pakistan, Egypt, and Jordan) and to the OIC.

September 7
Prime Minister Fredrik Reinfeldt of Sweden meets with ambassadors from twenty-two Muslim nations to discuss the Vilks incident.

November 26–28
British schoolteacher Gillian Gibbons is arrested and charged in Khartoum by Sudanese authorities for "insulting religion, inciting hatred and showing contempt for religious beliefs" for allowing her elementary school class to name a teddy bear Muhammad as part of a school project. Gibbons is released on December 3 after two British Muslim peers, Lord Nazir Ahmed (Labour) and Baroness Sayeeda Warsi (Conservative), meet with the Sudanese president Omar al-Bashir.

2008

February 12
Danish security police arrest three men on charges of conspiracy to murder cartoonist Kurt Westergaard, who drew the image of Muhammad wearing a turban containing a bomb. One suspect is a Danish citizen of Moroccan origin, and the other two are Tunisians.

February 13
Sixteen Danish newspapers reprint Westergaard's cartoon as a statement of solidarity.

February 19
Egypt bans international newspapers that reprinted the cartoons and cancels a handball tournament and other events planned with Denmark.

February 22
Pakistan blocks access to YouTube in anticipation of the promised release of a short film attacking Islam and Muslims by Dutch MP Geert Wilders. The Malaysian company hired by Pakistan to do the filtering accidentally cuts off Internet traffic to large parts of the Middle East and Asia. It takes weeks to repair the problem.

March 7
The official web site of the Islamic Emirate of Afghanistan (the Taliban) denounces Israel's attack on Gaza, the republication of the Danish cartoons, and Wilders's film. It calls for an end to all diplomatic relations with Denmark and the Netherlands.

March 20
Al-Qaeda's media company, Al-Sahab, releases an audiotape of a pronouncement by Osama bin Laden to mark the anniversary of the invasion of Iraq. On the tape, bin Laden says that the cartoons are part of a "new Crusade" against Islam, links them to Pope Benedict XVI's speech, and threatens reprisals against Europeans for joining up with President Bush. Bin Laden also attacks King Abdullah of Saudi Arabia for failing to deal with the insult of the cartoons.

March 27
After a long buildup, Geert Wilders releases his sixteen-minute-long film, titled *Fitna*, in which he compares the Koran to Hitler's *Mein Kampf* and predicts "the Islamization" of Europe. The film is released on the British web site LiveLeak but taken down forty-eight hours later after a British tabloid reveals the identities of the site's staff. The film is put up again on the Internet briefly on March 30 but removed after Danish cartoonist Kurt Westergaard sues Wilders for copyright violation for using the iconic cartoon of the bomb in the turban. A new version of the film omitting the cartoon is posted an April 6. Westergaard eventually wins ten thousand dollars in compensation against Wilders.

April 7
Arla Foods announces that Middle Eastern consumers continue to boycott its products. "Our turnover is only half the level that we had expected for this year," says a spokesman, who estimates the annual loss at €175 million ($223 million). "In 2006 our sales were at a complete stop," he adds.

April 9
Hundreds of students demonstrate against Wilders's film in front of the Dutch embassy in Tehran.

April 15
The Czech extremist Nationalist Party screens Wilders's film. Party leader Pavel Sedlacek warns against "the Islamization of Europe." Czech police announce an investigation to determine if the film complies with Czech law. News sources report that only twenty people attend the screening.

April 26

In an event organized by Jamaat-i-Islami, four thousand women demonstrate against the cartoons and Wilders's film in Karachi, Pakistan. The party calls for the end of diplomatic relations with Denmark and the Netherlands.

May 13

Dutch cartoonist Gregorius Nekschot (a pseudonym) is arrested following a complaint lodged by a Dutch imam. The public prosecutor charges Nekschot with exceeding the limits of free speech for posting eight cartoons depicting Muslims on his web site. He is released three days later.

June 2

A car bomb explodes outside the Danish embassy in Islamabad, Pakistan. The next day Al-Qaeda claims responsibility for the bombing, calling it revenge for the "insulting drawings."

NOTES

INTRODUCTION

1. Pew Global Attitudes Project, *The Great Divide: How Westerners and Muslims View Each Other; Europe's Muslims More Moderate,* released June 22, 2006, http://pewglobal.org/reports/display.php?PageID=832.

2. Charles F. Westoff and Tomas Frejka, "Religiousness and Fertility among European Muslims," *Population and Development Review* 33 (2007): 785–810.

3. Rahsaan Maxwell, "Muslims, South Asians and the British Mainstream: A National Identity Crisis?" *West European Politics* 29 (2006): 736–756; Dalia Mogahed and Zsolt Nyiri, "Reinventing Integration: Muslims in the West," *Harvard International Review* 29 (2007); see tables at http://www.harvardir .org/articles/1619/. See also the publications of the Gallup Center for Muslim Studies (available at http://gallup.com/consulting/worldpoll/26410/ gallup-center-muslim-studies.aspx).

4. See, e.g., "Timeline: How the Cartoon Crisis Unfolded," *Financial Times,* February 6, 2006.

5. The oil crisis was caused by the oil-producing countries' decision to raise oil prices drastically. On October 17, 1973, the Arab OPEC members additionally imposed a full oil embargo against Denmark and the Netherlands in retribution for Danish and Dutch government leaders' vocal support of Israel in the Yom Kippur War.

6. The Dreyfus Affair also inspired cartoonists: see Mark Bryant, " 'J'Accuse . . . !': Cartoons of the Dreyfus Affair," *History Today* 57, no. 9 (2007): 60–61.

7. For different perspectives on the events, see Salman Rushdie, "The Book Burning," *New York Review of Books,* March 2, 1989, 25; Tariq Modood, "Brit-

ish Asians and Muslims and the Rushdie Affair," *Political Quarterly* 61 (1990): 143–160; and Bernard Lewis, "Behind the Rushdie Affair," *American Scholar* 60, no. 2 (1991): 185–196.

8. The *Wall Street Journal* accepted the Danish imams' version: see Andrew Higgins, "How Muslim Clerics Stirred Arab World against Denmark," *Wall Street Journal*, February 7, 2006.

9. Pew Global Attitudes Project, *Great Divide*.

10. See http://www.djh.dk/ejour/52/52Tegninger1.html.

11. An Egyptian newspaper, *Al-Fagr*, printed one of the cartoons on its front page on October 17, 2005. The issue is now removed from the newspaper's web site, but otherwise the editors faced no reprisals. Jordanian, Moroccan, and Yemeni newspapers, and even a Saudi newspaper, also reprinted the cartoons. The Saudi newspaper was shut down, and the Jordanian editors were arrested.

12. Interview, Baku, Azerbaijan, April 26, 2007.

13. Jytte Klausen, "Rotten Judgment in the State of Denmark," *Salon*, February 8, 2006, http://www.salon.com/opinion/feature/2006/02/08/denmark/.

14. The results of this research were published in *The Islamic Challenge: Politics and Religion in Western Europe* (Oxford: Oxford University Press, 2005). The book was published in German as *Europas muslimische Eliten: Wer sie sind und was sie wollen* (Frankfurt: Campus, 2006). It was published in Turkish in 2008.

15. The *Brussels Journal* copied the cartoons from a Danish site, and the English translations of the captions are in some cases inaccurate; see http://www.brusselsjournal.com/node/382.

CHAPTER 1. THE EDITORS AND THE CARTOONISTS

1. The editorial is reprinted in a collection of documents put together by the Danish PEN Club: Anders Jerichow and Mille Rode, eds., *Profet-affæren* (Copenhagen: Dansk PEN, 2006).

2. A standard for criminal speech was set in 1997 when Mogens Glistrup, a far-right politician, was sentenced to seven days in prison for saying that "everyone who has ever studied Muhammadism [a slur for Islam] know that they [meaning Muslims] are here only to insinuate themselves long enough until they are strong enough to kill us." The highest court upheld the verdict in 2000. *Højesteret*, sag 44/5/1999, August 23, 2000, http://www.domstol.dk/hojesteret/nyheder/pressemeddelser/Pages/Sag4451999.aspx.

3. A copy of the letter soliciting the illustrations can be found in John Hansen and Kim Hundevadt, *Provoen og profeten* (Århus: Jyllands-Postens forlag, 2006), 15.

4. Ibid., 17.

5. Interview, Copenhagen, October 22, 2007.

6. "De zware beproevingen van een moslimmeisje," *Volkskrant*, September 30, 2006.

7. BBC, December 19, 2004.

8. The experiment was carried out about one month after *Jyllands-Posten*'s original "test." Rune Englebreth Larsen and Tøger Sidenfaden, *Karikaturkrisen: En Undersøgelse af baggrund og ansvar* (Copenhagen: Gyldendal, 2006), 46.

9. On July 23, 2008, I found the clip on this web site: http://jp.youtube.com/watch?v=sVwXONnQ4og.

10. Stephen L. Carter, *Civility: Manners, Morals, and the Etiquette of Democracy* (New York: Basic Books,1998).

11. Ian Buruma, *Murder in Amsterdam: The Death of Theo van Gogh and the Limits of Tolerance* (New York: Penguin, 2006).

12. Interview, Copenhagen, October 22, 2007.

13. This account of the discussions between the editors and the journalists builds on Hansen and Hundevadt, *Provoen og profeten*, and personal interviews with Carsten Juste and Flemming Rose.

14. Hansen and Hundevadt, *Provoen og profeten*, 17.

15. Marion G. Müller and Esra Özca, "The Political Iconography of Muhammad Cartoons: Understanding Cultural Conflict and Political Action," *PS: Political Science and Politics* 40 (2007): 287–291.

16. Art Spiegelman, "Drawing Blood: Outrageous Cartoons and the Art of Outrage," *Harper's*, June 2006, 43–52.

17. The Holocaust Museum's archive contains an anti-Semitic drawing from a children's book that uses a surprisingly similar iconography. The Danish cartoonist used the nose and the bushy eyebrows in much the same ways, but where the original squishes the Semitic face into the Star of David, the Danish cartoonist updated the imagery by using the crescent and star; see http://www.ushmm.org/uia-cgi/uia—doc/query/87?uf=uia—QJEpKL.

18. The European Union Monitoring Center on racism and xenophobia uses the term exclusively to connote anti-Jewish stereotyping and uses "Islamophobia" as the parallel designation for the denigration of Muslims. See http://www.european-forum-on-antisemitism.org/working-definition-of-antisemitism/.

19. The quotations are from "Vi stod meget alene." Interviews conducted by Arne Hardis, Jesper Vind Jensen, and Klaus Wivel, *Weekendavisen*, September 28–October 4, 2007.

20. Interview, Copenhagen, October 22, 2007.

21. The sermon took place February 18, 2005. An English version of the news story is available in the newspaper's online archive at http://jp.dk/arkiv/?id=277531.

22. *Jyllands-Posten*, May 22, 2005.

23. Margit Warburg and Brian Jacobsen, eds., *Tørre tal om troen: Religionsdemografi i det 21. århundrede* (Højbjerg, Denmark: Univers, 2007), 143–165. I thank Jørgen S. Nielsen for this reference.

24. The editor was Jens Kaiser, not one of the editors responsible for publishing the cartoons. When confronted with the old rejection letter, Kaiser said, "It is

ridiculous to bring this forward now. It has nothing to do with the Muhammad cartoons." Few people were persuaded by his explanation. "In the Muhammad drawings case, we asked the illustrators to do it. I did not ask for these cartoons. That's the difference." *Guardian*, February 6, 2006.

25. *America Morning*, February 8, 2006.

26. In an interview with a Danish Christian daily, Rose described how he felt that his world collapsed because of his own mistake in the CNN interview. Flemming Rose, "Jeg havde følelsen af, at hele verden faldt sammen om mig," *Kristelig Dagblad*, September 29, 2007.

27. Interview with Carsten Juste, October 23, 2007.

28. Interview with Flemming Rose, October 22, 2007.

29. An English version of the letter can be found in the newspaper's online archive, see at http://jp.dk/arkiv/?id=177649.

30. The letter is still posted on the web sites of many Danish embassies; see, e.g., http://www.ambnewdelhi.um.dk/en/servicemenu/NEWS/OpenLetter FromTheEditorinchiefOfTheDanishNewspaperJyllandspostenOnTheDrawin gsOfTheProphetMohammed.htm.

31. "Udenrigsministeriet lukker for Muhammed-protester," *Dagbladet Information*, March 10, 2006.

32. Udenrigsministeriet (Danish foreign ministry), Exportrådet, *Dansk Export*, 2007. June 2008, 20.

33. "Jeg kan ikke fortryde," *Information*, May 2, 2008.

34. *Politiken*, December 4, 2006.

35. *Jyllands-Posten*, September 13, 2007.

CHAPTER 2. THE PATH TO A SHOWDOWN

1. Sidney G. Tarrow, "Cycles of Collective Action: Between Moments of Madness and the Repertoire of Contention," *Social Science History* 17 (1993): 281–307, and *Power in Movement: Social Movements, Collective Action and Mass Politics in the Modern State* (Cambridge: Cambridge University Press, 1994).

2. "Massive Cartoon Protest in Beirut: Iran, Syria Deny U.S. Claim They Are Inciting Violence," *CNN World*, Thursday, February 9, 2006, http://www .cnn.com/2006/WORLD/asiapcf/02/09/cartoon.protests/index.html.

3. There has been no evidence that anyone has tried to claim the reward, which has not been withdrawn. "Fatwa for Danish Cartoonist's Killing Won't Be Withdrawn," *Daily Times* (Pakistan), December 14, 2006.

4. The manifesto was released March 1, 2006. The full text is available on the BBC News web site at http://news.bbc.co.uk/2/hi/europe/4764730.stm.

5. "Anders Fogh Rasmussens interview til Al Arabiya," February 2, 2006. See http://www.stm.dk/Index/dokumenter.asp?o=2&n=0&d=2508&s=1&str= stor. Transcription in Danish published by DR Nyheder. Author's translation to English.

6. Statement by the secretary-general at the opening session of the second

meeting of the High Level Group for the Alliance of Civilizations, Doha, Qatar, February 26, 2006.

7. Personal communication, Ambassador Ömür Orhun, permanent representative of Turkey to the OSCE, Baku, Azerbaijan, April 27, 2007.

8. For a definition of contentious politics and associated repertoires of protest, see Doug McAdam, Sidney Tarrow, and Charles Tilly, *Dynamics of Contention* (Cambridge: Cambridge University Press, 2001), 5, 162.

9. Peer C. Fiss and Paul M. Hirsch, "The Discourse of Globalization: Framing and Sensemaking of an Emerging Concept," *American Sociological Review* 70 (2005): 29–52.

10. For a description of a prototypical European protest movement, see Herbert P. Kitschelt, "Political Opportunity Structures and Political Protest: Anti-Nuclear Movements in Four Democracies," *British Journal of Political Science* 16 (1986): 57–85.

11. Robin Cohen, "Diasporas and the Nation-State: From Victims to Challengers," *International Affairs* 72 (1996): 507–520.

12. "New 'Bin Laden Tape' Threatens EU," *BBC News,* March 20, 2008, http://news.bbc.co.uk/1/hi/world/europe/7306002.stm.

13. "Bomb Hits Pakistan Danish Embassy," *BBC News,* June 2, 2008, http://news.bbc.co.uk/2/hi/south—asia/7430721.stm.

14. "Danish Embassy Blast," *Dawn* (Pakistani English-language daily), June 4, 2008.

15. Available at http://www.nefafoundation.org/miscellaneous/FeaturedDocs/nefadenmarkpakistan0608.pdf. In its own words, the NEFA Foundation is "a non-profit organization created after the attacks of September 11, 2001. The Foundation strives to help prevent future tragedies in the U.S. and abroad by exposing those responsible for planning, funding, and executing terrorist activities, with a particular emphasis on Islamic militant organizations."

16. The interview is available at http://anikah.wordpress.com/2008/07/23/geo-tv-interview-with-sheikh-mustafa-abu-al-yazid/. See also *Voice of America,* July 22, 2008, http://www.voanews.com/english/2008–07–22-voa20.cfm.

17. See note 1, above. See also Sidney G. Tarrow, *Power in Movement: Social Movements and Contentious Politics,* 2nd ed. (New York: Cambridge University Press, 1998). On violence, see Donatella della Porta, "Research on Social Movements and Political Violence," *Qualitative Sociology* 31 (2008): 221–230. In another book Tarrow raises the possibility of nonnational social movements; see *The New Transnational Activism* (New York: Cambridge University Press, 2005).

18. Interview, Baku, Azerbaijan, April 26, 2007.

19. See www.elfagr.org. The page with the cartoons is available on another site, http://freedomforegyptians.blogspot.com/2006/02/egyptian-newspaper-pictures-that.html.

20. *Ejour,* see site citation in note 21, above.

21. *Weblog,* http://www.editorsweblog.org/analysis//2006/02/how—many—newspapers—published—mohammed—c.php#more.

22. AFP, February 3, 2005. Report available in Voice of America archives at http://www.voanews.com/english/archive/2006–02/2006–02–03-voa53 .cfm?CFID=116180428&CFTOKEN=78859018.

23. Transcript available at http://www.cbsnews.com/stories/2006/02/17/ 6ominutes/main1329944—page3.shtml.

24. *Economist,* January 5, 2006.

25. "BBC's Dilemma over Cartoons," *BBC News,* February 3, 2006, http://news .bbc.co.uk/newswatch/ukfs/hi/newsid—4670000/newsid—4678100/ 4678186.stm.

26. The listing of newspapers that reprinted the cartoons builds on the following accounts: Helle Nissen Kruse, "En digital tur rundt paa kloden," *eJour,* February 27, 2006, http://www.djh.dk/ejour/52/52Tegninger1.html; and Risto Kunelis et al., eds., *Reading the Mohammed Cartoons Controversy: An International Analysis of Press Discourses on Free Speech and Political Spin* (Bochum: ProjektVerlag, 2007). All information has been checked against two secondary sources and when available against the original.

27. They were *Essafir* (The Ambassador), *Iqra* (Read), which is a supplement to a weekly magazine called *Panorama,* and *Errissala* (The Letter).

28. *Yemen Observer, Al-Hurriya,* and *al-Rai al-Aam,* all weekly newsmagazines.

29. *Saudi Gazette* web site, *Jedda,* in English, February 22, 2006. Posted by BBC Monitoring. For a description of the newspaper and its publisher, see the web site of the Allied Media Corporation, a media market research company, http://www.allied-media.com/Arab-American/al—hayat.htm.

30. "Muslim Anger Hits SA: Religious Group Interdicts Press from Using 'Insulting' Prophet Cartoons," *Sunday Tribune* (South Africa), February 5, 2006.

31. Alain Navarro, "Enough Emotion over Cartoons, Time for Dialogue," *Middle East Times,* February 9, 2006.

32. The Vatican's web site posted the lecture with added disclaimers in the notes. In these, Benedict stresses that his use of the Byzantine quotation was intended only to support his observations about the essential theological superiority of the True Church. See http://www.vatican.va/holy—father/ benedict—xvi/speeches/2006/september/documents/hf—ben-xvi—spe— 20060912—university-regensburg—en.html.

33. "Prophet's Head Rolls, and Nobody Cares," *Spiegel Online,* December 19, 2006, http://www.spiegel.de/international/0,1518,455469,00.html.

34. One spoof compared Wilders to Donald Duck and alluded to his fleeting fame by way of Andy Warhol's remark about everyone being entitled to fifteen minutes of fame; see http://www.youtube.com/watch?v=fzKOTuB1CVQ.

35. "Dutch Film against Islam Is Released on Internet," *New York Times,* March 28, 2008, http://www.nytimes.com/2008/03/28/world/europe/28dutch .html?—r=1&fta=y&oref=slogin.

36. Flemming Rose, "Vejen til Gud," *Jyllands-Posten,* June 21, 2008.

37. The remark is taken from Bruce Bawer, *While Europe Slept: How Radical Islam Is Destroying the West from Within* (New York: Broadway Books, 2006), 233.

38. Henryk M. Broder, *Hurra, wir kapitulieren: Von der Lust am Einknicken* (Berlin: Wolf Jobst Siedler Verlag, 2006).

39. Martin Amis, *The Second Plane* (New York: Random House, 2008); Amis, "9/11 and the Cult of Death," *Times* (London), September 11, 2007. The essay has been removed from the *Times*'s archives but is still available on Martin Amis's web site, http://martinamisweb.com/commentary.shtml.

40. Richard Dawkins, *The God Delusion* (New York: Bantam Books, 2006); Christopher Hitchens, *God Is Not Great: How Religion Poisons Everything* (New York: Warner, 2006).

41. Daniel Pipes, "Europe's Stark Options," *National Interest*, March–April 2007.

42. Mark Steyn, *America Alone: The End of the World as We Know It* (Washington, DC: Regnery, 2006).

43. *Deutsche Welle* reported the 2050 estimate as a "rumor" and promptly discredited it. It was nonetheless reported as a fact in many publications and web sites, which all ignored the original disclaimer included in the source; see http://www.dw-world.de/dw/article/0,2144,2229744,00.html.

44. Charles F. Westoff and Tomas Frejka. "Religiousness and Fertility among European Muslims," *Population and Development Review* 4 (2007): 785–830.

45. Centraal Bureau voor de Statistiek, "More than 850 Thousand Muslims in the Netherlands," *Web Magazine; Statistics Netherlands*, October 25, 2007.

46. Charles F. Westoff and Tomas Frejka, "Religiousness and Fertility among European Muslims," *Population and Development Review* 33 (2007): 790.

47. Olivier Roy, *Secularism Confronts Islam* (New York: Columbia University Press, 2007); Ian Buruma, *Murder in Amsterdam: The Death of Theo van Gogh and the Limits of Tolerance* (New York: Penguin, 2006).

CHAPTER 3. THE DIPLOMATIC PROTEST
AGAINST THE CARTOONS

1. The list of member states includes African countries with mixed Muslim and Christian population, such as Ghana, Mozambique, and Ivory Coast. A new charter added in 1973 dedicated the organization to the strengthening of solidarity between Islamic states and promotion of economic, educational, cultural, and scientific cooperation.

2. A realist perspective on international relations can be found in Kenneth N. Waltz, *Realism and International Politics* (New York: Routledge, 2008).

3. The letter was published in *Politiken*, October 12, 2005.

4. The letter was reprinted in *Politiken*, April 3, 2006.

5. Interview, Århus, October 23, 2007.

6. The programming can be accessed online at http://www.livetvcenter.com/roj_tv_578.asp. Turkish papers reported in March 2008 that the Danish foreign minister had agreed to allow Turkish police to join the investigation of ROJ

TV in Copenhagen, but Per Stig Møller later denied the reports to Danish journalists. A meeting in July between Erdoğan and Fogh Rasmussen in Paris also failed to change Rasmussen's mind.

7. *Chechnya Weekly* (The Jamestown Foundation), vol. 7, nos. 6 and 7 (February 9 and 16, 2006).

8. "Dansk besøg i Moskva markerer tøbrud," *Jyllands-Posten,* February 18, 2006.

9. *Agence France-Presse* (Paris), November 4, 2005.

10. Anders Jerichow and Mille Rode, eds., *Profet-affæren* (Copenhagen: Dansk PEN, 2006), 34.

11. Rune Englebreth Larsen and Tøger Seidenfaden, *Karikatur krisen: En undersøgelse af baggrund og ansvar* (Copenhagen: Gyldendal, 2006).

12. Det Udenrigspolitiske Nævn, UPN FT-del Bilag 59. "Brev til Folketinget's formand vedr. Muhammed-sagen," March 8, 2006.

13. The final communiqué from the summit meeting is available at the OIC's web site, at http://www.oic-oci.org/oicnew/ex-summit/english/fc-exsumm-en.htm; "At Mecca Meeting, Cartoon Outrage Crystallized," *New York Times,* February 9, 2006. The recommendations from the civil society groups prepared in collaboration with the American Bar Association were published.

14. January 30, 2006. A chain of UAE supermarkets, the Consumer Cooperative Union, began a boycott of Danish products. *Middle East Journal* 60 (2006): 567–568.

15. "Something's Rotting from the State of Denmark," *Business Today Egypt,* March 2006.

16. Interview, Baku, Azerbaijan, April 25, 2006.

17. "Mohammed-brevet Norge ikke skulle se," *Dagbladet,* January 26, 2006.

18. *First OIC Observatory Report on Islamophobia,* May 2007–March 2008, presented at meeting held in Dakar, Senegal, March 13–14, 2008. The report is available at the OIC's web site: http://www.oic-oci.org/oicnew/is11/english/Islamophobia-rep-en.pdf.

19. CNN's interview with Vilks is available on YouTube, at http://www.youtube.com/watch?v=eeIgpZdM4As. As it turned out, the loudest threats to Vilks came from a Swedish woman living nearby and from Al-Qaeda.

20. Interview, Cairo, February 16, 2008.

21. An Internet petition supporting Amr Moussa's candidacy for the presidency circulated in Egypt before the 2005 presidential election.

22. Available on YouTube at http://www.youtube.com/watch?v=0pciRGoBd30.

23. Remarks by Ambassador Ömer Orhun, personal representative of the OSCE chairman-in-office on Combating Intolerance and Discrimination against Muslims, Freedom of the Media: Protection of Journalists and Access to Information, Vienna, July 13–14, 2006.

24. One Internet-based study concluded, "A time series analysis of related blog postings suggests that the Danish cartoons issue attracted little attention in the English-speaking world for four months after the initial publication of the cartoons, exploding only after the simultaneous start of diplomatic sanc-

tions and a commercial boycott." See "Blog Searching: The First General-Purpose Source of Retrospective Public Opinion in the Social Sciences?" *Online Information Review* 31 (2007): 277–289.

25. The initiatives were discussed at the G8 Gleneagles Meeting in July 2005, which was interrupted by the 7/7 attacks on the London Underground. The civil society initiatives, including the recommendations for legal reform of civil society activities, are listed on the web site for the meeting; see http://www.g8.gov.uk/servlet/Front?pagename=OpenMarket/Xcelerate/Show Page&c=Page&cid=1122476777415. An official statement from the Rabat meeting is available at the U.S. State Department's web site, http://www.state.gov/r/pa/prs/ps/2004/39676.htm.

CHAPTER 4. MUSLIMS' "DAY OF RAGE"

1. Pia Kjærsgaard's weekly newsletter (ugebrev), February 6, 2006.
2. Phone interview, Jeddah, July 12, 2006. On Abdul Haqq Baker's work with the 9/11 families, see Carie Lemack, "Victims of Terrorism Unite," *International Herald Tribune*, April 14, 2008.
3. Natana J. DeLong-Bas, *Wahhabi Islam: From Revival and Reform to Global Jihad* (Oxford: Oxford University Press, 2004).
4. Mary Habeck, *Knowing the Enemy: Jihadist Ideology and the War on Terror* (New Haven and London: Yale University Press, 2006).
5. John Hansen and Kim Hundevadt, *Provoen og profeten* (Århus: Jyllands-Postens forlag, 2006), 28.
6. Interview, Copenhagen, November 3, 2006.
7. Interview, Århus, October 23, 2007.
8. David Rennie, " 'Extra' Cartoons: More Evidence," *Daily Telegraph* (blog), February 6, 2006.
9. Lene Kühle, *Moskeer i Danmark: Islam og muslimske bedesteder* (Gylling, Denmark: Forlaget Univers, 2006), 127.
10. Ibid., 118.
11. Ibid., 122.
12. "Jeg taler ikke med tyve tunger—kun én," *Berlingske Tidende*, August 1, 2006.
13. Hlayhel reportedly also wanted relief money collected at the mosque to go to his village outside Tripoli, whereas other members of the committee wanted the money to go to refugees from Baalbek, where most came from. On his departure, Hlayhel mentioned nothing of the disagreements but cited the continued absence of an "apology" from Danes for the cartoons as his reason.
14. Rebecca Bloom, "Backgrounder: Fatah al-Islam," June 8, 2007, http://www.cfr.org/publication/13391/.
15. The were cited in the English-language Egyptian newspaper *Arab News*, but other Middle Eastern newspapers and Al Jazeera ignored them. "Imamer udsender forsonlige signaler i arabiske medier," *Politiken*, February 2, 2006.
16. "Hver tiende muslim accepterer flagafbrænding," *Ugebladet A4*, March 13, 2006.

17. Ibid.

18. "Toneangivende muslimer har kun få med sig," *Ugebrevet A4*, March 20, 2006.

19. "Suspect in German Bomb Plot Killed in Lebanon Fighting," *Deutsche Welle*, May 21, 2007.

20. "Prophet Drawings Motivated by Suspects behind Failed German Train Bombings, Investigator Says," *International Herald Tribune*, September 2, 2006.

21. Gilles Kepel, *Beyond Terror and Martyrdom: The Future of the Middle East* (Cambridge, MA: Harvard University Press, 2008), 222–223.

22. The report is based on public testimonies from the police's investigations in 1994 and contemporary Danish newspaper accounts. Michael Taarnby Jensen, *Jihad in Denmark: An Overview and Analysis of Jihadi Activity in Denmark, 1990–2006* (Copenhagen: Danish Institute for International Studies, 2006), available at http://www.flwi.ugent.be/cie/documenten/jihad-dk.pdf.

23. Jane Mayer, "Outsourcing Torture: The Secret History of America's 'Extraordinary Rendition' Program," *New Yorker*, February 14, 2005.

24. See Lorenzo Vidino, *Al Qaeda in Europe: The New Battleground for International Jihad* (New York: Prometheus Books, 2006).

25. Lorenzo Vidino, "Creating Outrage: Meet the Imam behind the Cartoon Overreaction," *National Review OnLine*, February 6, 2007, http://www.nationalreview.com/comment/vidino200602060735.asp.

26. Hans Jørgen Bonnichsen, *Frygt og fornuft: I terrorens tidsalder* (Copenhagen: People's Press, 2008), 55.

27. Krekar's real name is Najmuddin Faraj Ahmad. Iraqi authorities have sought his extradition since 2003.

28. "Moroccan-born Dane Sentenced to Prison for Promoting Terrorism," *International Herald Tribune*, April 11, 2007.

29. The *Wall Street Journal* accepted the Danish imams' version: see Andrew Higgins, "How Muslim Clerics Stirred Arab World against Denmark," *Wall Street Journal*, February 7, 2006.

30. Mosaic News is a thirty-minute news program broadcast on the U.S.-based satellite station LinkTV. It brings daily excerpts from Middle Eastern television news program translated into English. The cartoons were first featured on the January 27, 2006, summary and the folder shown on the January 30, 2006. Available at http://www.youtube.com/watch?v=—pMDrhnbHHc.

31. Ramzy Baroud, "Punishing Denmark," *Al-Ahram Weekly*, February 5, 2006.

32. Translation provided by MEMRI, Special Dispatch Series, no. 1089, February 9, 2006.

33. El-Houdaiby is a columnist for the Egyptian Muslim Brotherhood's English web site and has a blog where he posts his articles in English for various Arab newspapers; see http://ihoudaiby.blogspot.com.

34. Telephone interview, February 8, 2008.

35. *Declaration of Fatwa by World Islamic Scholars about Danish Cartoons*, posted February 20, 2006. Available at the American Muslim web site as part of a

collection titled *Muslim Voices against Extremism and Terrorism*, Part 1, *Fatwas*, compiled by Sheila Musaji; see http://www.theamericanmuslim.org.

36. He made it on *Time; Al-Ahram Weekly*, May 17–23, 2007.

37. "Muhammad Cartoons 'Global Crisis,'" *BBC*, February 7, 2006, http://news .bbc.co.uk/1/hi/world/south—asia/4690338.stm.

38. Alison Pargeter, "Libya: Reforming the Impossible?" *Review of African Political Economy* 33 (2006): 219–235. For an account blaming the cartoons, see "Off with His T-Shirt!" *Al-Ahram Weekly*, February 23–March 1, 2006.

39. "Forty-five Die as Nigeria Protests against Cartoons," *Cape Times* (South Africa), February 20, 2006.

40. "Lebanon's New War?" *Al-Ahram Weekly*, May 24–30, 2007.

41. An innocuous example was a flash mob happening at Grand Central Station in New York City, where the participants were instructed to "freeze" in the central hall; see http://www.youtube.com/watch?v=jwMj3PJDxuo.

42. *The News* (Pakistan), February 27, 2006. Reporting by Mayed Ali, Salman Aslam, Arslan Rafiq Bhatti, and Asim Hussein.

43. For a recent summary of social science theory on violence and contentious action, see Charles Tilly, "Terror, Terrorism, Terrorists," *Sociological Theory* 22 (2004): 5–13. An excellent discussion of Western images of the Arab street protest phenomenon is contained in Asef Bayat, "The 'Street' and the Politics of Dissent in the Arab World," *Middle East Report* (2003): 10–17.

CHAPTER 5. SEEKING THE THIRD WAY

1. See http://news.bbc.co.uk/1/hi/technology/4692518.stm.

2. For the channel's own estimates of viewer demographics, see Al Jazeera's web site, http://allied-media.com/aljazeera/JAZdemog.html.

3. "Aftermath from the Prophet Muhammad Protests: Three Weeks After," posted February 16, 2006, available at http://www.zone-h.org/content/ view/4445/31/.

4. Pictures from the demonstration circulate on many anti-Muslim sites and are available on YouTube, at http://www.youtube.com/watch?v=UufTBjgEE5Q.

5. "Four Men Jailed over Cartoon Demo," *BBC News*, July 18, 2007, http://news .bbc.co.uk/1/hi/uk/6904622.stm.

6. Footage from the February 11 demonstration can be seen at http://www.you tube.com/watch?v=52skWZjOv28.

7. Go to http://blogs.salaam.co.uk/article.php?story=20060212181916448.

8. Munira Mirza, Abi Senthikumaran, and Zein Ja'far, *Living Apart Together: British Muslims and the Paradox of Multiculturalism* (London: Policy Exchange, 2007), 74–75.

9. Testimony of Steven Emerson to the U.S. House of Representatives Permanent Select Committee on Intelligence, April 9, 2008, available at http:// intelligence.house.gov/Media/PDFS/Emerson040908.pdf; Robert S. Leiken and Steven Brooke, "The Moderate Muslim Brotherhood," *Foreign Affairs* 86 (March–April 2007): 107–121.

10. Carrie Rosefsky Wickham, *Mobilizing Islam: Religion, Activism, and Political Change in Egypt* (New York: Columbia University Press, 2002), 226.

11. European Parliament resolution of January 17, 2008, on the situation in Egypt (RC-B6–0023/2008), http://www.europarl.europa.eu//sides/getDoc .do?pubRef=-//EP//TEXT+TA+P6-TA-2008–0023+0+DOC+XML+V0// EN&language=EN.

12. Tarek Masoud, "Are They Democrats? Does It Matter?" *Journal of Democracy* 19 (2008): 19–24.

13. Interview with Lhaj Thami Brèze, Paris, December 12, 2006.

14. L'UOIF, "Réalisations et orientations," speech by Lhaj Thami Brèze, president of UOIF at the 23rd Annual Meeting of French Muslims at the Parc d'Expositions, Paris-Le Bourget, May 7, 2006.

15. Olivier Roy, *Globalized Islam: The Search for a New Ummah* (New York: Columbia University Press, 2004).

16. Stefan Simons, "Danish Caricatures on Trial in France: Cartoons 1: Muhammad 0," *Spiegel International*, February 17, 2007.

17. The FIOE's web site is www.euro-Muslim.net. The charter and a map listing the national member organizations are posted on the site.

18. "Four Hundred Groups Sign Charter for European Muslims," *EUobserver*, January 14, 2008, http://euobserver.com/9/25444?rss—rk=1.

19. The Pew Global Attitudes Project, *Muslims in Europe: Economic Worries Top Concerns about Religious and Cultural Identity*. Released July 6, 2006. Research carried out April 2006.

20. Paul M. Sniderman and Louk Hagendoorn, *When Ways of Life Collide: Multiculturalism and Its Discontents in the Netherlands* (Princeton, NJ: Princeton University Press, 2007).

21. Press release available at http://www.neareastconsulting.com/cartoons/ files/nec-pr-en.pdf. Raw data and cross-tabulations available on the web site.

22. "Thousands of Palestinians Protest Bomb-Attired Prophet Cartoon," Associated Press, February 10, 2006.

23. Data available at http://www.ipsos-mori.com/content/perception-of-cartoons-of-prophet-muhammad.ashx.

24. "Publics in Western Countries Disapprove of Muhammad Cartoons but Right to Publish Widely Defended," Angela Stephens, World Public Opinion, http://www.worldpublicopinion.org/pipa/articles/home—page/171.php? nid=&id=&pnt=171&lb=hmpg2.

25. "Epinion: Ingen skal undskylde Muhammed tegninger," *DR Nyheder*, January 28, 2006.

26. When Danish papers reprinted the cartoons in February 2008, 59 percent of the respondents in a Danish survey said that the paper was wrong to do it again. "Måling: Forkert at bringe tegningerne anden gang," *Jyllands-Posten*, March 16, 2008.

27. Mustafa Akyol and Zeyno Baran, "A Muslim Manifesto: Rejecting the Bad," *National Review Online*, March 1, 2006.

28. Tariq Ramadan, "Cartoon Conflicts: Comment," *Guardian*, February 6, 2006.

29. For a description of the cross-national networks sustaining the religious lives of Irish and Brazilian Catholics and Gujarati Hindus living in Boston, see Peggy Levitt, "Redefining the Boundaries of Belonging: The Institutional Character of Transnational Religious Life," *Sociology of Religion* 65 (2004): 1–18.

30. Fatima Mernissi, "Place Fundamentalism and Liberal Democracy," in *The New Crusaders: Constructing the Muslim Enemy*, ed. Emran Quereshi and Michael A. Shells (New York: Columbia University Press, 2003), 51–67.

31. Anna Tsing, "The Global Situation," *Cultural Anthropology* 15 (2000): 327–360.

32. Amartya Sen, "What Clash of Civilizations? Why Religious Identity Isn't Destiny," *Slate*, March 29, 2006, http://www.slate.com/id/2138731/.

CHAPTER 6. MUSLIM ICONOCLASM AND CHRISTIAN BLASPHEMY

1. Anonymous, *Canto XXVIII, Circle 8, Bolgia 9, "The Sowers of Religious Discord, Punished by Mutilation (Mahomet),"* 1491 (woodcut).

2. Mormons refer to Smith and Muhammad in the same way, as "Prophets." Joseph Smith is reported to have compared himself to Muhammad in a speech from 1838: "I will be to this generation a second Mohammed, whose motto in treating for peace was 'the Alcoran [Koran] or the Sword.' So shall it eventually be with us—'Joseph Smith or the Sword!'" Fawn M. Brodie, *No Man Knows My History* (New York: Alfred A. Knopf, 1971), 230–231.

3. Anthony Quinn, who was best known as "the Greek" from his success in *Zorba the Greek* (1964), was in fact of Irish and Mexican descent and grew up a Catholic.

4. *The Message* (1976), director, Moustapha Akkad. It is a popular clip on YouTube; see http://www.youtube.com/watch?v=iV7wRcQcD5k.

5. Tariq Ramadan, *Western Muslims and the Future of Islam* (Oxford: Oxford University Press,2004).

6. On the "ticking bomb" scenario, see Stephen Holmes, "Is Defiance of Law a Proof of Success? Magical Thinking in the War on Terror," in *The Torture Debate in America*, ed. Karen J. Greenberg (New York: Cambridge University Press, 2006), 118–135.

7. "Muslims Rip '24' for Renewed Terror Role," Associated Press, January 18, 2007.

8. The Zombie Image Archive started collecting images of Muhammad and posting them. Michelle Malkin, a blogger, picked up the argument suggested by the pictures and the mainstream media took it from her.

9. A rare exception to the general absence of public exhibitions, the British Library put an illustration from the poem on display in fall 2007. It can still be viewed on the exhibit's web site, http://www.bl.uk/onlinegallery/sacred texts/nizami.html.

10. I am grateful to Ünver Rüstem for pointing out the differences in the symbolic style language between this and other manuscripts.

11. Reza Aslan, "Depicting Mohammed: Why I'm Offended by the Danish Cartoons of the Prophet," *Slate*, February 8, 2006, http://www.slate.com/id/2135661/.

12. See http://www.allposters.com/gallery.asp?startat=/getposter.asp&A PNum=1874068&CID=AA6BoD3E17D64F06A474F82AB9BF7914&PPID=1&search=Muhammad&f=t&FindID=0&P=1&PP=4&sortby=RD&cname=&SearchID=.

13. Oleg Grabar, "The Story of Portraits of the Prophet Muhammad," *Studia Islamica, Écriture, Calligraphie et Peinture* 96 (2003): 19–38, pls. 6–9; Eva Baer, "The Human Figure in Early Islamic Art: Some Preliminary Remarks," *Muqarnas* 16 (1999): 32–41.

14. Sheila S. Blair and Jonathan M. Bloom, "Art and Architecture," in *The Oxford History of Islam*, ed. John L. Esposito (New York: Oxford University Press, 1999), 230.

15. Echoing statements by other high-ranking religious authorities in Egypt and Saudi Arabia, Abdel-Moeti Bayoumi, a member of Al-Azhar's Islamic Research Academy, said, "The boycott is the least Muslims could do to defend their Prophet after the majority of Danish people supported their government for not apologising for the offensive drawings." See "Cartoon Battle Turns Uglier," *Al-Ahram Weekly*, February 2–8, 2006.

16. Taha Jaber al-Alwani, " 'Fatwa' Concerning the United States Supreme Courtroom Frieze," *Journal of Law and Religion* 15 (2000–2001): 1–18. I thank my colleague Joseph Lumbard for bringing this article to my attention.

17. Ibid., 25.

18. SAAS is short for "Salla Allahu 'Alaihi Wa Sallam," meaning, "May the blessing and the peace of Allah be upon him." English-speakers commonly use PBUH, "Peace be upon him."

19. Chapter 272 of the Penal Code of the State of Massachusetts proscribes "crimes against chastity, decency, morality, and good order," and includes in section 36 the following injunction, "Whoever willfully blasphemes the holy name of God by denying, cursing or contumeliously reproaching God, his creation, government or final judging of the world, or by cursing or contumeliously reproaching Jesus Christ or the Holy Ghost, or by cursing or contumeliously reproaching or exposing to contempt and ridicule, the holy word of God contained in the holy scriptures shall be punished by imprisonment in jail for not more than one year or by a fine of not more than three hundred dollars, and may also be bound to good behavior"; http://www.mass.gov/legis/laws/mgl/272-36.htm.

20. See http://www.opendemocracy.net/democracy-europe—islam/muslim—cartoons-3244.jsp#one.

21. Telephone interview, Abdul Haqq Baker, Jeddah, July 12, 2006.

22. "Afgørelse on eventual strafforfølgning i sagen om Jyllands-Postens artikel 'Muhammeds ansigt,' " Rigsadvokaten, March 15, 2006.

23. An Italian magazine has taken up Allievi's cause; see *Dialogues on Civiliza-tion. ResetDoc,* http://www.resetdoc.org/EN/Allievi-Freedom.php.

24. Council of Europe, Recommendation 1805 (2007): "Blasphemy, religious in-sults and hate speech against persons on grounds of their religion"; see http://assembly.coe.int/Main.asp?link=/Documents/AdoptedText/ta07/EREC1805.htm.

CHAPTER 7. DANISH INTOLERANCE AND FOREIGN RELATIONS

1. *Politiken,* March 3, 2006; "Anders Fogh holdt vigtigt brev tilbage," *DR Nyheder,* March 4, 2006.

2. Own translation, Anders Jerichow and Mille Rode, eds., *Profet-affæren* (Copenhagen: Dansk PEN, 2006), 28.

3. For the view that fragmentation leads to consensus-building, see Arend Lijp-hart, *Patterns of Democracy:Government Forms and Performance in Thirty-Six Countries* (New Haven and London:Yale University Press,1999). A more re-cent account is Wolfgang C. Müller and Kaare Strøm, eds., *Coalition Govern-ments in Western Europe* (New York:Oxford University Press, 2000).

4. See http://news.bbc.co.uk/2/hi/middle—east/6382675.stm.

5. "Muhammedtegninger har kostet en milliard i eksport," *Politiken,* Septem-ber 28, 2006; "Muhammed-krisen kostede Arla 450 mio.," *B.T.,* March 1, 2007.

6. Press releases regarding the contracts with Mærsk are available at the U.S. Navy's Military Sealift Command's web site: see "MSC Awards Special Mis-sion Ship Operating Contract," Press Release, March 16, 2005, http://www.msc.navy.mil/N00p/pressrel/press05/press10.htm.

7. The shipping company requested help from the Danish foreign minister in connection with a complaint from the Iraqi government over the company's doings in the oil harbor; Khor az-Zubayr, "Mærsk bad om hjælp i irakisk hav-nesag," *DR Nyheder,* May 18, 2006. In this case the company incurred severe criticism also from U.S. government sources.

8. Joseph S. Nye, *Soft Power: The Means to Success in World Politics* (New York: PublicAffairs, 2005).

9. *Dagbladet Information,* March 15, 2006. The newspaper concludes in this case that the foreign ministry called the shots, an interpretation that cannot be sustained in view of the big picture.

10. Poll conducted of 1,348 respondents by Morgenavisen Jyllands-Posten, May 20, 1997, http://www.dupi.dk/webtxt/dupidok/1997/del4—97.htm.

11. Ulf Hedetoft, "Denmark: Integrating Immigrants into a Homogeneous Wel-fare State," *Migration Information Source,* November 2006, Migration Policy Institute, http://www.migrationinformation.org/Profiles/display.cfm?ID=485.

12. International Migration and Denmark, *SOPEMI Report to OECD 2006,* Danish Ministry of Refugee, Immigration, and Integration Affairs, November 2006.

13. *Politiken*, January 2, 2007.
14. Kjærsgaard filed a defamation suit in 1999 against an activist who said in an interview on the Danish radio that her organization was reluctant to be associated with "Kjærsgaard's racist views." Both the lower court and the appeals court held with Kjærsgaard and fined the activist. In 2003, the supreme court found the activist's statement to be permissible as long as it was Kjærsgaard's views rather than her person that had been described as racist.
15. The party's web site is http://www.danskfolkeparti.dk/.
16. Pia Kjærsgaard's newsletter, February 25, 2002, http://www.danskfolkeparti.dk/sw/frontend/detail.asp?parent=19106&typeid=13&id=169&menu—parent=&layout=0.
17. Ulrik Høy, "Kulturkamp?" *Weekendavisen*, September 30, 2005, 12.
18. "Denmark Targets Extremist Media," *BBCNews*, August 17, 2005, http://news.bbc.co.uk/2/hi/europe/4159220.stm. The station has programming in English: http://www.radioholger.dk/. Like Osama bin Laden, Radio Holger continues to milk the cartoons. A text version of a program on the cartoons and the failings of Islam can be found at this link, which had been defaced by an anti–far right group when I looked at it in August 2008, http://www.radioholger.dk/tekster/tekst158.htm.
19. "Frevert indhentet af porno-fortid," *B.T.*, November 14, 2005.
20. Her cleaned-up opinion pieces are available at http://louisefrevert.dk/artikler.php.
21. Ida Buhl, "Krarup: Kun kristne er rigtige danskere," *Berlingske Tidende*, January 14, 2004.
22. It is available on YouTube at http://www.youtube.com/watch?v=jBSoMiG94Es&NR=1.
23. "Nazistervelkomne i Dansk Folkeparti," *Ekstra Bladet*, August 21, 2006.
24. The group's web site is http://www.skrewdriver.org.
25. The videos can usually be found on YouTube but travel from site to site. I have found them on Spanish, Russian, and Japanese sites. Last accessed August 16, 2008, at http://www.buscatube.com/watch/y/dansk/1/tAjVQnStTzk/dansk-front-demonstration/ and http://www.youtube.com/watch?v=sVwXONnQ4og.
26. *Politiken*, October 15, 2005, and various newspapers. Available in Danish at http://www.humanisme.dk/debat/pro51215b.php.
27. The letter was published in Danish newspapers, including *Politiken*, December 19, 2005.
28. "Store virksomheder presser Jyllands-Posten," *DR Nyheder*, January 27, 2006.
29. Broadcast on ABC News on February 2, 2006, http://abcnews.go.com/International/story?id=1570095.
30. *Jyllands-Posten*, May 20, 2006.
31. Pia Kjærsgaard, during the opening debate of the Danish Folketing, October 4, 2001. Available at http://ft.dk/?/samling/20061/MENU/00000002.htm.

32. "Dashing Dane Anders Fogh Rasmussen Favourite for President of EU," *Times* (London), May 6, 2008.

33. Anonymous source.

34. The core statement was issued June 3, 1997, and signed by, among others, Dick Cheney, Jeb Bush, Donald Rumsfeld, Zalmay Khalilzad, Lewis Libby, Norman Podhoretz, and Paul Wolfowitz. It can be read at http://www.new americancentury.org/statementofprinciples.htm.

35. Statement available at http://www.um.dk/da/menu/OmOs/Udenrigsmin isteren/Taler/Arkiv2003/UdviklingsbistandSomEtInstrumentIForebyggel seAfTerrorisme.htm.

36. Available at the foreign ministry's web site, http://www.um.dk/Publikat ion er/Danida/English/DanishDevelopmentCooperation/PartnershipForPro gressAndReform/Det—Arabiske—Initiativ—ENG.pdf.

37. The two attacks were carried out by al- Zawahiri's Islamic Jihad, an Egyptian group that joined Al-Qaeda in 2001.

38. See http://jp.dk/indland/article1263173.ece.

39. Prime Minister Anders Fogh Rasmussen's speech at the opening of Folketin-get, Tuesday, October 3, 2006. My translation. Posted at http://www.stm.dk/ Index/dokumenter.asp?o=2&n=0&d=2691&s=1.

40. Udenrigsministeriet, *Det Arabiske Initiative: Status og resultater*, no date.

41. "U.S. Government Calls Anti-Islamic Cartoons 'Offensive,' " press release, February 3, 2006, http://usinfo.state.gov/mena/Archive/2006/Feb/04–274076.html.

42. *BBC News*, February 2, 2006.

43. Press release available at http://www.un.org/News/Press/docs/2006/ sg2105.doc.htm.

CHAPTER 8. THE FREEDOM AGENDA REBOUND

1. Interview, Ministry of Foreign Affairs, The Arab Republic of Egypt, Cairo, February 18, 2008.

2. Pew Global Attitudes Project, *Global Unease with Major World Powers and Leaders. 47-Nation Survey Finds Rising Environmental Concerns.* Released June 27, 2007. http://pewresearch.org/pubs/524/global-unease-with-major-world-powers-and-leaders

3. "Sitzkrieg" was the term used in Germany for the phase during World War II between the German invasion of Poland in September 1939 and the start of military operations in western Europe in April 1940. In the United King-dom, it was called the Phoney War. War had been declared, but active fight-ing had not yet begun.

4. John Hansen and Kim Hundevadt, "The Cartoon Crisis—How It Unfolded," posted March 11, 2008, *Jyllands-Posten* (web in English), http://jp.dk/ud land/article1292543.ece. Adam Hannestad, a journalist from the competing newspaper *Politiken*, advanced the same explanation in connection with an interview with the Egyptian foreign minister, Ahmed Aboul Gheit, who said

that the Egyptians had without success sought mediation with Fogh Rasmussen and nothing that would support the scapegoating claim. "Jeres udenrigsminister sagde nej, nej, og nej," *Politiken*, February 23, 2006.

5. "Egypt's Muslim Brotherhood Vows to Contest Local Elections," *Voice of America*, February 21, 2008.

6. "Look Who's Getting Votes," *Time*, December 12, 2005.

7. European Parliament resolution of January 17, 2008, on the situation in Egypt.

8. Interview, Cairo, February 17, 2008.

9. Marc Lynch, a political scientist, has written about the arrest of Hamza on his blog, http://abuaardvark.typepad.com/abuaardvark/2008/02/khaled-hamza.html.

10. Interview, Cairo, February 18, 2008.

11. Telephone interview, United Arab Emirates, February 8, 2008.

12. Dr. Rice Addresses War on Terror. Remarks by National Security Advisor Condoleezza Rice Followed by Question and Answer to the U.S. Institute of Peace, Washington, DC, August 19, 2004. The strategy was elaborated in a testimony by Michael Kozak, assistant secretary of state; see "Challenges to Democratization in the Middle East and Central Asia," Part 1—Oppressors vs. Reformers in the Middle East and Central Asia, Subcommittee on the Middle East and Central Asia of the House International Relations Committee, May 4, 2005, www.state.gov/g/drl/rls/spbr/45659.htm.

13. Joel Brinkley, "Rice Calls Off Mideast Visit after Arrest of Egyptian," *New York Times*, February 26, 2005. For an Egyptian perspective on Rice's visit, see Salama A. Salama, "Condoleezza's visit," *Al-Ahram News*, June 23–29, 2005.

14. This is what Rice said: "The Egyptian Government must fulfill the promise it has made to its people—and to the entire world—by giving its citizens the freedom to choose. Egypt's elections, including the Parliamentary elections, must meet objective standards that define every free election. Opposition groups must be free to assemble, and to participate, and to speak to the media. Voting should occur without violence or intimidation. And international election monitors and observers must have unrestricted access to do their jobs." Remarks at the American University in Cairo, June 20, 2005, available at http://www.state.gov/secretary/rm/2005/48328.htm.

15. See press conference with Liz Cheney and Daniel Fried, assistant secretary for Euro-Asian affairs, http://fpc.state.gov/fpc/56709.htm. When pressed by a journalist from the Egyptian television station Nile News about the Egyptian Brotherhood's likely win in an election, Cheney insisted that once Egyptian voters had the benefit of freedom they would support liberal parties, but Fried answered: "As Liz said, for a very long time there has been no place in most countries in the broader Middle East for the expression of and development of liberal opinion and liberal parties, that Islamism was the only opposition. And as societies open up, I suspect—I don't know, these are

independent places—but I suspect you will see two things: You will see as space develops, liberal parties of different varieties moving in to fill the space that is newly available.

"And secondly, I suspect that you will see so-called Islamist parties beginning to differentiate very widely from those who are genuinely extremist and those who move in a democratic direction."

16. Human Rights Watch, letter to Secretary of State Condoleeza Rice about Department of State Comments on Egyptian Elections, December 2, 2005; Mona El-Ghobashy, "Egypt's Paradoxical Elections," *Middle East Report* 238 (Spring 2006): 20–25.

17. The Egyptian Organization for Human Rights, 2005 Parliamentary Elections Run-Offs Initial Report, November 27, 2005; Assessment of the Electoral Framework, Final Report, The Arab Republic of Egypt, May 14, 2007, http://www.eohr.org/report/2007/reo514.shtml.

18. Available at http://mepi.state.gov/outreach/index.htm#strategic.

19. President Bush Discusses Freedom in Iraq and Middle East. Remarks by the President at the Twentieth Anniversary of the National Endowment for Democracy. Washington, D.C., Office of the Press Secretary, November 6, 2003.

20. For a link to the statement and a list of names, see chapter 7, note 34. The statement spoke of four "consequences"—so labeled to recall Franklin D. Roosevelt's four freedoms—for securing American security and greatness in the twenty-first century: increased military spending and modernization, a war of "values" against hostile regimes, the promotion of political and economic freedom abroad, and building American security by building an international order "friendly to our security, our prosperity, and our principles." Elliott Abrams et al., "Statement of Principles," June 3, 1997. The statement used to be available at the web site, newamericancentury.org, but is no longer available.

21. See note 19, above.

22. For European and Middle Eastern reactions, see " 'It Would Be Laughable, Were It Not So Pathetic': Reactions to His Pro-Democracy Speech Are Mixed," *Guardian*, November 10, 2003. Reactions were also summarized by GlobalSecurity.org, http://www.globalsecurity.org/military/library/news/2003/11/wwwh31110.htm.

23. See note 15, above.

24. The foundation's web site lists current projects and staff, as well as the member states, http://www.foundationforfuture.org.

25. "Ms. Rice's Retreat: The Secretary of State, Who Once Championed Reform in Egypt, Waives Human Rights Restrictions on U.S. Aid," *Washington Post*, March 11, 2008.

26. Per Bech Thomsen, *Muhammedkrisen: Hvad skete der, hvad har vi lært* (Copenhagen: People's Press, 2006), 87.

27. Michael E. O'Hanlon, "Iraqi Elections: Time for Flexibility," *Washington Times*, August 4, 2008.

28. Mehmet Ali Birand, "Don't Trust Every Promise Obama Makes," *Hürriyet* (online edition), April 7, 2009.

Index